WRITING AN IDENTITY
NOT YOUR OWN

WRITING AN IDENTITY NOT YOUR OWN

A GUIDE FOR CREATIVE WRITERS

ALEX TEMBLADOR

ST. MARTIN'S
ESSENTIALS
NEW YORK

First published in the United States by St. Martin's Essentials,
an imprint of St. Martin's Publishing Group

www.stmartins.com

Designed by Steven Seighman

The Library of Congress Cataloging-in-Publication Data is available
upon request.

ISBN 978-1-250-90711-0 (trade paperback)
ISBN 978-1-250-90712-7 (ebook)

Our books may be purchased in bulk for promotional, educational,
or business use. Please contact your local bookseller or the Macmillan
Corporate and Premium Sales Department at 1-800-221-7945, extension
5442, or by email at MacmillanSpecialMarkets@macmillan.com.

First Edition: 2024

10 9 8 7 6 5 4 3 2 1

For folks who are willing to sit in discomfort
so they might learn and grow.
To the friends who reminded me of who
I am when I forgot.
For those fighting to make creative writing more
diverse, inclusive, and representative.

CONTENTS

AUTHOR'S NOTE

As you read through this book, you will notice that I have used excerpts from creative writing works as examples. Some of these examples are from books written by authors writing characters with identities different from their own; however, most are writers writing within their own identities. If I have used an excerpt to demonstrate how an author accomplished something well in one part of their work, that is not necessarily a personal stamp of approval for the rest of the piece. My goal is to only provide specific positive examples, not to give my opinion on the rest of their work.

I have also pointed out some books that are widely known for having problematic portrayals and storylines relating to historically marginalized communities. I tried to only include books that have been so vastly discussed in the news, at conferences, and within the literary and reading communities that most writers and readers will be aware of the discussion surrounding these problematic portrayals. It is not my intent to criticize anyone callously; rather, I intend to use these examples as a means to add to the discussion of writing identities not your own.

Most of the stereotypes, tropes, and terms presented in this book are such that we would use in the U.S. While I believe that many writers from around the world will benefit from this book, I hope they do understand that I wrote this book with a U.S. perspective and that some things may not apply to their societies.

At times, I will use terms like BIPOC, people of color, gender-queer folks, or the LGBTQIA+ community as a shorthand to discuss specific groups. I understand that these acronyms or terms are not liked by all and that, in some instances, they are reductive to the communities they represent. For the sake of this book, I will be using them to make the reading experience easier. It is not my intent to cause offense, but to easily convey all of the information I can without making things any more complicated. If there comes a time when the majority of the population decides that such terms or acronyms should be removed from our usage completely, the book will be updated to reflect that shift.

I tried my best to include the most up-to-date information, statistics, and perspectives to help you write other identities well. I sourced information from people who have more knowledge than I do in specific areas, and at other times, I used logic and my own personal experience to provide insight and advice. Despite my attempt to write and design this book in a way that would help most creative writers, I will be the first to admit that I am biased and imperfect, and so there may be topics, questions, or discussions that I could not or did not anticipate. My friend reminded me that this book is not the Ten Commandments. In other words, we must remember that the tips or rules I have presented here are free to change and evolve. Language, society, and the industries related to creative writing are ever-changing and so there is always something new to discover about this topic. Please keep this in mind when utilizing this book, as you might have to do additional research to help you answer specific questions you have about your creative writing piece. I hope that I will have the opportunity to update this book over time and continue to contribute to this conversation.

Last, but most importantly, this book is for writers who wish to write identities not their own. Many of the subjects I will discuss *cannot* and *should not* be applied to writers who write within their own identities. For instance, if a writer of color wishes to write a story about someone with their same racial/ethnic identity who goes through a struggle similar to one they have faced or could face in reality, we would not call that trauma porn. The rules, advice, and suggestions presented in this book will not usually apply to historically marginalized writers writing characters with their same identity; writers writing outside of their identities should remember this.

Introduction

MY JOURNEY TO *WRITING AN IDENTITY NOT YOUR OWN*

dentity has always been at the forefront of my mind. It had to be when kids didn't believe that my Mexican American father and white mother were my parents or that my lighter-skinned Mixed brother was my full-blooded sibling. I couldn't *not* think about identity, especially when I watched how people behaved around my sister, who has intellectual and physical disabilities—people never speaking directly to her or shuffling with their backs against the wall out of a fast-food joint because my sister made verbal noises as a means of expressing her joy for lunch. I considered how the world vilifies certain identities when kids bullied my brother for having a seizure and later for coming out as queer. I thought about identity every time kids and adults told me that because I was a girl, I couldn't be better than boys at sports (which I often was), or when I read *The Handmaid's Tale* in high school and cried in my closet because I understood that many of the things that happen to women and girls in the novel have occurred, do occur, or could occur in this world. I faced the privileges of identity often, like when my ex-boyfriend who was Black was pulled over by the cops and was visibly scared, or after I wrote my first article on transgender rights and a transgender woman who was experiencing houselessness reached out to me on social media to share some current struggles she was facing. I even mulled over the oddities and ironies of identity every time someone asked me "What are you?" or when people of color assumed my racial and ethnic background as Native American, Black, Indian, or even Balinese, and I had to recognize what was happening and then uncomfortably correct them.

I have long been acquainted with the intricacies of identity, so of course, it made its way into my writing career early on. Latine, Black, and Mixed characters were prevalent in my creative work, a reflection of the community of friends and family I grew up with in North Texas. Similarly, I wrote gay characters and characters with disabilities because my siblings had these identities. Even in my career as a journalist, I covered racism, gender discrimination, LGBTQIA+ rights, and diverse family dynamics.

By the time I started writing my second novel, *Half Outlaw*, in 2017, I felt confident creating characters with identities not my own. That confidence increased by the time my literary agent took *Half Outlaw* out on submission to publishers in 2019 because within those two years, I'd written even more articles on diversity, inclusion, and equity, and I felt assured that I was crafting holistic and authentic characters with historically marginalized identities.

Two months after George Floyd was killed by police officers

in 2020, *Half Outlaw* was acquired by Blackstone Publishing. By the time I was assigned an editor a year later, in 2021, my perspective on writing characters with differing identities had shifted completely.

Between 2020 and 2021, our society began picking apart the nuances of prejudice and biases, learning new vocabulary concerning discrimination, and educating ourselves about the ways in which these things unconsciously crawl into our thoughts, behaviors, and writing.

I'd been a part of the conversation myself. Editors at magazines had asked me to write articles on topics relating to diversity, and others had invited me to join national and international panels, both as an author and a freelance journalist, to offer my insight and advice on how we could diversify the publishing and journalism industries. In that time, I won a Bessie Award for the Most Impactful Piece of Writing for an article I wrote for *Condé Nast Traveler* titled "Questions Every Anti-Racist Traveler Should Ask on a Trip," and spoke to countless associations and organizations, as well as at conferences on how to make libraries, schools, publishing, newsrooms, tourism, the outdoors, design and architecture, and art scenes more inclusive and equitable.

I was becoming known as an expert in diversity, equity, and inclusion in certain communities, and it was because of this that I was asked to teach a seminar for WritingWorkshops .com that would instruct writers on how to write characters with identities other than their own—especially those from historically marginalized communities. I had plenty of teaching experience at that time, but I knew that this class, which I titled "Writing an Identity Other Than Your Own," wasn't something I could or would take lightly. What I taught or didn't teach in that class wouldn't just affect the literary world; it could have measurable effects well beyond it.

Before the pandemic hit, a book called *American Dirt* was published in January 2020. Unbeknownst to some, a conversation about diversity and inclusion in the publishing world had been boiling for years, and it spilled over with the publication of this book.

Jeanine Cummins, the author of *American Dirt*, identified as a white woman and then began to identify with her one-quarter Puerto Rican heritage during the lead-up to publication. The novel was about a Mexican mother and child who escaped a drug cartel by crossing into the U.S. as undocumented noncitizens. Cummins herself said she wrote the book "to help readers see Mexican migrants as human beings."[1]

Before the book hit the market, it was shared with reviewers and notable book clubs. Months before it came out, it was being touted as a hit, a bestseller from an exciting new voice who would spark conversations about immigration across America. Not everyone saw *American Dirt* in this way.

Myriam Gurba, a Mexican American writer and book reviewer, published a review on an academic blog called *Tropics of Meta*.[2] What she found in the pages of *American Dirt* was alarming. She explained it was filled with stereotypes, was riddled with cultural inaccuracies, idolized the U.S., and turned the Mexican migrant experience into trauma porn. Later, other readers would point out passages that eerily resembled the work of famed Latino author Luis Alberto Urrea.[3]

Gurba's piece sparked a huge discussion in the literary community about the way we tell stories of people from historically marginalized communities. Arguably, Cummins prompted the conversation when she wrote in her author's note, "I worried that, as a non-migrant and non-Mexican, I had no business writing a book set almost entirely in Mexico, set entirely among migrants. I wished someone slightly browner than me would write it."[4]

Here's the thing: many "browner" people had written this story, but they didn't receive the kind of support or financial incentive that Cummins—who called her family white "in every practical way"—did.[5]

Cummins received a seven-figure advance and a six-figure marketing budget (which is uncommon). Ten thousand early copies were sent to bookstores, a book party was hosted by her publisher, and a first print run consisted of half a million copies. Such a deal was nearly unheard of for most authors—much less Latine ones writing about Latine experiences.[6]

Latine/x/o/a and Hispanic writers have written many fiction and nonfiction books about the immigrant experience. Some of us have been published; many of us have not. I can tell you that most of us haven't received seven-figure deals and we sure as hell didn't receive the type of marketing or publishing support that Cummins did. Not only that, but Cummins was a debut author, and there have been many Latine debut authors who have received no more than small four-figure debut deals and less than $20,000 for second book advances—even when we've won awards.

Latine authors weren't the only ones distraught over the *American Dirt* debacle. Many writers of other historically marginalized identities had experienced the same thing—and we were tired of it happening time and time again. *The Help* by Kathryn Stockett, *The Cricket in Times Square* by George Selden, *The Seventh Sun* by Lani Forbes, *The Continent* by

Keira Drake, *A Fine Dessert* by Emily Jenkins, *Disclosure* by Michael Crichton, and *Blood Heir* by Amélie Wen Zhao have prompted similar discussions. So how and why had this happened so many times?

Publishing has a diversity problem, and it's something you need to be aware of, because it's connected directly to the subject of this book. Stick with me for a moment.

Ninety-five percent of novels published between 1950 and 2018 were written by white authors. In 2018 alone, white authors penned 89 percent of adult books.[7] The Ripped Bodice's report on racial diversity in romance publishing shows that in 2022, only 12.3 percent of traditionally published romance authors fall under the BIPOC (Black, Indigenous, and people of color) umbrella.[8] As for studies relating to LGBTQIA+ and disability representation in publishing, there is little up-to-date information, especially as it relates to author representation. What we know is that in 2019, the Cooperative Children's Book Center found that 3.4 percent of all children's books featured a main character with a disability, whereas 3.1 percent highlighted an LGBTQIA+ main character.[9] It is unclear if these characters were written by authors with the same identity.

The lack of diversity among authors is due in part to the fact that the publishing industry—from boards, editors, and literary agents to staff at review journals—is overwhelmingly white. In 2019, the publishing industry was 76 percent white, editorial departments were 85 percent white, and the executive level was 78 percent white, according to a study by Lee & Low.[10] Eleven percent of publishing staff identified as having a disability in 2019.[11]

Suffice it to say that in comparison to people of historically marginalized identities writing within their own identities, people with privileged identities are more likely to get published when they write stories that feature historically marginalized identities that are not their own. If you ask me, that's pretty messed up.

The backlash against *American Dirt* entered the public sphere and became one of the biggest conversations in the news until Covid-19 hit. With this national spotlight on publishing, Latine authors David Bowles, Myriam Gurba, and Roberto Lovato of #DignidadLiteraria, as well as Matt Nelson, the executive director of Presente.org, met with Flatiron Books on February 3, 2020. They discussed the lack of diversity and inclusion in publishing and how that affects the books that get published, as well as the advances and marketing efforts for privileged authors compared to those who are not.

Because of this conversation, the publisher agreed to hire a Latinx in Publishing board member as an editor at large, use sensitivity readers, audit its catalog to see how many books had been written by authors of color, and review advances for authors of color and the language used in their marketing materials. (It's unclear as to what extent Flatiron Books has followed through on all of this.)

You're probably wondering, "What is the point of all this conversation about *American Dirt*? Why do I care?" Because despite the backlash and the work by Presente.org, *American Dirt* was a *New York Times* bestseller for thirty-six weeks and a bestselling adult novel in 2020. That means thousands of people read a book that is full of harmful stereotypes and tropes and reinforces biases about Mexican people, undocumented noncitizens, and the U.S. (and many of these readers did so knowing full well the type of negative press the book received).

Can you imagine the kind of repercussions that might have in a society? I can.

This is why I don't take the subject of writing an identity not your own lightly—and neither can you.

For Cummins's part, I think she may have had good intentions, but it's hard to consider good intentions when your writing has major consequences. I'd wager to guess that Cummins believed her literary agent and editor would catch her mistakes, or that publishers wouldn't have published the book if it were filled with negative misrepresentations. Most authors believe the same. However, the reality is editors and publishers are human—and usually straight, white, abled, and cis—and they didn't seem to recognize or understand the bias, misrepresentations, and problems in her story. Instead, they focused on Cummins's storytelling skills and ignored (maybe subconsciously, maybe not) the harmful portrayals.

The lesson here: you can't trust that publishers, editors, literary agents, sensitivity readers, or critique partners will catch these things; it is your responsibility to recognize and fix them yourself, because when your work is published, it's your name that's listed in big bold letters below the title, not anyone else's.

It wasn't long after *American Dirt* was published that I was asked to teach the seminar on writing identities other than your own. Writers feared writing something that would further racism, discrimination, ableism, homophobia, sexism, and other forms of prejudice. (Some only wanted permission to write characters of identities other than their own. I'm not here to give you permission. This is your journey, so do it or don't, and take responsibility for your choices.)

Writers were looking for answers, and answers weren't easy to find on the internet. A few websites existed that discussed the topic, but they were outdated and not being managed any-more. The handful of craft books on this subject were either outdated or limited in their scope. It was difficult for people to even find these limited resources. How can you find information on the topic if you don't know the right terms to use in the Google search bar?

No one seemed to have the answers, and I sure as hell didn't have them all, but I'd been writing and talking about representation for years and had experienced the lack of inclusion and equity in publishing as a Mixed Latine author myself. I wanted to at least try to teach a class on the subject of writing an identity not your own.

So, I taught the three-hour seminar, and let me tell you, I had more attendees in that one class than I had ever had before. Although the class was held virtually in the summer of 2020, I could feel the tension of the attendees emanating from my laptop. The participants were nervous, and I was too, because if I said the wrong thing, if I didn't get my point across correctly, then more writers might go out in the world not understanding why writing an identity not your own is a big task, one that takes responsibility and care to achieve.

When I started editing *Half Outlaw* with my editor at Blackstone Publishing in 2021, I had already taught the seminar quite a few times for a variety of writing workshop companies, organizations, and private writing groups. As I taught the class more frequently, I couldn't help but examine how I'd portrayed characters who were Indigenous, gay, Black, Asian, or Latine, and/or who had disabilities, or substance use disorders. Had I done it correctly? I owed it to those characters and readers who were of those identities to write those characters with the respect and care they deserved.

I had two months to edit my *Half Outlaw* characters, to catch any stereotypes and tropes that had unconsciously made their way into the text. Friends and colleagues were surprised when I told them how stressed and anxious I was editing the book. I heard "But you're Mexican American, Mixed, Latina, a woman with a lot of connections to historically marginalized communities. In your job, you talk about diversity all the time; surely you won't make a mistake."

This is a problematic mindset, because these friends and colleagues assumed that because I identify with historically marginalized identities, I'm free of biases or privilege—and I'm not. No one is.

I know this to be true because I found mistakes in my manuscript. I found stereotypes and colonized language; I found instances of othering and unconscious bias. With a laser-eyed focus, I found these mistakes and I fixed them. I'm sure I didn't catch them all, because if I've learned anything, it's that there might be some mistakes still in the text that even my obsessive editing could not catch—or that my editors and sensitivity reader did not notice (because they're humans who make mistakes and have biases too). There might even be mistakes in the text that won't be apparent to me until five or ten years from now, when we've gained new insights and education on identity—and I had to be okay with that.

During the editing process of *Half Outlaw*, I utilized all the information that I had gathered for my three-hour class presentation on writing other identities, but I quickly realized that it wasn't enough. I needed more information on certain aspects of writing an identity not your own, so I had to go and find it. By the time I was done, I realized that editing my novel would have been a lot easier if I'd had a checklist, a guide, or even a writing craft book on the subject that I could reference.

The idea of creating my own guide or writing a craft book on writing identities not your own was something that I had thought about in the past. The thought first came about when I taught the class and students asked for reading suggestions on the subject. I couldn't find a craft book that spoke in-depth about a range of historically marginalized identities and had been published within the last five years.

Every time the conversation about authors writing other identities poorly came up on social media, at literary festivals, at conferences, and in online panels, I thought, "Wouldn't it be nice if we had something to refer to when talking about writing other identities? Something that cleared up some of this confusion? Or a book we could push toward writers and publishers and say, 'Start reading, hon'?"

I don't know exactly what made me go to my literary agent and say I wanted to write this book. My friend recently told me she thought the subject of writing identities intrigued me, and rather than move forward without any direction, I sought to name, identify, and get as many concrete answers on the subject as I could. I think she was right.

I'm tired of us giving fifteen minutes to this subject during a writing panel or no time at all in an MFA program's creative writing class. I want us to talk about writing other identities, and not just in a state of frustration after another novel that gets it wholly wrong has been published. Let's get ahead of the problem. Maybe we can start with a writing craft book.

I'll begin this book by saying that I acknowledge that all writers have and/or will write an identity other than their own. It's likely you've written a character with a different gender identity, age, or career. You may have done well in some aspects of that process, and not so well in others. This book, however, is meant to focus on writers who want to write characters with historically marginalized identities and/or communities (or at the very least, writers who want to write about a world where those identities and communities exist).

Writing other identities is a polarizing topic in the literary sphere. I know many people will not like that I have written this book. Some will be upset or angry at me, ironically for different reasons. Some will say that by writing this book I have given indiscriminate permission to people to write other identities. Others will say that I'm a "politically correct" millennial who is making too big a deal out of nothing, that anyone can write any identity without "rules." Some will feel that these tips and tricks will elevate privileged creative writers over writers of historically marginalized identities. And still, some others will be thankful for some guidance.

To be honest, I have mixed feelings on this subject too. (Trust me, there were a few times during the writing process of this book when I thought, "Why the hell did you take this on, Alex?")

So, here are my current thoughts: I believe people can write characters of different identities, including historically marginalized identities, but I don't think many writers are equipped to do so. Let's say they have the writing knowledge or skills to take on that task—I don't think many writers succeed in doing it well, at least not without creating problematic representations, including their own unconscious biases in the characterization and text, and/or developing a stereotypical and harmful trope storyline.

I'm always amazed by how many published authors continue to publish book after book with problematic portrayals or storylines and don't ever seem to fix their mistakes—even when the literary community offers considerable feedback on the topic. Which brings me to my next point: the people who allow these stories to continue to be published—editors, literary agents, and publishing staff—are also wholly uninformed on how to write or edit identities not their own.

All of this has ultimately resulted in a long and ugly cycle of problematic pieces entering the world—and I'm over it. I've amassed a lot of knowledge on this subject over the years, and I want to share it with my fellow creative writers and industry professionals so they can do better and we can stop harming historically marginalized identities with creative works that disseminate stereotypes and problematic depictions.

Even as I share this information with you, I want to be clear that publishers should be publishing more work by authors who are writing about their own identities. For instance, there shouldn't be more published books by white authors that feature mostly characters of color and/or protagonists of color than those written by authors of color themselves. That's a problem—one that authors of privileged backgrounds need to be mindful of because it directly affects authors of historically marginalized backgrounds in ways they wouldn't expect.

Here's an example: Years ago, a publisher randomly reached out to ask me to read, for free, a new manuscript by a white author who had received poor coverage in the past for misrepresenting Latine cultures and communities. It took me two weeks to craft a response to the publisher explaining why it was a great initiative to get a sensitivity reader for this author, yet the manner in which they were going about it was wrong, to say the least.

The publisher didn't want to pay me for a job that sensitivity readers get paid to do, and yet they wanted me, a Latine writer, to expend my energy for a white woman I did not know, who was writing about my identity and had done so incorrectly in the past. If I gave my stamp of approval or suggestions to fix the piece, the author would get a new book deal with a large advance and the publisher would make money, but I, the Latine writer, would get nothing.

My thoughts on writing identities not your own may change on a day-to-day basis, but I know that writers will write characters with identities other than their own, and if they're going to do it, they should have a guidebook that teaches them to make fewer mistakes. At the very least, a guidebook would not allow writers, literary agents, editors, or publishers the excuse of "Well, I didn't know. There's no guidebook on this topic." I also hope a book like this shows literary agents and editors why it's so beneficial to work with authors of historically marginalized identities who are writing about their own identities.

Before you begin reading this book and working through the exercises, I want you to move forward with one thing in mind: You're going to make mistakes in this process. You're going to get something wrong. Accept it. However, you might get some things right. You might do the hard work that this journey will require. You might become more aware of your biases, which will allow you to dismantle them and become a better person, if not a better writer. You might learn what it means to be an ally and an accomplice in the fight to increase diversity, inclusion, and representation in creative writing. You might write stories that are as inclusive and representative as the world around you. The only way that is going to happen is if you put in the hard work.

This is not something that you practice for some years and become an expert in. It's a lifetime commitment. Realistically, you might not ever get it right. It might not be a success. You might have to put the story that features characters of marginalized identities in the back of your desk drawer because it could cause more harm than good in the world. That's okay too.

Whatever you decide to do, I am glad that you are reading this book (hopefully thoroughly) and using it in a way that I hope you do—as a guide that you refer to over and over throughout your writing process. I hope you share it with other writers and help them understand why we should be extremely mindful of how we write characters with different identities from our own. I hope you have more conversations on this subject with fellow writers.

Once again, I hope you remind yourself repeatedly that mistakes will be made because you're human. Accept them, claim them, own up to them, and do the work necessary to better yourself as a writer and a human, because that's the least we can do.

SECTION ONE

BEFORE YOU WRITE

1

IDENTITY

Years ago, I was going through a box of things from my childhood when I found a stack of drawings I had done of a little brown girl and her white, blond-haired, blue-eyed mother. The drawings dated to when I was between the ages of three and six.

Holding those drawings in my hand, I couldn't help but think of how early I'd recognized the differences between my mother and me. Perhaps I shouldn't have been surprised. I have had to defend my Mixed identity for as long as I can remember. "That's not your mom. She's white," was said too many times for me to count.

Identity has been something that I've been thinking about since I was a child. You have to when you're a brown-skinned Mixed girl who always has to explain why she looks more like her Mexican American father and her light-skinned Mixed brother looks more like their white mother. Race and ethnicity were not the only identity dynamics that played a role in my childhood.

In my late teens, my brother would come out as queer, but before that, there was my sister and her identity. Tiffany is my father's first daughter, a Mexican American woman who was born with tuberous sclerosis, which played a role in her having physical and intellectual disabilities and being unable to communicate through language or hand gestures.

Tiffany's inability to communicate with language or hand gestures meant that my family and I had to learn to read her subtle body language to know what she needed. My sister simply scratching her ear could mean she has an ear infection. How long she stares at me could tell me whether she is thirsty or if she wants to lie down. To help take care of her, I had to ask myself all sorts of questions: Is she hungry? Is something about her wheelchair making her uncomfortable? Is she too hot or cold? Is that bug bite on her arm itchy, and does she need an ointment for it?

At the same time that I was learning my sister's form of communication through body language, I asked other questions about what was going on in her mind and heart to learn more about the girl she was and the woman she became. How does it feel for her to be in a wheelchair and pushed around by other people? What makes her laugh? Does she need a hug? What does she think about the world she lives in? Does it annoy her that people talk around her and not to her? What scares her? What makes her happy?

I didn't realize it as a child, but not everyone was asking these sorts of questions about my sister—much less about other people who may have a different disability, racial or ethnic background, sexual orientation, nationality, class, or body type. After a while, the questions that I had for my sister began to form for other people. I wanted to know how they thought, what they felt, and their experiences, so I began to ask others to tell me about the things I couldn't possibly know about them. I asked about their past, the happiest and saddest moments in their lives, why they did the things they did, and what it was like for them to move about in the world.

Those questions that I asked myself as a little girl about my own racial/ethnic identity, that of my family's multiculturality, and my siblings' various identities, in some way led me to ask a big question: How do we write other identities?

WHAT IS IDENTITY?

When it comes to defining identity, I've always been partial to the following definition in *Psychology Today*: "Identity encompasses the memories, experiences, relationships, and values that create one's sense of self. This amalgamation creates a steady sense of who one is over time, even as new facets are developed and incorporated into one's identity."[1]

I like how the writers of *Psychology Today* see identity as something that's created over time from our memories, experiences, relationships, and values. They hint to the fact that identity can be fluid and ultimately results in our sense of self.

The social and political systems of the society we live in also play a role in the shaping of our identities. The world defines us, and that definition may differ from or affect how we see ourselves or the way we are perceived by others. Ultimately the concept of identity is not limited to a character's own perspective of themselves, but how others view them too.

The title of this book, *Writing an Identity Not Your Own*, is a bit of a misdirection because it indicates that you'll only be crafting a character who has one identity that differs from you. The reality is, you'll likely be creating a character or characters who have many different identities from your own.

Below, I've written a short (but not exhaustive) list of the different types of identities that you will likely consider when developing a character:

- Race and Ethnicity
- Gender Identity
- Sexual and Romantic Orientation
- Disability
- Age/Generation
- Origin
- Location
- Political Beliefs
- Religious Beliefs
- Culture
- Relationship Status
- Family
- Nationality
- Class

If you've ever written a creative writing piece, I'd wager you've already tried your hand at writing a character with a different background. Maybe it was an identity you felt more comfortable with, like class or political beliefs. Even if you have the same race or gender identity, your character could be older or younger, have different religious beliefs, or have been born in a different place than you. There is ultimately no way to avoid writing other identities, unless you create a piece of work in which every character has every single identity you do. What a rare piece of work that would be.

HISTORICALLY MARGINALIZED IDENTITIES

Most of you have picked up this book because you want to learn how to craft a character with a historically marginalized identity.

According to the National Collaborating Centre for Determinants of Health at St. Francis Xavier University in Nova Scotia, historically marginalized populations are defined as "groups and communities that experience discrimination and exclusion (social, political, and economic) because of unequal power relationships across economic, political, social, and cultural dimensions."[2]

To be Black, queer, transgender, a woman, or have a disability is to be part of a historically marginalized identity. These are but a few examples, but we know these to be historically marginalized identities because there are countless studies, histories, and first-person accounts that prove that these populations of people have historically been marginalized—whether that's in relation to economic status, by the passage of discriminatory laws, or through societal exclusion.

THIS IS AN EMOTIONAL JOURNEY

When I say that writing an identity other than your own is a "journey," it's because "journey" is the best word I can think of to describe what you're about to experience. You're starting out in a place where you may know some things about writing other identities—like how stereotypes and stock characters are bad—but there is still so much to learn.

This book may break down what you think you know about writing other identities. It may tell you that you've made major mistakes in the past, or it may reinforce what you already know. (Writing the book did both for me!) This book will challenge you to think about identity in ways that you haven't thought about before. Likely, it will help you confront your biases and better understand your prejudices, and how they may appear in your work.

Reading this book and incorporating the suggestions I've provided into your work will not be an easy task, and it will likely cause different emotions to arise. Let yourself feel uncomfortable, embarrassed, awful, angry, sad, confused, upset, whatever it may be. Take many breaks from reading this book if necessary. However, I ask that you please not throw this book aside.

I can't guarantee that by reading this book and learning these skills, you will get to your desired destination—the ability to write other identities well. You may get lost a time or two or never reach your goal. Or perhaps you will. The journey is equally as important as getting to the destination, and no matter what, you'll learn a lot about yourself, identity, and writing along the way.

"THIS PROCESS IS OVERKILL AND IT'S STIFLING MY CREATIVITY"

I'm aware that there will be people who pick up this book and say the likes of:

"She wants us to do too much. I'm going to use some of the advice and ignore the rest," or even perhaps "This is stifling my creativity."

Throughout this book I will continually say, "This is not an easy task and not all writers will be able to write a character with an identity not their own." If you are a writer who does not want to undergo this process, then don't. Own your decision when and if an editor says you have a problematic scene, a literary agent doesn't feel comfortable moving forward with a storyline, your readers leave negative Goodreads or Amazon reviews, book bloggers analyze your book for stereotypes and tropes, or you read your book ten years from now and feel bad that it contributed to harmful representations.

Some of this may happen. None of it may happen. I'm writing this book to help end the cycle of harmful representation first and foremost, but if I can help writers not have to go through these situations—I'd like that too. It's up to you on what you want to do.

I expect many writers will read this book and feel like I'm stifling their creativity. Yes, I will ask you to change your writing process, edit your work more than you ever have, use different words, describe your characters in ways you might not initially describe them, and write alternative scenes. I will challenge you to do better. It's not necessarily fun.

This book is not meant to stifle creativity but to open your eyes to how you've written in the past and how you can write in the future. It'll provide you with more creative tools and encourage you to get out of your comfort zone and try new ways of approaching a storyline, a scene, a character, and an identity. It may ask you to kill your darlings, but any good writer knows that we must let go of things that do not work for the story—and harmful representations, stereotypes, tropes, and biases will not benefit your work in the long run. This is a challenging process, one that I hope will help you to grow and improve as a writer.

Again—if you don't want to use this book, then don't. When and if you're asked about your decision to represent other identities in your work, own your choices and take the feedback you receive from the literary community with grace.

2

UNINTENTIONALLY WRITING A PROBLEMATIC PIECE

Memoirs of a Geisha by Arthur Golden is a tale about a Japanese geisha named Chiyo/Sayuri who lives and works in the Gion district of Kyoto, Japan, in the 1930s and 1940s. The story follows Sayuri from her childhood, through her years as a geisha, and ends with Sayuri reuniting with her "true love," the Chairman, and moving to the United States with him.

By the time I got to graduate school, I had read *Memoirs of a Geisha* a few times and watched the film, but something about it nagged at me. With the help of research by others and a deeper look at the text, I learned how writing an identity not your own can result in a problematic piece—one that a writer did not set out to intentionally write.

Not only did Golden write Sayuri's story in a way that describes Asia and its cultures through a Eurocentric and white Western lens, Golden exoticized Sayuri's Japanese culture and her experience as a geisha. Sayuri makes comments throughout the novel that portray Japan and its culture as abnormal and immoral, especially when compared to that of the U.S., a country that is described in a more positive light and as having a "richer" culture.

For instance, Sayuri uses certain terms like "slavery" and "mistress" to describe her experience as a geisha, terms that Japanese people would likely not use (especially at that time). In the U.S., such terms are more impactful to readers because of our history and culture. By having Sayuri use these words, Golden distances the Japanese culture and country from the American reader and further paints Japan as this foreign, mysterious, and immoral country with "exotic" practices.

If all that wasn't enough, Golden fashioned the novel as a Cinderella story with Sayuri as Cinderella and the Chairman as the prince. This is not a typical story trope in Japanese literature, but a Western trope used to romanticize the geisha life and make it "consumer friendly" for the American reader.

The best proof of this novel being a primary example in

exoticization came after *Memoirs of a Geisha* was published and a geisha named Mineko Iwasaki, whom Golden had interviewed, sued Golden for using falsified details concerning her experience as a geisha. She claimed that the coming-of-age ceremony for geisha known as mizuage had been incorrectly portrayed by Golden as selling a geisha's virginity to the highest bidder. Iwasaki went on to publish her own autobiography to try to reverse the negative effects of Golden's novel.

Golden, a white American man, argued that the book was based on his interview with Iwasaki, his experience living in Kyoto during the 1960s and 1970s, and extensive research on geisha life in the 1930s and 1940s. Despite all his research and even his experiences living in Kyoto, there is too much evidence that shows that Golden wrote an entire novel that exoticized the Japanese and geisha culture and he seemed to do so without realizing it.

Memoirs of a Geisha was published in 1999, during a time when awareness around writing other identities wasn't widely discussed. Because neither Golden nor his editors recognized the harmful portrayals in the book, it became a widely popular, bestselling book—and still is today. It also led to a film that took Golden's problematic depictions and further disseminated them to new audiences.

Unfortunately, readers who pick up this book do not always realize or perceive the highly problematic depictions and exoticization of the main character and her culture. It took me a few reads and some thorough research to grasp the full extent of the misrepresentation in the novel. Almost three decades later, this misinformation, misrepresentation, and tropic story continues to permeate among readers.

Golden did extensive research for his novel and yet he

fell into the trap of exoticization among many other stereo-typical forms of writing. Why? If I had to wager, I'd guess that Golden was not aware of his unconscious biases prior to writing *Memoirs of a Geisha*. So that is where we will start—with biases.

DEFINING UNCONSCIOUS BIAS AND BIAS BLOCKS

One of the best definitions for unconscious bias comes from the University of California San Francisco: "Unconscious bi-ases are social stereotypes about certain groups of people that individuals form outside their own conscious awareness. Everyone holds unconscious beliefs about various social and identity groups, and these biases stem from one's tendency to organize social worlds by categorizing."[1]

In other words, biases are something that we are not con-sciously aware of having. They are unconscious beliefs about certain groups of people and identities that have formed through humanity's need to organize and categorize our so-cial world. We form these unconscious biases from child-hood onward. Our parents, schools, places of worship, social groups, and the era we grew up in impacted the way we think about our own and other identities. As we grew older, these unconscious biases continued to exist in our minds and were reinforced, impacted, or added to by personal experiences or a lack thereof, as well as educational pursuits, the changing of times, new people who entered our lives, and more.

In 2002, the term "bias blind spot" was coined by researchers Emily Pronin, Daniel Lin, and Lee Ross at Stanford University.[2] Over the years, it has become a more widely understood phenomenon by many.

Study.com defines blind spots as "things that are overlooked systematically, either intentionally or subconsciously."[3] This means that even if you are aware of your unconscious bias, there still may exist a bias blind spot, an incorrect belief, judgment, or portrayal that you do not see as being biased, despite it being so. The bias blind spot is much harder to recognize and is the most dangerous to your writing.

Because "blind spot" is an ableist term, I will not be using it throughout the rest of this book. Instead, I'll call it a "bias block," and for all intents and purposes, it will have the same definition as the term "blind spot."

To reiterate, the writer's definition of a bias block is a difficult-to-recognize unconscious belief about certain groups of people that can appear in your portrayal of a character, in your discussion of a certain identity, in an overall storyline dialogue, setting, and more.

WHO HAS UNCONSCIOUS BIAS AND BIAS BLOCKS?

After I wrote my third novel, I sent it to a few different people to gather critiques, suggestions, and feedback. My protagonist was sexually attracted to people of all gender identities, and I had a scene in which she has sex with a woman. I wanted someone who had a similar sexual orientation to read my book and see if I'd portrayed my main character's sexual interaction with a woman authentically. Through my literary agent, I found a beta reader to whom I had given feedback on their novel the year before. They could personally relate to my protagonist's sexual orientation, so I was very excited when they agreed to read my manuscript.

There was a scene in my novel in which my protagonist goes to the home of a woman she meets at a bar to have sex. During the scene, my first-person narrator explains how she came to sleep with people of all gender identities, despite growing up in the 1500s when the Catholic Church and societal norms villainized non-heteronormative relationships.

When I received the manuscript from the beta reader, they made a note about a single line in that section of the text.

My protagonist had said the following: "As a cursed woman, it didn't take long for me to slough off the restraints of human moralities, the Church, and social norms."

In a comment box, the beta reader wrote, "This is a little homophobic, but if that's the way you want the character to be, that's okay, too. It's not something straight people will pick up on as offensive, but queers will."

I looked at the line and at the beta reader's comment, then back at the line and the comment. I read the entire scene from start to finish. Offensive? I couldn't figure out what the beta reader meant. Did they think I was saying that the protagonist saw herself as cursed because she slept with women? That couldn't be. My main character was literally a cursed woman—cursed to never die because of a crime she'd committed centuries before. My beta reader understood that.

Over the course of the next three days, I returned to that line and my beta reader's comment, trying to see what I could not see. Until, finally, I did. (I should have asked the beta reader to explain further, but I was determined to figure it out on my own. Don't be as stubborn as I was. Just ask.)

When my protagonist says that after she became a cursed woman she sloughed off "the restraints of human moralities, the Church, and social norms," she was indicating that freeing herself from the restraints of human moralities allowed her to sleep with women. In effect, my character was saying that to be queer was to be immoral.

I thought that I was portraying a five-hundred-year-old woman explaining how she was letting go of all the restrictions her church and society had placed on her. However, the way I wrote that line did not say what I wanted it to say. It sounded like I, a straight author, was having my queer protagonist believe that sleeping with different gender identities, including her own, was immoral. My character wouldn't say that, and I would never want to say that.

I don't believe that being queer is immoral. However, as a straight woman writing a WLW (woman-loving woman) protagonist, I found myself writing something I do not believe and did not intend to write. But I did. I was writing outside of my identity, and I made a mistake, a subtle one for sure, but one that the community I was writing about would recognize (and did recognize) as offensive. If I had not done my due diligence to get someone from the identity I was writing to read my work, that line could have gone to print one day and caused harm that I didn't want to cause.

Everyone has unconscious bias and bias blocks. I have them. You have them. We all have them, no matter our race, age, ethnicity, sexual orientation, gender identity, or any other type of identifier. It may be hard to admit or even accept, but it's one of the things that make us human.

Social conditioning—your parents, places of worship, schooling, the time period in which you grew up, the movies you watched—all worked together to inform your idea of people with different identities. At times, you might not be aware of these unconscious biases or how they impact your behavior.

Bias comes in many forms, and for creative writers, it most definitely appears in our work, and not always in the ways we expect. It might appear in a single line, phrase, characterization, dialogue, description, or in the overall storyline that runs through the length of a novel. For me, it was a small section of a single line, and when it was pointed out, it took me days to see what I'd done wrong because I have bias blocks like everyone else.

It's at this point that some writers may ask themselves: If I write something unconsciously biased, does that make me a bad person, someone who is racist, homophobic, xenophobic, sexist, or discriminatory in some other way?

Joseph L. Graves Jr. and Alan H. Goodman, authors of *Racism Not Race: Answers to Frequently Asked Questions*, wrote in their book, "A single act does not make you a racist. As Ibram Kendi says, we all do racist stuff. For our culture, that is a norm. The point is to be more aware and, we hope, move from more to less."[4]

While the authors may be talking about race specifically, we can apply it to all forms of biases. We all have biases, but our integrity as writers—and humans—is determined by whether we seek them out and what we do when we realize them.

Unconscious biases and bias blocks can be recognized and broken down bit by bit. It will take a lot of work, self-reflection, self-education, and self-editing, but in doing so, you will be better equipped to write an identity different from your own.

HOW TO RECOGNIZE YOUR UNCONSCIOUS BIASES AND BIAS BLOCKS

They say there is a test for everything, and maybe there is, because, you guessed it, there is a test to recognize your biases, and it is called the Implicit Association Test, or the IAT.

Developed by Harvard researchers, the IAT "measures the strength of associations between concepts (e.g., Black people, gay people) and evaluations (e.g., good, bad) or stereotypes (e.g., athletic, clumsy)."[5]

The IAT is a good start toward understanding certain biases, but unfortunately it is not so thorough that it can inform you of all your biases. That will require work on your part.

Begin your bias recognition journey by taking the IAT test:

To begin recognizing your unconscious bias and bias blocks, start by reflecting on your childhood and what your parents, school, and social activities (places of worship, athletics, clubs, etc.) told you pointedly or subtly about other communities and identity groups. Did you live in a neighborhood that was diverse in terms of race and class, or did you grow up in a bubble with people who had similar experiences as you? Did the leaders at your place of worship preach negative viewpoints about queer people or share sexist messages about how "women should adhere to male family members"? Consider how you were shaped as a child to believe certain things that informed your behavior or words as a teen, young adult, and adult.

From there, examine the media—TV, film, podcasts, books, social media—you consume, and diversify it. Seek out voices that are different from your own within different forms of media. For instance, if you want to diversify the TV shows you watch, look at their showrunners and producers. Are they people with different identities from yours? Do the actors have different identities from yours? Does the show depict life experiences that you did not have? Do the writers and actors have the same lived experiences as the identity presented? Creators who portray their own identities—whether it's through writing or acting—can bring a more realistic and usually accurate perspective to a show (or any kind of media) and that makes an immeasurable difference.

Through the consumption of diversified media, you will begin to slowly see how your perception of certain communities differs from what you are watching, reading, or listening to. Such moments can be a great jumping-off point when it comes to dismantling your biases.

At the same time, you can learn about the history and current social structures that contribute to unconscious bias across communities. This includes educating yourself on things like racism, sexism, anti-LGBTQIA+ initiatives, the patriarchy, and institutional discrimination.

The best way to dismantle your biases is to expand your network to include more individuals with different identities. We know that stories are powerful in changing minds,[6] and what better way to learn about different identities and change your perception of other people than to hear their stories?

BEWARE OF CONFIRMATION BIAS

As you go through the process of dismantling your unconscious biases and recognizing your bias blocks, be careful that you do not unwittingly or wittingly commit confirmation bias.

In an article in *The New Yorker*, writer Elizabeth Kolbert wrote that confirmation bias is "the tendency people have to embrace information that supports their beliefs and reject information that contradicts them."[7]

If you have the belief that all gay men are effeminate and you only seek out information that showcases this idea, you are confirming your own bias. To an extent, you're trying to make yourself feel good about having certain beliefs and preventing yourself from realizing and/or admitting that you are wrong. This is reductive and does not help you in the process of writing other identities.

WILL I EVER BE FREE OF UNCONSCIOUS BIAS OR BIAS BLOCKS?

It's unlikely that you'll ever be free of any form of unconscious bias or bias blocks, which means that you'll have to be diligent in the writing and editing process for every piece of work you produce and wish to share with the world.

You are not alone on this journey. Every writer, no matter who they are, no matter their identity, is (or should be) going through the same thing.

CAN I WRITE SOMETHING THAT IS 100 PERCENT FREE OF ANY PROBLEMATIC PORTRAYALS, STEREOTYPES, OR BIASES?

There is a lot of fear among writers who want to go on this journey of writing an identity not their own. "What if I make a mistake and get crucified on social media?" I can't lie—that may happen. It's not an experience that anyone wants to go through, but it's a reality that all creatives might face when they put their work out in the world.

I was fearful when I was editing *Half Outlaw* (and writing this book!), but I tried to look at that fear as a tool to push me to get outside of my comfort zone and do the hard work necessary to write other identities well.

While it is not my intent to assuage all your fears, you could follow this guide to a tee and still make mistakes in terms of problematic portrayals, inclusions of stereotypes or harmful tropes, biased perspectives, and more. You are human and you will make mistakes—as will beta and sensitivity readers, literary agents, and editors. Those mistakes may not be realized until after something has been published.

If you make a mistake, own it, fix it, and try your damnedest not to do it again. That is within your control. None of us can control the feedback we receive from the literary community about our work—whether it is about the plot or a depiction of an identity not our own. That is what comes with being a published writer. I wrote this book to help you on this journey, to make it a safe space to explore this topic and learn about it in all its facets. Read this guide all the way through, try your hand at the exercises and suggestions, and you'll come away having learned something.

EXERCISE

Start your bias recognition process with a quick and easy activity. It's sometimes called the "Circle of Trust," but no matter what you call it, this activity may bring some of your unconscious biases to the forefront and encourage you to think further about how you approach writing identities not your own.

This exercise will not work unless you are honest about your answers. I should also mention that this exercise is usually done with a facilitator reading out the instructions, so do the exercise as you go. Reading ahead could affect the results.

Begin by filling out the following list for yourself. For instance, if you identify as a cisgender man, write "cisgender man" next to "Gender Identity."

- Gender Identity:
- Sexual and Romantic Orientation:
- Race/Ethnicity:
- Disabilities:
- Nationality:
- Age Group (Gen Z, Millennial, Gen X, Boomer, etc.):
- Class:
- Religion:
- Political Views:
- Education Level:

On another piece of paper, list at least seven people whom you trust the most. These people cannot be family members.

List them vertically (on the y-axis) on the left side of the paper. At the top of the paper (on the x-axis), horizontally list the following categories: Gender Identity, Sexual and Romantic Orientation, Race/Ethnicity, Disabilities, Nationality, Age Group, Class, Religion, Political Views, and Education Level.

Your paper should look like this:

	Gender Identity	Sexual and Romantic Orientation	Race/Ethnicity	Disabilities	Nationality	Age Group	Class	Religion	Political Views	Education Level
Person #1										
Person #2										
Person #3										
Person #4										
Person #5										
Person #6										
Person #7										

Next to each name, place a check mark if they have the same gender identity, sexual orientation, race/ethnicity, disabilities, nationality, age group, class, religion, political views, and education level as you. For instance, if you are a white person, you will place a check mark next to all the individuals who are also white.

Now look at the chart. What do you notice? How different—in terms of identity—are the most trusted people within your inner circle? Do they have backgrounds that are like yours?

Most people tend to have a group of trusted friends who have similar identities, appearances, and interests to their own. This is called affinity or in-group bias; in other words, it's an unconscious preference for people who have similar backgrounds to yours. In-group or affinity bias can also contribute to the development of unconscious negative biases toward people who are seen as being part of the "out group." In other words, people with different identities.

Let's think about how that could play out in your creative approach to writing characters of different identities. Here are some questions to ask yourself:

- In looking at this chart, what is your perceived "in group"? Once you've determined the perceived in group, can you determine what the perceived out group might be?
- How might being part of your in group contribute to unconscious biases about other identities?
- Do any of the people in your trusted circle have an identity that you wish to write that is not your own? How might having more personal connections to

people of that identity help you better write other identities?

- Do you have zero close, personal connections to the identity you wish to write? What kinds of obstacles might that produce in your writing journey?

3

THE "BEFORE YOU WRITE" CHECKLIST

STEP 1: READ CREATIVE WORKS BY AUTHORS OF THE IDENTITY YOU WISH TO WRITE

Cynthia Leitich Smith, author and citizen of the Muscogee Nation, once said:

> Before trying to write any character outside one's
> lived experience, I recommend reading at least 100

books by authors from that community . . . to start. It sounds daunting. It should be daunting. But it's only a foothold. An opportunity to begin shrugging off societal misconceptions and miseducation. A way to more fully consider an authentic perspective rather than rushing to regurgitate bite-sized nuggets of misrepresentation.[1]

Leitich Smith's advice is a good starting point for writing an identity different from your own, as it forces you to audit your physical and digital libraries to see how much you've invested in the stories of the people you wish to write about.

Go ahead, audit your library now. Have you read fiction, nonfiction, poetry, screenplays, or other types of creative works by authors of the identity you wish to write? Not nearly enough? Make a list and get to reading. If you want to write about other authors' identities, at the very least, support them, buy their books, review their work, highlight them on social media—be their allies.

> Do you want to portray Chicano/a/x characters? Check out this website: A Visual History of Chicano/a/x Literature. This amazing resource lists books written by Chicano/a/x authors that were published from 1610 to present day.[2]
>
>

STEP 2: RESEARCH OTHER FORMS OF MEDIA

Books should be the first step in your research, but not the last. Dive into historical and cultural research about the community that you hope to represent, as well as their personal narratives. Here are different forms of media you can seek out:

- Articles
- Scientific studies
- Autobiographies
- Recordings
- Essays
- Films
- Documentaries
- Photographs
- Music
- YouTube videos
- Social media accounts
- Podcasts

Always research your sources. Who created the source? For what purpose? When was it created, and is it out of date? Is it full of biases or stereotypes? Does it confirm a bias that you have about the community, and if so, can you find something that offers a different perspective?

> Book influencers who identify with a historically marginalized background are a great resource in your journey to

writing an identity not your own. Not only do they share extensive reading lists that feature authors of historically marginalized identities, but many of them break down problematic depictions and misrepresentations in creative works in ways that are easy to understand. The more you see how writers make mistakes and the ways in which they make them, the better you can recognize them in your own work.

In the past, I've heard writers make negative comments about book influencers, concluding that they're "bitter readers who don't write" and thus are unable to offer in-depth analytical feedback about creative pieces and how well an author portrays other identities. A mindset like this will not benefit you on your writing journey and is likely an insecure response to having to face your own biases. Book influencers read widely and those who identify with historically marginalized communities have personal information and insight that could be helpful to you in the future. You never know what kind of useful feedback they might offer.

STEP 3: BUILD AUTHENTIC RELATIONSHIPS

How can you write a character with an identity not your own unless you intimately know someone of that identity?

In the early 1990s, James Ransome was asked at a conference for the Cooperative Children's Book Center why he hadn't illustrated any books with Native American characters and his response was so poignant: "I haven't held their babies."[3]

If you haven't built a strong enough relationship with someone in the community that you wish to portray—to the point that they'd let you hold their babies—then why should they trust you with their story?

Forging meaningful bonds with community members of the identity you are going to write is the most important step in the entire prewriting process. These must be two-way relationships, ones in which the other person is comfortable sharing personal details with you. This is not an interviewer-interviewee relationship (though that can be an additional step in your research and writing process), nor should this be an associate who you only see at work, a place of worship, mutual friends' parties, and sporting events, who has never invited you to a dinner party or an important moment in their life like a birthday or a funeral.

Investment in the community is necessary because it ensures that writers understand what's at stake if they exploit historically marginalized communities and/or further stereotypes through their work.

EXERCISE

In Alexander Chee's 2019 *Vulture* article, "How to Unlearn Everything When It Comes to Writing the 'Other,' What Questions Are We Not Asking?" he shares a small anecdote between himself and one of his students:

> I once advised a young white writer who believed that because she had loved a novel written by a writer from a certain background that she, too, could write about a family from that background. Her country had colonized this country, but a condition of being a colonizer is that you do not know the country you are taking possession of, or the culture—you don't have to. I knew the questions this student still had to answer because I knew people from this community. I had to draw her attention to everything she didn't know. She seemed resentful throughout.[4]

The line "I had to draw her attention to everything she didn't know" is particularly profound because it makes a good point about what we know and don't know in relation to our characters. This chapter's exercise is inspired by that one line.

The "Know vs. Don't Know" exercise is meant to help you discover what things you still don't know about the identity of your character. The results will hopefully guide you toward the kind of research you still need to do.

Set up a graph as shown on the following page. Under each column, answer the questions as you see fit (as a list or in full sentences).

KNOW	DON'T KNOW
What do you know about your character's identity? In terms of history? Socially? Culturally?	What are you unsure about or uncomfortable writing as it relates to your character's identity?
How does your character's identity present when it is intersected with their other identities like class, age, etc.?	What are historical, social, and cultural aspects of the identity that you know nothing about?
What harsh realities may a person from that identity face because of their identity?	What are the tropes, stereotypes, and clichés relating to your character? As they relate to your literary genre?
What are some of the beautiful elements relating to a person from that identity?	Do you understand how institutional discrimination affects people of your character's identity?

After you've developed your graph, take some time to look at it. In the "Know" column, are you confident in your answers? Are they limited in scope? Can you point to where you got your answers? Are they something that you've gathered from TV, film, your family, or your upbringing? Or were these answers obtained from books written by authors of that identity, scientific studies, and essays in the *Atlantic*? Are your answers biased?

There may be some aspects on the "Know" column that you will need to add to the "Don't Know" column until you do additional research. Once you've critiqued your answers, determine what else you need to research as it relates to your character. Then make a written plan as to how you can better understand those topics or gather more insight on your character's community.

SECTION TWO

AS YOU WRITE

4

CHARACTERIZATION

In college, I wrote a short story set in the early twentieth century at a psychiatric hospital in East Texas. There were two main characters—a Black janitor and a Mexican woman who had intellectual and physical disabilities. The two formed an unlikely bond in the hospital cafeteria one day over music. In addition to these two main characters, there was a third villainous character, best described as a Nurse Ratched type.

When I first wrote the short story, it was clear that the plot was

stronger than the characterization. The two main characters—
who had very different marginalized identities than my own—
fell a little flat. When I started to rework the piece, I tried to
focus on the characters' backgrounds and histories, and how
their marginalized identities would be perceived by others and
would affect them in their personal experience.

Arguably, the Black janitor was the lead protagonist because it was through his first-person account that the story
was told. I would need to inhabit his thoughts and emotions
and do something similar for the Mexican woman with physical and intellectual disabilities. My goal was to make these
characters feel authentic to the period, their situation, and
their identities. This was not as easy as I hoped it would be.

I quickly realized that I was not a strong enough writer to
write a main character who was a Black man in his forties in
the early twentieth century. So instead, I made the character
half Mexican, half Black, hoping that as a Mixed woman who
is half Mexican, I might be better able to inhabit his character
and characterize him in a more authentic way. That didn't work
either, and eventually, I made him fully Mexican, but I soon realized that his race was not my only, or biggest, concern.

I struggled with figuring out his motivation for connecting
with the Mexican woman with intellectual and physical disabilities, so I gave him a brother who had had intellectual disabilities and had died at a young age. What kind of message
did that send? Only people with siblings who had intellectual
disabilities would be more willing to connect with people who
have intellectual disabilities?

Then there was the Nurse Ratched character. She was clearly
a stock character—too evil, without nuance. And the woman
with disabilities? I felt like I had painted her as a victim in need

of saving and had her undergo traumatic experiences that were not well handled. I feared she was becoming a plot device to help the janitor work through the guilt he had about his younger brother's death. I worked on the short story for nine years, and as I look back on it now, I realize that the problems I was having with the characterization were directly bleeding into issues with the overall plot—admittedly a poorly written savior story with traumatic and stereotypical elements. The characterization directly affected the storyline and vice versa. I learned that if my characterization was poor and filled with misrepresentations and problematic portrayals, my storyline would be too.

I'm very glad that my story never made it out into the world and that I've let it die a deserved death on a hard drive that clutters my desk. Such a short story does not need to exist in the public sphere, as it would have contributed to all the things that I stand against.

I tell this story not because it's easy for me to (it isn't), but to showcase the importance of character building, especially as it relates to writing characters with historically marginalized identities. No matter if your character is a protagonist or a secondary or tertiary character, how you characterize them can impact your story in myriad ways, whether you intend it or not.

> You cannot "relax" on the characterization of a tertiary character any more than you can a protagonist. You will have to put in the same levels of effort toward authentically building out all characters of historically marginalized identities. Anything less could be disastrous.

THE MOST IMPORTANT THING: INTERSECTIONALITY

If you take one thing away from this book, it should be this: characters are not the sum of one singular identity—they are an amalgamation of many identities and experiences. This is called intersectionality.

Intersectionality as it relates to writing is how a character's different identities overlap, interconnect, combine, and intersect, resulting in a unique way in which the character perceives the world, and the world perceives them. That's confusing, I know, so let's break it down further.

Consider the idea of creating a character who is an Asian woman. When crafting the character, you can't just consider the woman's race—Asian—because her race is not the only identity that she inhabits. You must keep in mind her race and her gender identity and how both identities can affect her characterization. Now consider the stereotypes associated with those identities. There are stereotypes about Asian people (e.g., they are naturally intelligent) and stereotypes about women (e.g., they are better at parenting), and then there are stereotypes that are specific to Asian women (e.g., they are small and submissive).

Now let's throw some other identities into the mix. The Asian woman is specifically Chinese, bisexual, and hard of hearing. As the writer, you must consider what the perspective and experience would be for a hard-of-hearing bisexual Chinese woman—because it will be entirely different from that of a straight, abled Chinese woman or even an Indian cisgender man who is asexual and uses a wheelchair.

Writing with intersectionality in mind means knowing all your characters' identities from the most important to the most mundane, and figuring out how they intersect, combine, overlap, and ultimately come together to form a unique and believable character on the page. When we don't consider intersectionality, we run the risk of creating a stock character, or one that's stereotypical, cliché, inauthentic, or misrepresentative.

CHARACTERS ARE HUMAN

It can be a daunting task to write characters of different identities, especially when you start to dive into their personality, emotions, past, and what has shaped them into a complicated character. To help with this, I like to remind writers that their character is human and that like you, they may fall in love, have a family, a job, dreams, hopes, and fears. (Even if your character isn't human, I'd wager to guess that they have humanistic thoughts, beliefs, and behaviors.)

We know that humans are driven by their needs (food, drink, shelter, community, safety, and sex) and their emotions (love, joy, anger, grief, fear, etc.), so if you understand that a character's decisions and actions are usually based off a mix of emotions, logic, and needs, then you have a better chance of creating a fully formed character whose thoughts and actions make sense.

You may be different from your character in terms of race, sexual orientation, gender identity, disabilities, or nationality, but if you can remember that you and your character are both human, with similar human needs and wants, you'll have a starting point in the characterization process.

BASING CHARACTERS ON PEOPLE YOU KNOW

It's no secret that as writers, we tend to base characters on people we know. However, when it comes to writing characters of a different identity, be wary of basing those characters on real-life people with historically marginalized identities.

I've heard people say, "This is a true representation because I based it on someone I know." The problem with that? Our perception of people of historically marginalized identities is not free of our unconscious biases and bias blocks, especially if we haven't done consistent and long-term work to break free of those biased chains.

Basing a character on someone you know with a historically marginalized identity could result in you unknowingly creating a stereotypical or inauthentic character. If you don't recognize your bias about a certain community or identity, who is to say that your perception of the person you know in real life is not free of those biases? If that's the case, won't that appear in your characterization?

Even worse, what if the person that you based the character on recognizes themselves in your work and sees your representation of them as biased? What then? It could turn out terribly—read the 2021 *New York Times* feature by Robert Kolker, "Who Is the Bad Art Friend?" It's about one author basing a character on another writer, and while the author did not base the character on a person from a historically marginalized identity, the results were still disastrous.[1]

It is usually not a good idea to write yourself into the character of a different identity. By this, I mean, do not substitute one of your identities with a historically marginalized identity and say, "Ta-da! I've created a fictional character." For instance, if you are white and want a character to be Black, do not create a character that is like you in most senses except that they're Black. Doing so will generally lead to mischaracterization and misrepresentation. The way you move in the world is not the same way a Black person moves in the world, which means you'll likely add your own biases into the character's perspective, which would be inauthentic and misrepresentative.

OTHERING

Othering, as it relates to creative writing, is the process by which a writer presents a character in a way that they are perceived as an "other" or a member of the "out group," while the reader is a member of the "in group."

This happens when the writer places negative associations on the character's identity through their dialogue, behavior, or appearance. The writer creates so much space between the reader and the character that the reader is unable to connect with the character on a human level and sees the character and their identity as alien, odd, fantastical, and ultimately lesser than their own. Othering puts a massive wall between the reader and the character, creating an us-versus-them dynamic.

When writing an identity not your own, othering is a big concern because it can contribute to discrimination toward historically marginalized identities, including the spreading of stereotypes, tropes, and misrepresentation.

Othering is somewhat difficult to explain, and equally as difficult to recognize in our writing. When talking about this topic, writers might ask: Am I othering my character if my character is unlikeable? Not necessarily. You can have an unlikeable or unreliable character whose identity isn't being othered. And that's the key—othering occurs when you add negative associations to elements of their identity in such a way that readers see their own identities as right and the character and their identity as wrong.

A good example of othering occurs throughout a novel many of us had to read in school—*Heart of Darkness* by Joseph Conrad.

Let's take a look at this passage:

> We were wanderers on a prehistoric earth, on an
> earth that wore the aspect of an unknown planet. We
> could have fancied ourselves the first of men taking
> possession of an accursed inheritance, to be subdued at
> the cost of profound anguish and of excessive toil. But
> suddenly, as we struggled round a bend, there would be
> a glimpse of rush walls, of peaked grass-roofs, a burst of
> yells, a whirl of black limbs, a mass of hands clapping,
> of feet stamping, of bodies swaying, of eyes rolling,

under the droop of heavy and motionless foliage. The steamer toiled along slowly on the edge of a black and incomprehensible frenzy. The prehistoric man was cursing us, praying to us, welcoming us—who could tell? We were cut off from the comprehension of our surroundings; we glided past like phantoms, wondering and secretly appalled, as sane men would be before an enthusiastic outbreak in a madhouse. We could not understand because we were too far and could not remember because we were travelling in the night of first ages, of those ages that are gone, leaving hardly a sign—and no memories.[2]

In the passage above, Conrad describes Europeans on a steamboat going down the Congo River and the Africans they encounter. He refers to these Africans as "the prehistoric man" and removes their humanity and individuality by describing them as "a burst of yells, a whirl of black limbs, a mass of hands clapping . . ." Africans, in this scene, are made to seem alien, inhuman, odd, beastly—"a black and incomprehensible frenzy."

When an author others a group or another character, they do so by putting a wall between two groups, creating an us-versus-them dynamic. This is exceptionally clear in the final line of the passage: "We could not understand because we were too far and could not remember because we were travelling in the night of first ages."

The "we" that Conrad is referring to are not just the Europeans on the steamboat, but what he considers to be the "civilized" society of Europe, and the exact audience he intended to read his novel. In this way, he is saying that the Africans are so unlike himself, the West, "civilized society," and his readers, and therefore the readers cannot connect or understand Africans because they are "ahead" of them in terms of civilization. Conrad erects the wall in this way, resulting in a perfect example of othering.

Now, if you've read *Heart of Darkness*, you might say that this perspective of Africans was coming from the narrator, Marlow, and not Conrad himself. Author Chinua Achebe explains why this is not the case in an essay titled "An Image of Africa: Racism in Conrad's *Heart of Darkness*":

> It might be contended, of course, that the attitude to the African in *Heart of Darkness* is not Conrad's but that of his fictional narrator, Marlow, and that far from endorsing it, Conrad might indeed be holding it up to irony and criticism. Certainly, Conrad appears to go to considerable pains to set up layers of insulation between himself and the moral universe of his story. He has, for example, a narrator behind a narrator. The primary narrator is Marlow, but his account is given to us through the filter of a second, shadowy person. But if Conrad's intention is to draw a cordon sanitaire between himself and the moral and psychological malaise of his narrator, his care seems to me totally wasted because he neglects to hint however subtly or tentatively at an alternative frame of reference by which we may judge the actions and opinions of his characters. It would not have been beyond Conrad's power to make that provision if he had thought it necessary. Marlow seems to me to enjoy Conrad's complete confidence—a feeling reinforced by the close similarities between their careers.[3]

Conrad did nothing to show the reader that Marlow's perspective was not his own, which is another nail in the othering coffin.

The passage shared above, and many others like it in the novel, is a perfect example of othering and what *not* to do in your creative writing. The othering within *Heart of Darkness* contributed to the spreading of racist and colonialist thoughts about Africa and the people who lived there (as well as toward all Black people). This is why othering is such a dangerous thing in creative writing.

To prevent othering from occurring in your creative piece, you'll need to ground your characters (or the communities you are describing), humanize them, showcase their individuality, and develop their identities through the practice of intersectionality and authenticity. The more well-rounded, detailed, and complex your character, the better your readers can connect to them. Removing harmful stereotypes and tropes, negative associations, problematic plots, and stock characterization will help too.

MYTHS ASSOCIATED WITH WRITING CHARACTERS WITH HISTORICALLY MARGINALIZED IDENTITIES

Before we move forward, we need to remove any myths or misconceptions about writing characters of a different identity from your brain. Let's do that through a game of True or False.

True or False: You're more likely to be published if you have written characters who identify with a historically marginalized identity.

FALSE.

We don't have any research that showcases how many books have ever been published that feature characters with historically marginalized identities. What we know is that the New York Times *reported that between 1950 and 2018, 95 percent of all novels published were written by white authors,[4] and between 2019 and 2021, 76 percent of Penguin Random House's authors were white.[5] The identities of authors tend to reflect the characters they create, so it's unlikely that a majority of books in the past or even in recent times featured a majority of diverse characters in terms of race, disabilities, sexual orientation, or any other historically marginalized background.*

We also know that only 3.1 percent of the books that the Cooperative Children's Book Center (CCBC) received in 2019 featured an LGBTQIA+ main character, while 3.4 percent had a main character with a disability.[6] And from 2020 to 2021, WordsRated found that the percentage of Black characters decreased by 23 percent in children's bestsellers.[7]

In 2022, 39 percent of children's books that the Cooperative Children's Book Center received (which was a total of 3,450) featured a primary character of a historically marginalized race and 46 percent had significant content about historically marginalized races.[8] These statistics seem to show an improvement in terms of diversity in the children's book world. However, it should be noted that these statistics are limited by the number of books that the CCBC receives from authors and publishers, not the entirety of what the publishing industry publishes each year. There could be an argument made that the increase in BIPOC protagonists in children's books is because there has been some increase in BIPOC authorship (40 percent) who tend to write characters that reflect their own experiences.

All in all, I feel fairly confident in saying that writing a character with a historically marginalized identity is not going to increase your chances of getting published. The publishing industry is still primarily made up of white, cisgender, abled, and heteronormative employees, which is one of the reasons why a lack of diversity in creative writing exists. We only need to look to authors of historically marginalized identities who continue to discuss publishing's lack of interest in their stories that feature characters like themselves.

True or False: People of historically marginalized backgrounds are inherently better at writing a character of a different marginalized identity.

FALSE.

Having a historically marginalized identity does not make someone better at writing a character of a different historically marginalized background. Why? Because we all have biases and bias blocks, especially toward identities that are not our own. There is racism in the queer community, homophobia in many communities of color, and ableism across many groups. No one is free of biases.

True or False: I need to keep in mind all my characters' identities—not just their race—when trying to build them out.

TRUE.

Intersectionality is the key to creating a well-rounded character. We are not the sum of one identity, but an amalgamation of many. You must discover how the intersection of those identities affects your character.

True or False: A story with a character from a historically marginalized background needs to feature discrimination of some kind.

FALSE.

Yes, people of historically marginalized backgrounds face discrimination, but a story does not have to include discrimination to be realistic. In fact, a character of a marginalized background can face many other adversities relating to the human condition—losing a loved one, searching for a job, a breakup, or an argument with a friend—which would still make for a well-rounded story.

True or False: Not everything that happens to characters with historically marginalized identities will be or should be negative.

TRUE.

Have you heard the term "trauma porn"? It's sometimes called misery literature, and it refers to a type of writing that dwells on the trauma of a character. Trauma porn typically presents itself as a story in which a character faces harrowing trials and tribulations, particularly relating to physical, mental, emotional, or sexual abuse and destitution, rape, and torture.

If you write a story in which everything (or most things) that happens to a character with a historically marginalized identity is negative, it will likely result in trauma porn. Not only can this be triggering to readers who identify with that same historically marginalized community, it can look like you're exploiting the experiences of people from historically marginalized identities and playing on the emotions of the reader.

Ultimately, you want to aim for a story that is balanced. Yes, bad things may happen to your character, but not everything in their life will be negative. They need joy, hope, fun, and happiness. A balanced story makes for a more complex and authentic piece.

As a reminder—we would not typically consider the work of historically marginalized writers who write stories with characters that have their own identity to be trauma porn. If the writer should show their character going through harrowing trials and tribulations, it is likely because this is something they themselves could experience, and thus is not exploitative, but a personal connection.

EXERCISE

In this exercise, you are going to learn about your character of a different identity. You can choose to create a brand-new character or do the exercise with a character that's already part of a working draft. Fill out the following list as if your character were filling it out. Be as specific as possible.

- Name
- Age
- Birthday
- Gender identity
- Race and ethnicity
- Sexual and romantic orientation
- Physical description
- Health history
- Address and home type (house, apartment, mansion, houseboat, etc.)
- Previous addresses and home types
- Nationality
- Disabilities
- Relationship status and relationship history
- Family and family history
- Job
- Career goals
- Personal goals
- Hobbies
- Notable talents
- Closest friends
- Enemies

- Fears
- Insecurities
- Traumas
- Bad habits
- Religious beliefs
- Political stance
- Moral beliefs
- Favorite color
- Music interests
- Favorite TV shows, films, or genre of film and TV
- Favorite books

What did you discover about your character after filling out this list? What else do you need to learn about your character? How can knowing this information help you?

It's my hope that you realize there is more to your character than one or even two identities. You don't have to use all this information in your work. In fact, I doubt you'll use half of it. However, having this information on hand and keeping it in mind when crafting your character can help you to develop a more intersectional, complex, and dynamic person.

WRITING DISCRIMINATION

Sometimes when we speak about people with historically marginalized backgrounds, we focus on the pain and trauma they've been through. However, their identity is not completely centered on the discrimination they face. Their life is very likely full of joy and basic aspects of the human experience—work, family, love, bills, travel, and friendships.

Sure, discrimination, sexism, racism, queerphobia, fatphobia, and ableism can be devastating—they even result in lifelong trauma—but those discriminatory experiences are a drop in a lake of what someone might experience daily. Think of it like this: a new homophobic law in Florida is devastating to a gay man, and while he may take time to be upset, hurt, and process any other emotions that arise, he still must go to work, pay bills, take that vacation he planned months ago, and show up for his relationships. He has responsibilities and a life beyond the discrimination. (This is not to diminish the discrimination or the feelings that arise for people of historically marginalized identities; the aim is to show that our lives are complex and full with other meaningful and mundane things that require our attention too.)

This might seem like an odd way to start off a chapter titled "Writing Discrimination," but it's something you need to keep in mind as a writer when crafting characters of historically marginalized identities, because it should never be your intention to tell a trauma story. This chapter is designed to give you the tools to write discrimination with strategy, care, and forethought, all the while keeping in mind that a character is far more than the discrimination they may or may not face.

Characters from diverse identities must be as dynamic as possible, which means a writer must show us the joys in their life as much as (if not more than) the pain.

DO I NEED A DISCRIMINATION SCENE?

If you are writing a creative piece that features a historically marginalized identity, you *do not* have to write a discrimination scene. There is absolutely no rule that says you must have a discrimination scene just because your character is Indigenous or has a disability or identifies as queer. In fact, many would say that it would be a welcome change if there were fewer scenes or no scenes that showcased discrimination.

So why include this chapter?

You may want to write a story that will feature discrimination of some sort, and you should have the tools to do that well. Perhaps even by learning the different forms of discrimination, you'll see that your story doesn't need a discrimination scene or that you're not yet prepared to write one.

At the least, you'll learn more about discrimination and how it is present in our society for various identities, which could lead toward you better understanding your own biases as a person and writer.

SUBTLE VS. OVERT DISCRIMINATION

When it comes to writing scenes that display discrimination, you'll have to ask yourself a few questions. The first: Should the discrimination be subtle or overt?

For a long time, the world understood discrimination to be overt and intentional. It was the Nazi who hated the Jew, one person yelling a slur at another person, or a landlord kicking out a couple because they were in a relationship with someone who had the same gender identity.

Overt discrimination is an intentional action by one party against another, and there is no real confusion as to what's been said or done. While overt discrimination does occur, it does not occur as frequently as subtle forms of discrimination.

Those who decide to write overt discriminatory scenes should be aware that they might cause intense emotions in your readers. If not handled properly, it can feel like you're manipulating the reader's emotions, which may pull the reader out of the scene. Overt forms of discrimination must fit with the story and be handled sensitively.

Subtle forms of discrimination are types of prejudices that are less noticeable (unless you're the person who they're directed at). While subtle forms of discrimination can be intentional, they may also present themselves as an unconscious form of bias—a discriminatory statement or action by a party who is not fully aware of the impact the statement or action has on a person of a marginalized background. It can appear as tokenism, profiling, and microaggressions, and it most definitely occurs in structural or systematic forms of discrimination like institutional racism, patriarchal systems, and ableist laws.

For scenes that depict subtle discrimination, you may need to showcase the discrimination through body language, words, and actions, and help your character acknowledge or process what has happened.

I believe that overt discrimination scenes are a lot more difficult to write than subtle scenes of discrimination. I do not say this to dissuade you from writing them. On the contrary, I'm all for challenging yourself as a writer, but I do believe that if you can master subtle scenes of discrimination, you will understand the nuances required for creating an overt discrimination scene.

Ask yourself: Why do you want your
character to experience discrimination?
What is the purpose?

You need to know the answer to this
question, and when you do, analyze
whether it's a good answer.

LITERARY EXAMPLE:

The Memory Keeper's Daughter by Kim Edwards
Overt Discrimination

"Mentally retarded is a pejorative term," Ron Stone replied evenly. "These children are delayed, yes, no one's questioning that. But they are *not* stupid. No one in this room knows what they can achieve. The best hope for their growth and development, as for all children, is an educational environment without predetermined limits. We only ask for equity today."

"Ah. Equity, yes. But we haven't got the resources," said another man, thin, with sparse graying hair. "To be equitable, we would have to accept them all, a flood of retarded individuals that would overwhelm the system. Take a look."

Despite being told that the term
"mentally retarded" is pejorative or
a derogatory term by Ron, the other
man in this scene continues to use
the term for people with intellectual

> disabilities. Not only that, he uses the term while he justifies why individuals with intellectual disabilities should not receive an education in schools. There is no question of his overt discrimination.

Subtle Discrimination

"It's an allergic reaction. We need to see a doctor *now*."

The nurse was older, a bit heavyset, her gray hair turned under in a pageboy. She led them through a set of steel doors where Al put Phoebe gently, gently, on the gurney. Phoebe was struggling to breathe now, her lips faintly blue. Caroline, too, was having trouble breathing, fear pulled so tightly in her chest. The nurse swept Phoebe's hair back, touching her fingers to the pulse in her neck. And then Caroline watched her see Phoebe as Dr. Henry had seen her on that snowy night so long ago. She saw the nurse taking in the beautifully sloped eyes, the small hands that had gripped the net so hard as she ran after butterflies, saw her eyes narrow slightly. Still, she was not prepared.

"Are you sure?" the nurse asked, looking up and meeting her eyes. "Are you really sure you want me to call a doctor?"

Caroline stood fixed in place.

> In the third paragraph, the nurse asks Caroline if she really wants her to call the doctor. There is subtext to that question

that we need to examine. In the previous paragraph, the nurse notices that Phoebe has Down syndrome. By asking Caroline whether she wants the nurse to call the doctor, the nurse is showing her discriminatory beliefs—that people with intellectual disabilities do not deserve to live simply because of their disabilities. While the nurse does not verbalize her discrimination explicitly, it is implied through her question and actions, which is why this is a subtle discrimination scene.

MICROAGGRESSIONS

Microaggressions are negative, hostile, derogatory, or offensive statements and actions against someone from a marginalized community. Sometimes they're unconsciously done on the part of one party to another, and other times, they're intentional passive-aggressive forms of discrimination. Although microaggressions occur in various ways, they all have the same impact upon the person they're directed at: they cause pain.

Microaggressions can be hard for some people to recognize, especially if their identity differs from the person the discrimination is being directed toward. Even if you don't know what a microaggression exactly is, when you read it in a narrative, you will likely realize that something is wrong. You may feel a little queasy or completely uncomfortable.

I've experienced microaggressions before, like how people who are full Latine have said I'm a "bad Latine" because I'm not fluent in Spanish (my grandmother didn't teach my dad, who in turn couldn't teach me). They've falsely assumed that language is a determinable factor of identity, and they have attempted to shame me through these microaggressive statements.

Then there are the non-Latinos who have looked at my tan skin and asked, "Where were your parents born?" When I've said, "Texas," they've replied, "Where were your grandparents born?" They've looked confused when I've answered, "California and Texas." Questions like these go to show that some people assume those of Latine heritage are first-generation Americans, when in reality, my family has lived in California and Texas for over a century. Their inquiries into my heritage in this manner are a microaggression because they question my "American-ness."

Microaggressions happen daily—probably around you, and you might not even recognize them. They're not exclusive to people's racial identities. They occur toward people with lower incomes or differing body shapes, sexual orientations, gender identities, religious beliefs, and so on. As someone who has experienced microaggressions, I can tell you they don't feel good. In fact, they stick with you, inform your understanding of the world and the people around you, sometimes make you feel unsafe, and can even affect your own perceptions about yourself.

Sometimes the best way to understand something is to see an example. The following are a handful of microaggressive statements and actions:

- A person squats down next to someone in a wheelchair to speak to them. (It infantilizes the person in the wheelchair.)
- A gay man is told "You don't really seem gay." (Indicates that there is a right or wrong way for gay men to act.)
- Someone tells a person who is fat or plus-size, "You have a pretty face. But if you worked out, you'd look better." (This is an assumption that people of a certain size do not work out and a fatphobic statement that indicates the person isn't attractive or worthy of love as they are.)
- A person assumes all Muslim women are made to wear head coverings and conveys this to a Muslim woman. (This is false and exhibits a deep lack of understanding of the Islamic faith. It also indicates that the microaggressor believes all Muslim women to be "weak" or that they experience subjugation from their religion, community, or family members.)
- Someone tries to touch a Black woman's hair. (During slavery, Black people did not have the rights to their own bodies and could be touched indiscriminately by white people. Even after slavery, Black people were still subjected to these rules. Attempting to touch a Black woman's hair without her permission is a nod to this traumatizing time in history.)
- A Jewish person is told they "don't really look Jewish." (This speaks to offensive physical stereotypes associated with Jewish people.)
- An Asian person is told they speak English really well. (The microaggressor assumes the Asian person was not born in the U.S. and that English is their second language.)

- A trans person is asked if they've had gender affirmation surgeries. (Not only is it invasive to ask someone about their medical history, it assumes that to be trans, one must undergo surgery, or that they can afford to. Surgery does not determine a transgender person.)

So how exactly do you portray a microaggression in a creative piece? Here is one simple way to do it:

1. Consider your character's identity. What are the stereotypes, assumptions, or discrimination that people of that same identity experience? You will need to research this.
2. Use this knowledge of stereotypes and discrimination to create a microaggression that your character will experience.
3. Choose a secondary character that will commit the microaggression. Why are they the best person to commit the microaggression? Is it because of the power dynamics between the two characters? Is it someone that the character needs to stand up to? Are you trying to show how this character has created a toxic relationship with your main character? Asking yourself these questions is imperative to creating a complex scene.
4. Write the microaggression. This is a subtle form of discrimination, so you'll need to decide how aware the microaggressor is of their offense and how the character experiencing the microaggression will react.
5. When considering the character who experiences the microaggression, ask yourself: How do they feel about it? What do they do? How do they respond? (No response

is also a response.) How the character responds to the microaggression will tell us more about them.

6. Decide if the person who said or did the microaggression recognizes what they did. Their recognition, or lack thereof, can affect your character and the scene.

7. How does that microaggression contribute to your character's journey through the book? Will it come up later in the story?

8. Is the microaggression necessary? What is the purpose?

LITERARY EXAMPLE:

Luster by Raven Leilani

The guest room is hotter than the other rooms, and so I head downstairs to gather myself, but while I'm on the stairs I hear Pradeep say, a monkey could do this, and all I can see is the back of Akila's head, the halo of green, synthetic frizz.

"I'm trying," she says, a tremor in her voice.

"You're not. It's simple math," he says, and I go down there and start looking for the Captain Planet mug, though it is just an excuse to linger. I glance at Akila and she looks upset, though I can sense that my looking at her makes it worse.

"Hey," I say, turning to Pradeep, my small voice back again. "You can't—"

"Can you not?" Akila says, and so I don't.

Let's set the scene: the narrator and Akila are Black; Pradeep is not. There is a long and ugly history of non-Black people referring to Black people as primates—monkeys, apes, and gorillas. When Pradeep says "a monkey could do this," he is not only calling upon a Black stereotype, he's insinuating that Akila is less intelligent than a monkey, which is an offensive, hostile, and derogatory statement. Because he did not directly call her "a monkey" or "stupid," Pradeep's statement is passive-aggressive and therefore a microaggression. Both Akila and the narrator recognize his statement as such, even if Pradeep does not. In this way, Leilani has written a perfect example of a microaggression.

TOKENISM

Years ago, I attended a literary discussion with a white speaker whom I knew. The audience was a crowd of thirty people, and I sat in the middle of the center row. At one point in the presentation, the speaker was discussing immigration as it relates to the Latine population. She gave a statistic, and then looked at me and asked, "Isn't that right, Alex?" It was a genuine plea for me to verify her statement, but the problem was that she'd singled me out—the only Latine person in the room—to give credence to her statement. As a white woman, she wasn't confident enough to discuss such matters, despite having written a novel that focused on that very subject.

It was a little embarrassing to be put on the spot. I wasn't being asked the question because I was the most intelligent or successful person in the bunch, nor the wisest or smartest. No—the question was only being asked of me because it related to one of my identities, and I was the only one in the room who had that identity. In that realization, I recognized how inappropriate the question was and that I felt called out to speak for every single Latine in a room full of people who had no understanding of what it feels to be Latine. (Also, how ridiculous is it to assume that people of color walk around with statistics about their community on hand?) I had been tokenized by the speaker, and it was awkward and uncomfortable, to say the least.

MasterClass defines tokenism as "the act of prioritizing diversity only symbolically, often by including only a small number of people from marginalized groups as a way to appear diverse without actually striving for it."

They go on to say: "Tokenism is a form of covert prejudice and only reinforces existing hierarchical power structures. It affects all marginalized groups . . . and it exists in all systems, including workplaces and hiring practices, media representation, cultural influencers, education and academia, and politics."[1]

In terms of discriminatory behavior, I've always found tokenization to be one of the hardest for people to understand, and that has to do with the fact that most people who tokenize others truly believe they're being inclusive. Unfortunately, their tokenization is a half-assed effort toward diversity that can negatively affect the person and/or the community being tokenized.

Here are some examples of tokenization:

- A company lacking employee diversity uses their only employee with Down syndrome on their marketing materials. (This creates a false impression that the company is inclusive and puts pressure on the person with Down syndrome to be the face of diversity for the whole company.)
- Event organizers have one (usually white) woman and one person of color (usually a man) on a list of twenty speakers (the rest of whom are all white men) to achieve their "diversity quota." (This is a half-hearted act of inclusion that uses the man of color and the white woman as symbols of the event's inclusivity.)
- A magazine publishes one queer-focused story each June. (The publication of a queer-focused article during Pride Month—and the lack of other queer stories throughout the rest of the year—points to a false and empty sense of inclusion and diversity.)
- Someone says, "I understand. My uncle is gay," or "I'm not racist; I dated an Indian man once," or a politician says he understands women's experiences "because I have a daughter/mother/wife/sister." (If they're saying this, they don't really understand. They're trying to erase their own biases and discrimination through their proximity to someone of a historically marginalized identity, and they're subsequently tokenizing that individual.)
- The only Arab person at a dinner party is asked for their thoughts on the apartheid and genocide of Palestine. (Others have singled out this individual's Arab identity and assumed that they are Palestinian, are well-informed of the experiences of a people related to their identity, or feel comfortable sharing their thoughts on the subject

with others. Would they have asked a random white person or an Asian person the same question?)

- A monoracial person is in a relationship with a Mixed person and, through subtle actions and statements, uses their partner either to gain status within their partner's racial/cultural community or to prove to the outside world how "open-minded" they are. (Depending on the situation, specific aspects of the Mixed person's identity or physical features might be used to the advantage of their partner's image.)

So how do you write a scene in which tokenism is on display?

1. Showcase how one character tokenizes another character and a specific identity they have.
2. Explain how the character being tokenized feels about it through their actions, inner thoughts, dialogue, etc.

   Characters who are being tokenized may feel on display and othered or recognize how they stand out in comparison to everyone around them. Other reactions might include feeling awkward, embarrassed, icky, angry, frustrated, annoyed, sad, upset, confused, or hurt. It can even lead to insecurity about who they are, and their capabilities.

   How your character reacts to being tokenized will wholly depend on the character you've created. Their inner dialogue may show how upset and hurt they are by being tokenized, but they may be outwardly silent about what's happening around them. Perhaps they'll be fed up and remark sarcastically, "Why are you asking me? Is it because I'm the only woman here?" Or maybe they'll be more direct: "I'm more than my racial and ethnic identity, and you're making me feel like that's all you see in me."

Internal and external dialogue can easily convey how your characters feel about the tokenization. Don't forget to focus on descriptions of their body language, which can be used to indicate what someone is thinking or feeling and create tension in the scene.

3. Depending on how the character who is being tokenized reacts, you may be able to present a reaction from the tokenizer.

The character who is initiating the tokenism is usually doing it unconsciously (though not always). They're generally not aware of how their actions or words are affecting another character or a community they're tokenizing. You might exhibit their genuine excitement, pride, or contentment with what they see as an inclusive behavior or their indifference or lack of total awareness of the situation.

I've created a tokenization scene below as an example:

A group of people are standing together at an art show talking about new art gallery openings. A woman named Ellen says, "There's this phenomenal new show by a queer artist from the Southside." Ellen then points to the only non-binary polysexual person in the group and says enthusiastically, "Angel, you have to see it. You'd love it." Angel, who is taking a drink of wine, lightly chokes and coughs a few times before wiping their mouth. When they compose themselves, the whole group is awaiting their response. Angel's cheeks redden, and they stutter, "Uh, yeah. Maybe." They nervously play with the bracelet on their wrist. The group gets quiet, Ellen's smile falters, and she starts twisting her hair nervously. Finally, Greg makes an awkward joke about how "queer" used to be a slur when he was growing up, and the conversation continues. Angel leaves the group and walks outside to get some fresh air.

While there is a little bit of dialogue in this scene, it's the behaviors and actions of Ellen and Angel that exemplify the effects of tokenization. Angel is caught off guard when Ellen points out their queer identity to a group of heteronormative cisgender people. Not only do they choke on their wine, their cheeks redden, and they stutter, indicating that Ellen has made them feel incredibly uncomfortable and put on the spot. Ellen assumes that because everyone else is cisgender and straight, they wouldn't connect to the art show like Angel would. Ellen may not entirely understand how she made Angel feel, but it's clear from the description that she recognizes that Angel does not exhibit the positive reaction she expected. We see Ellen's smile falter, which hints to the reader that Ellen feels bad about her behavior. To make things worse for Angel, Greg makes a tasteless joke that further others Angel to the group. While we don't get Angel's inner thoughts here, we know they are upset by the conversation by their decision to get fresh air away from people who make them feel uncomfortable.

I understand that many people who read this section may not have previously understood or recognized a scene like this as tokenization. Perhaps you've found yourself in the same situation and didn't fully grasp what had happened. We've all likely committed this mistake a time or two. Like I said, tokenization is one of the hardest forms of discrimination to understand. We like to think that inclusive efforts should be praised, even if they fall short, but that's a privileged mindset when we consider the person or community being harmed by tokenization.

If you are going to depict any type of subtle form of discrimination in your writing, I would challenge you to try your hand at tokenization. It's such a complex and nuanced experience, and if you can master it in scene work, you'll find that the other forms of discrimination presented in this chapter will be easier to grasp.

LITERARY EXAMPLE:

The Other Black Girl by Zakiya Dalila Harris

Nella looked up from her desktop at Sophie, who happened to be one of these Very Specific People, and who was still chattering on. Over the course of just a few minutes, Sophie'd managed to talk herself onto a train of social awareness, and it was clear she had no intention of getting off anytime soon. "It reminds me of that anonymous op-ed *BookCenter* article I sent you last week—the one I swore you *had* to have written, because it just sounded so *you*—about being Black in a white workplace. Remember that piece?"

"Yeah, I do . . . and for the tenth time, I definitely

didn't write that article," Nella reminded her, "even though I can obviously relate to a lot of the stuff that was in it."

Sophie is a white woman who thinks that Nella, a Black woman, wrote the anonymous op-ed. She tokenizes Nella by placing her into a role or position—in this case as the anonymous writer—of which she had no part.

Why would Sophie think that Nella wrote the article? Is Nella the only Black person to ever have worked in a white workplace? Of course not. Sophie is tokenizing the only Black person, Nella, in her workplace so she can appear to be socially conscious.

INSTITUTIONAL DISCRIMINATION

Institutional discrimination is the process by which institutions have been designed in a way that causes harm to people from marginalized groups through a lack of opportunities, resources, and mistreatment. It is through the passage of laws and policies that institutional discrimination can occur.

There are many different forms of institutional discrimination, though you may be most familiar with patriarchal systems and systemic racism.

The patriarchal system places men in a position of authority over other gender identities. You may recall that up until recently, laws were in place that prevented women from voting, opening a bank account, getting divorced, or doing anything without their fathers', brothers', or husbands' permission. While many of these laws have been repealed in the U.S., the patriarchal system continues to affect women and other gender identities today. You can see this in the gender wage gap, the tampon tax, the repeal of *Roe v. Wade*, and the rise of anti-trans laws.

Systemic racism is a type of racism that has been legalized and implemented in various systems and institutions (like politics, housing, education, and the workplace). In the U.S., racism was legalized through laws, such as those relating to slavery, the Indian Removal Act of 1830, the Japanese American Internment of 1942, Operation Wetback, anti-miscegenation laws, and the Chinese Exclusion Act.

When these laws went into effect and legalized racism toward a specific racial or ethnic community, they made it so that various institutions—police, education, housing, etc.—were allowed to be racist too. Unfortunately, repealing the laws did nothing to fix the racism that had been securely integrated into such institutions. Institutional racism is why police still profile (and kill) Black and Latino men at a higher rate than any other race or ethnicity.[2] It's why people of Indigenous communities continue to have their land stolen by the U.S. government for oil pipelines and why Black mothers die more often in pregnancy and postpartum than any other race.[3]

Systemic racism and patriarchal systems are not the only types of institutional discrimination found in our world. Discrimination toward people based on their age, sexual orientation, gender identity, and physical and intellectual disabilities has also been built into our systems and institutions.

For instance, many believe that the Americans with Disabilities Act has made it so that all buildings must be accessible to those who use wheelchairs. However, you might be surprised to learn there is a caveat that allows building owners to install accessible ramps only when it is "readily achievable."[4] This means a lot of buildings are not compliant with the ADA and people who use wheelchairs cannot enter easily, because owners can claim that it's not "readily achievable" to add a ramp. When the law allows building owners to deny access to (discriminate against) those who use wheelchairs, that's institutional discrimination.

Here are some examples of institutional discrimination:

- High rates of Covid-19 deaths among Indigenous peoples
- School-to-prison pipelines
- Medical biases toward women and their pain
- Higher healthcare costs for people over certain ages
- High rates of LGBTQIA+ teens experiencing houselessness
- Gentrification of neighborhoods with people who make lesser incomes
- Higher rates of poverty for people with disabilities

Institutional discrimination can be presented in creative works in a variety of ways. Those who write dystopian fiction have built fictional worlds that critique these very systems. Where *The Handmaid's Tale* by Margaret Atwood critiques patriarchal systems, *Lakewood* by Megan Giddings highlights the intersection of systemic racism and patriarchal systems.

However, you don't need to write genre fiction that is dystopian, science fiction, fantasy, or horror to showcase these forms of discrimination in your work. Look at *The Hate U Give* by Angie Thomas. Systemic discrimination that Black people face from the police is on full display in the novel.

Writers can have their character experience systemic discrimination. For instance, your character may be a transgender woman who calls the police for assistance with a domestic dispute. For background, this is a state that has passed anti-trans bathroom bills and policies that persecute the parents of trans children; it also makes it incredibly difficult for trans people to change their gender markers on their driver's licenses. The police come and, upon seeing that a trans woman was the caller, do not make her threatening partner leave the property. They treat the situation as nonserious, and a few days later, the trans woman is reported missing. The police put little effort into solving the case, instead focusing on another missing person, a white cisgender woman with blond hair and blue eyes. The law in this state has determined that trans people can be discriminated against, and it has trickled into institutions like law enforcement.

I think it's important for every writer to inform themselves on the types of institutional discrimination that their diverse characters might face. Whether they use them in the story or not, it's imperative to understand how their characters move in a world that has made it legally more difficult for them to thrive. In doing this type of research, you'll be better informed of your characters and their identities, which may be helpful in unexpected ways.

LITERARY EXAMPLE:

Ayesha at Last by Uzma Jalaluddin

"Termination is a last resort, and proper protocols must be followed. We wouldn't want Livetech to be involved in any legal unpleasantness." Sheila gave Clara an arch look. "Let's start with Khalid Mirza. I want you to prepare a file on his work habits, how often he misses deadlines, and his inappropriate behavior toward women."

Clara was typing furiously but slowed down at Sheila's words. "Is this about what happened in the hallway earlier?"

Sheila lowered her voice. "You saw what he did," she said. "He's clearly one of those extremist *Moslems*."

Clara leaned back, fighting to appear calm. The chair pinched her shoulder and she winced. "I'm not sure what you mean."

Sheila's tinkling laugh rang out. "You are so innocent. I love working with a blank slate."

Clara's sense of unease grew.

"I was headhunted by a big conglomerate in Riyadh, the capital city of Saudi Arabia, a few years ago. I lasted six months." Sheila's teeth gleamed. "Khalid would fit in with my former employers perfectly, right down to the bedsheets and dirty beard."

Clara's stomach clenched. "You can't get rid of someone because of their religious beliefs," she said carefully. "And his beard looks presentable to me. He told me he dry-cleans his robes every week."

Sheila's eyes narrowed. "Livetech is a growing global

player. Our senior team must maintain a certain professionalism, and that includes a uniformity of dress." She leaned across the desk. "Sweetheart, you'll find this type of behavior the higher you climb. Men afraid of a woman with power; men who can't handle a woman's ambition. There are limits to religious accommodation—and it's your job to find those limits. I've set up a meeting with Khalid for next week, which is more than enough time for you to compile your report. I do hope your promotion was the right decision for Livetech."

In this scene, we see Sheila, a boss at Livetech, trying to use the company's human resources guidelines to discriminate against Khalid Mirza. Why? Because Khalid is a Muslim employee who did not shake Sheila's hand per the guidelines of his faith. It is well within the workplace rules to keep files on employees and their behavior. However, Sheila wants to use "the system" to justify her prejudiced perception of Khalid. She may very well be successful in this endeavor if Clara goes along with it.

By saying "There are limits to religious accommodation," Sheila makes a good point as to how the workplace is an institution where discrimination has been woven into the fabric and can be used to harm people of certain racial, ethnic, and religious backgrounds.

Work environments have a history of discriminating against people of color and people of various faiths with restrictive dress codes that target people from such groups. We can see this at play here in how Sheila wants Clara to take note of Khalid's beard and robe. If his clothes and beard are flagged—both of which are part of his religion and culture—as "inappropriate" under the rules of HR, Khalid's job may be at risk.

SLURS AND BAD WORDS

When we think of discrimination, our minds go to the most outrageous and harmful forms—like slurs and bad words that demean a person's identity. For example, when a person calls another person a racial or ethnic slur, it's a clear-cut indication that they are a racist, and we like when racism is clear-cut and overt because it doesn't leave us confused.

As you may know, slurs are specific words and phrases that are meant to insult, degrade, or offend someone from a specific group. Slurs may seem like an easy way to indicate discrimination or prejudice in your creative work, but ironically, they're the most controversial form of discrimination to write, which makes using them a very difficult task indeed.

The biggest issue with slurs is that they shock readers. Whether the bad word is directed at us or someone else, hearing a slur makes for an emotionally charged moment. While it may seem like a good thing to shock your audience, your readers may think you're trying to manipulate their emotions. This can result in a sentimental scene—a faux pas in the writing world that occurs when a writer creates a scene that is excessive or exaggerated to invoke an emotional response in the reader that is not authentic.

Sentimentality

As mentioned above, sentimentality, as it relates to creative writing, occurs when a writer creates an emotional scene that is excessive, exaggerated, or self-indulgent to trigger an emotional response in the reader that is not authentic.

In an article for *Electric Literature*, Elisa Gabbert says it best: "It's not sentiment or emotion itself that's bad, it's misused or overused emotion, and this is what writers, maybe especially poets, need to watch out for: unearned sentiment that feels mawkish, cloying, or cheap. In other words, laying it on too thick, or using emotional tropes to trick the reader into thinking they're feeling something, when actually they're just recognizing the outlines of a familiar emotion."[5]

Be careful that you don't use your character's historically marginalized identity as a tool to make your reader feel sorry for them. In doing this, it actually displays the writer's own bias toward the identity—as something to be pitied.

It also shows that the writer hasn't put enough work into the scene to trust the reader to make up their own opinion on how they feel or don't feel.

I'm not here to tell you to not use a slur in your creative piece. I went back and forth on whether to use them in certain scenes in my second novel. Was I trying to shock the reader? Manipulate their emotions? Was I trying to exemplify how racism was integral to the community of outlaw bikers in the 1970s–1990s? Was it a purposeful tactic to show people how slurs toward Mexican people, which are sometimes so casually used in comedy, films, or schoolyards, are just as bad as any other slurs? These were questions I asked myself repeatedly.

I like to think that I exemplified the demoralizing environment that my main character—a Mixed woman—grew up in, and part of that environment involved the people who raised her using slurs. However, I know that by using slurs in specific scenes, I might have unknowingly hurt readers who are triggered by such words.

Some people will tell you to not use slurs in your creative

writing, even if the people you depict in the book would have used them or it was more common to hear them in the time period in which the story is set. As writers, I think we should consider our readers and how our work will impact them. Isn't that what this book is about?

I don't take this concern over slurs to mean that we shouldn't ever include them in our work. In my last book, I ultimately decided to remove some slurs and bad words and left others in. Slurs existed in the past, they exist today, and there will be new slurs created in the future. I don't necessarily think we need to ignore this. Scenes with slurs may be used to critique a specific character or illuminate historical, cultural, and social practices and movements. Like everything, using slurs in your creative writing pieces requires a lot of care.

If you write a scene that features a slur or bad word, get feedback from another writer or two about how the slur is handled. Is it thrown about without care? Has it been used authentically? Are your characters fully developed? (If not, using a slur or bad word will likely not go well.) Is there a better form of discrimination that can be used in its place? Is it manipulating the emotions of your readers? This is one of those instances where hiring a sensitivity reader might be crucial.

Reading Slurs Aloud

I would not advise a writer who is writing an identity not their own to read slurs from any creative work aloud. This is something that I feel should not need explaining; however, I have seen an author do this, and it resulted in an uncomfortable experience for the audience (to say the least).

If you include a slur in your creative work and find yourself asked to read a section from your work aloud at a literary reading, conference, or some other event, you may not want to read the section that features the slur, especially if you are writing a character with a different identity, one who is from a historically marginalized group. This can result in a poor experience for audience members of that identity, as well as backlash against you, the author.

LITERARY EXAMPLE:

"The Plunge of the Brave" in *Love Medicine*
by Louise Erdrich

"Ask the chief if he'd like to work for me," she said to her man up front. So her man, a buffalo soldier, did.

"Doing what?" I asked.

"I want him to model for my masterpiece. Tell him all he has to do is stand still and let me paint his picture."

By itself, "chief" is not necessarily a bad word if used in the right contexts. However, in this instance, a white woman is referring to an Indigenous man as "chief," which is a derogatory stereotype. By having the white woman use this derogatory term in the scene, Erdrich is telling readers a lot about the white woman's perspective and mindset toward Indigenous peoples.

LITERARY EXAMPLE:

"Welcome to Your Authentic Indian Experience"
by Rebecca Roanhorse

Squaw Fantasy is Boss's latest idea, his way to get the numbers up and impress Management. DarAnne and a few others have complained about the use of the ugly slur, the inclusion of a sexual fantasy as an Experience at all. But Boss is unmoved, especially when the first week's numbers roll in. Biggest seller yet.

Boss looks over at you. "What do you think?"

Boss is Pima, with a bushy mustache and a thick head of still-dark hair. You admire that about him. Virility. Boss makes being a man look easy. Makes everything look easy. Real authentic-like.

DarAnne tilts her head, long beaded earrings swinging, and waits. Her painted nails click impatiently against the Formica lunch table. You can smell the onion in her sandwich.

Your mouth is dry like the red rock desert you can see outside your window. If you say Squaw Fantasy is demeaning, Boss will mock you, call you a pussy, or worse. If you say you think it's okay, DarAnne and her crew will put you on the guys-who-are-assholes list and you'll deserve it.

You sip your bottled water, stalling. Decide that in the wake of the Crazy Horse debacle that Boss's approval means more than DarAnne's, and venture, "I mean, if the Tourists like it . . ."

Boss slaps the table, triumphant. DarAnne's face twists in disgust. "What does Theresa think of that, eh, Jesse?" she spits at you. "You tell her Boss is thinking of adding Savage Braves to the menu next? He's gonna have you in a loincloth and hair down to your ass, see how you like it."

The word "squaw" is a racial and sexual slur used to refer to Indigenous women as sexually "loose" or "whores." It's such a demeaning slur that the U.S. Department of the Interior is working to change 650 place-names across the country that include the word.[6]

In this speculative fiction piece, Boss has created a tourist experience called "Squaw Fantasy," which is both racist and misogynistic toward Indigenous peoples, especially Indigenous women. The fact that Boss is part of the Pima Indigenous community makes the situation more complex and illustrates why this is a good example of handling a slur in a scene.

Rather than having someone from outside of the identity use the slur against an Indigenous person, which would create a very emotionally charged scene, the author had a Pima man use the slur, which complicates the situation and makes the piece more dynamic.

At the end of the scene, DarAnne tries to explain to Jesse why he should be upset about "Squaw Fantasy" by sarcastically saying that the next experience Boss offers will be "Savage Braves." The term "savage" is a slur that labels Indigenous people as violent, uneducated, and uncultured. "Brave" was historically used by Europeans to refer to Native American warriors—and not in a positive way.

DarAnne is Indigenous and is trying to make a point to Jesse by creating a hypothetical experience with a similarly offensive name. Again, we have one Indigenous person using a slur to explain something to another Indigenous person. While the slur is still uncomfortable to read, it has been handled in a way that doesn't overpower all other elements of the scene.

Last but not least, it should be noted that this story was written by an author who is both Black and Indigenous, and she is writing within her own identity. If this story had been written by a non-Indigenous writer, it might have been hard for readers to remove that from the context of the story or the scenes in which the slurs are presented.

EXOTICISM

You've probably heard the word "exotic" thrown around a time or two, and you might not have thought anything of it. Whether it's being used to describe a person or place, "exotic" is a word that can cause a lot of unintentional harm.

To exoticize someone or something is to portray them as unusual, foreign, alien, or fantastical, typically in a stereotypical, superficial, or romanticized way. (It's a type of othering.) In discussing exoticization, we usually point out how it affects people of color as well as various nationalities and cultures, but it can absolutely be directed at disabled people or people of different gender identities, sexual orientations, sizes, religions, and so on.

The main problem with exoticization is that it creates a distance between an "in group," which is seen as "normal," and an "out group," which is perceived as "abnormal." So, what does exoticization look like? Here are some examples:

- A Mixed person is asked, "What are you?" or someone says, "Mixed babies are the prettiest babies." (Pointing out the "uniqueness" of the physical characteristics of the

Mixed person is reducing that person to their looks and distancing them from monoracial people.)

- Arranged marriages among people who practice Hinduism or Islam are romanticized. (Marriage is marriage no matter how it occurs. Placing a romantic element on one type of marriage over another is exoticization.)
- Travelers are fascinated and obsessed with seeing kathoey (transgender) performers in Bangkok, Thailand. (This is a mix of queer and racial exoticization that begins with the romanticizing and glamorization of kathoey people and their looks. Visitors to Thailand typically have positive interactions with these Thai individuals and tend to behave as if kathoey performers are a tourist attraction to experience. It's also important to point out that tourists don't usually have the same positive thoughts or interactions with trans, non-binary, or queer people in their own country.)
- Other senses of blind or Deaf people are poeticized. For example, a blind person might be asked if their touch or hearing senses are heightened. (Focusing on a disabled person's possible "abilities" rather than their disabilities is a form of exoticization. It's alluding to the magical disability stereotype, which attempts to make a disability seem "less bad" by hinting at other enhanced abilities. In reality, it showcases the idea that there is something bad about having a disability and conveys the false idea that disabilities are "abnormal" and to be abled is "normal.")
- There is a positive focus on the accent of a European. (It's reducing the individual to their accent; also, it might display how the person sees only certain accents as "acceptable" or "attractive" compared to others. This

tends to intersect with race, ethnicity, and culture. An example: a Black man from London is seen as more favorable or "attractive" than a Black man from Nigeria.)

Now let's talk about how to write a scene that features an occurrence of exoticization between two characters.

The exoticizer (or the character who is doing the exoticizing) may not be aware of what they're doing. This should be made very clear to the reader. The exoticizer will usually fixate on a particular identity trait, cultural aspect, physical feature, or clothing item and romanticize, glamorize, or point out its unusualness or foreignness.

The character who is being exoticized will behave very differently. Once they realize they're being exoticized, they're usually uncomfortable, embarrassed, frustrated, or annoyed by the false attention. They may feel othered, or "abnormal" in some sense. This can impact their self-perception and make them feel dehumanized, and it can put them in a position where they recognize how they are continually exoticized, stereotyped, or harassed by others.

You would typically approach writing an exoticization scene in a similar way to how you would portray scenes that contain microaggressions or tokenism.

LITERARY EXAMPLE:

The Henna Wars by Adiba Jaigirdar

"I wanted to show you something." Flávia extends her hands toward me on the table in front of us. For a moment, I think she's going to take my hand, until I notice it. The red wrapped around her palms, weaving up and down her skin. "You inspired me at the wedding. Well, everything there did, really. And then Chyna told me about an Asian shop in town where we could probably get a tube of henna."

Discomfort flutters around in my stomach that I don't really understand. It's how I feel when Priti comes into my room in the middle of the night and pushes into my bed and steals almost all of the duvet. Annoyance? But annoyance verging onto anger almost.

"How did you . . . ?" I begin, not sure exactly what question I should be asking.

"I just wanted to try it, you know," Flávia says, extending her palm out in front of her. She's looking at her hand and not at me anymore. She isn't even asking for my opinion, just admiring her own handiwork. "I think I did a pretty good job, what do you think?"

I frown. "I . . . I guess."

She looks at me, her smile still in place. But instead of the usual butterflies that smile sends fluttering in my stomach, the gnawing discomfort grows.

"I really thought it would be more difficult than it was," she says. "But once I had that picture your sister put up on Insta . . . it was simple, really."

The gnawing grows from annoyance to all-out anger. Flávia can't just do henna because she saw it at the wedding and because she saw Priti's Instagram picture. How can she sit in front of me and act like there aren't a million things wrong here?

In this scene, we meet Flávia, a Brazilian Irish girl, who has done henna on her hands and arms after attending a Bangladeshi wedding where Nishat, a Bangladeshi Irish teenager, was in attendance. Nishat, who has a crush on Flávia feels immediately uncomfortable upon learning that Flávia has gone to an "Asian shop" and hennaed her hands on her own. What we are witnessing in this scene is cultural appropriation, which is a form of exoticism.

Cultural appropriation occurs when one person, who is not part of the community, appropriates—or takes for their own use—a cultural element of another group. It is a form of exoticism because the person is romanticizing another's culture and using it for their own means. In this instance, Flávia has romanticized the Bangladeshi practice of henna.

If Flávia had gotten her hands hennaed by a Bangladeshi person for a Bangladeshi event, and even better, had paid a Bangladeshi person to do it, it would not be considered cultural appropriation or exoticism. However, because Flávia does henna to share on Instagram and start her own henna side hustle (which is explained as the chapter goes on), we see that this action is cultural appropriation and exoticism. Author Adiba Jaigirdar does a great job exhibiting how exoticism in this scene makes Nishat uncomfortable.

EXERCISE

This two-part exercise will help you examine how perspective plays a big role in scenes of discrimination.

First part:

Write a scene in which you depict tokenization, a microaggression, or exoticization. Write from the perspective of the person who is experiencing the discrimination. Be sure to convey how your main character feels about this form of discrimination through words, body language, and internal thoughts. Then show how the person doing the discriminating responds (or doesn't) to your character's reaction. Play out the full situation until there is a natural ending to the scene.

Second part:

Take that same scene and write from the perspective of the person committing the tokenization, microaggression, or exoticization. Convey their thought process leading up to the discriminatory action and the response (body language and/ or words) they receive from the person they discriminated against. Show their internal thoughts. Play out the full situation until there is a natural ending to the scene.

Now examine both scenes and reflect on what you've written. You might ask yourself:

- Which part was easier or harder to write? Why?
- What are the most notable differences between the two scenes in your creative approach?
- In the first part of the exercise, did you focus more on internal thoughts, words, or body language descriptions? Was it different in the second scene?
- Do you notice mood shifts depending on which perspective you're writing from?
- What did you learn? How can that inform your writing in the future?

6

DIALOGUE

n 2017, nearly one thousand film scripts were analyzed by researchers at the University of Southern California to see how stereotypes relating to gender, race, and aging are reinforced through dialogue. Their findings illustrate exactly why dialogue is an important factor to consider when writing an identity other than your own.

When it came to race, the researchers found that Latine and Mixed characters used more sexualized language than characters of other races, and Black characters used a higher percentage of swear words. This comes as no surprise when we consider the most common stereotypes of those racial identities: the "spicy and sexual Latina," the "exotic" Mixed person, and the "thuggish," "ghetto," crass, and violent Black person.

The researchers looked at women's and men's dialogue too (no other gender identities were examined). Women's dialogue tended to have a more positive affect and used language that was associated to family values, whereas men used words related to achievement and death and swore more frequently than women characters.

Again, not shocking. Women are commonly assumed to be proper and focused on families and raising children and men are success-driven, rougher around the edges, and allowed to be flawed. Of course these stereotypes made it into their dialogue.

The dialogue of older characters (regardless of gender identity) contained fewer mentions of sexual topics and appeared more intelligent, calm, and religious. Congruently, their dialogue had similar traits to men. As a society, we assume that people grow wiser—and less sexual—as they age, hence the reason their dialogue was focused on calm, intelligent, and religious topics.

The USC researchers didn't examine the dialogue of other identities, but it's likely that stereotypes appear in their dialogue too. If this study proves anything, it's that most writers' rooms have been and are still overwhelmingly dominated by cis, straight, able-bodied white men, even when the movie or TV show features main characters of color, queer characters, women, and characters with disabilities. Sounds a lot like the publishing world, no?

What we can take from this study is that stereotypes associated with various identities tend to find their way into the dialogue that we create for those characters. For instance, we know that there are stereotypes associated with the language of gay men, which is sometimes known as "gay speak," and that disabled people often have their dialogue made to sound simple and/or stiff to indicate stereotypical assumptions about their intelligence levels. Although the study looked at scripts, we know these gaffes occur in short stories, books, and poems too. Thankfully, there are plenty of tips and tricks to identify and steer clear of stereotypes in dialogue.

CAN A CHARACTER "SOUND" LIKE AN IDENTITY?

In creative writing workshops and seminars, I've heard writers say, "I want my character to sound like [insert specific identities]," or "This character doesn't sound like a [insert specific identity]." Such statements are giant signposts revealing our assumptions and biases about different communities.

A character's race, ethnicity, sexual orientation, or gender identity is not a determining factor for the way they speak or how their voice may sound. To assume so is a first-class ticket to a stereotypical, cliché, stock character trap. Not to mention it can result in the character being othered by the audience.

The way we speak and the language we use are affected by many things—our historic period, our age, where we've lived, our parents' accents, our friends' dialects, how much we travel or don't travel, our culture, the media we consume, and more.

Culture no doubt plays a role in the language that people from certain identities use; however, culture is not a self-contained thing. The language of a Puerto Rican girl who lives in East Harlem today isn't exclusively influenced by other Puerto Ricans in that neighborhood. Her language will be influenced by the neighborhood's diverse set of residents including Cubans, Dominicans, Mexicans, and Asians—not to mention the vast amount of music, books, film, and TV she devours and the social media platforms she engages with.

Because the combinations of our full life experiences are so complicated—meaning not everyone in our identity groups will have the same experience—the way we speak is going to be diverse and particular for each person.

So, what does this mean for you as a writer? Take that notion of how a person from a particular identity should sound, crumple it in a ball, and throw it in the trash (and set it on fire, as my editor added), as it's unlikely to serve you in the long run.

There may be times when an editor or critique partner points out that your character's voice doesn't sound authentic. When you are told this, investigate further. Ask your critique partner to explain what they mean. What doesn't sound authentic? What don't they like? On one hand, your critique partner could be showing you their unconscious biases. We all have them.

On the other hand, they could be trying to convey that they want your character to use more words or phrases that speak to the character's childhood in southern Georgia, or that they noticed the character is using more modern slang rather than the kind that would have been used in 1877.

If the editor is someone from your character's identity

background, they may have more insight into language nuances of that identity. Like I mentioned, culture can play a role in the type of language most commonly used by certain groups of people, and you can keep this in mind when crafting your character. However, it shouldn't be the only thing you base a character's dialogue on.

WHERE TO FIND VOICE AND DIALOGUE INSPIRATION

In Chapter 3, I pointed out three things to do before you start writing an identity not your own:

1. Read books, poetry, screenplays, and other creative writing by writers of the identity that you wish to write.
2. Consume non-written forms of media relating to that identity.
3. Build authentic two-way relationships with communities you wish to represent.

If you did all three of these things, you'll have a wealth of inspiration to create authentic dialogue for your character. Again, reading books by authors from historically marginalized identities can be very helpful in understanding how identity may or may not affect a person's dialogue. However, in my opinion, the third point—building authentic two-way relationships—is by far the best method for developing voice.

Although I think the second point—consuming other forms of media beyond literature—is necessary for gathering an understanding of the history and culture of a person from a certain identity, some media can reinforce stereotypical dialogue. You only have to look at the study I mentioned at the beginning of this chapter to see exactly why that's been a problem.

A great example of this is the popular TV show called *Kim's Convenience* about a Korean Canadian family in Toronto. After the show finished five seasons, actors on the show like Simu Liu (also the star of *Shang-Chi and the Legend of the Ten Rings*) and Jean Yoon revealed how the white scriptwriters refused input from Asian cast members when it came to cultural portrayals, dialogue, and storylines.[1] In fact, Yoon wrote on social media that the writers had "overtly racist" and "extremely culturally inaccurate" storylines and created a toxic work environment where the actors—some of whom were Korean— were not able to provide input on the glaring inaccuracies, stereotyping, and misrepresentations in the script.

Therefore, TV and film can be a little tricky to use when researching authentic dialogue and voice. However, if you do use TV and film, seek out works that have a diverse writing and production staff. A great example of this is Issa Rae's *Insecure*. Credits for such shows can be found on IMDb.

That said, don't assume that all Black characters will speak the same way as the Black characters on *Insecure*. Again, location, age, interests, cultural background, and other experiential factors will affect a character's dialogue.

Podcasts and radio shows are a better type of media than film and TV when it comes to finding dialogue inspiration, because generally the hosts of the show write their own scripts, and they usually present themselves exactly as they are (i.e., they aren't acting).

FORMATTING OTHER LANGUAGES

How do you format other languages in your creative work? The answer is simple: don't format it any differently from English.

In my first novel, *Secrets of the Casa Rosada*, the Spanish is italicized, and this was true for most books that have featured other languages until recently. Around 2018, we saw an industry-wide shift, one that began to treat other languages the same as English.

In the United States, we've had a long and ugly history surrounding immigration, and this was especially rampant under presidents like Donald Trump, who fostered hatred toward people of other countries through xenophobic statements and immigration policies.

People who speak other languages in addition to English have long been subjected to such prejudices. My Mexican American bilingual grandmother—who was born in the United States, mind you—felt the pressure of such discrimination, which is why she didn't teach my father to speak Spanish. In turn, I didn't grow up speaking Spanish.

When we italicize other languages in our creative work, we other those languages and the types of characters who speak those languages. By using the term "othering," I mean the process of treating a person or group of people as inherently different from yourself.

Why is this a big deal? Because people who write characters of diverse cultures generally want the reader to connect with that character, but when we other that character through things like italicizing another language, we erect a large wall between the reader and the character.

In italicizing other languages, we may also be reinforcing the idea that English is superior to other languages, which is not true. One language can't be better than another language, because they're squiggly drawings that we call letters and words, put together in a pattern that some long-dead person decided was a sentence.

So, if English is no better than any other language, then why would we format another language differently from English?

We wouldn't.

An Italic Exception

There are some good arguments for italicizing other languages, such as one that comes from Jumoke Verissimo. She wrote a piece for *LitHub* called "On the Politics of Italics" that explains why she uses italics in her work. She describes herself as a bilingual author who speaks English and Yoruba and sees italics as a stylistic choice to assert her bilingualism. Verissimo writes:

"The use of the italics is to in fact assert the privilege of my personhood, which I believe the italics announces in my writing. This is how I shift the gaze and force attention to the lingual hybridity as a state of my existence. This is found in the Yoruba that becomes English, the philosophy, the values, the generations of persons performing genealogy on my tongue; the city of multi-ethnic groups becoming a colloquial language that makes each day go by quickly. This cannot be a slant bowing down of a typeset representative of my language's subservience to another, it is I believe in this instance, a recognition of distinction in the world of the colonized; a perpetual reminder of the incompetence of English to assimilate and magnify/signify my worldview."

Verissimo uses italics as a "political statement on the real sense of language and borders, inclusions and exclusion, otherness and personhood." In fact, she says, "Italics, for me, as me, says this border where I'm standing is my side of the story and you're welcome to enter this world. Italics emphasize my world—the way I choose to introduce our language to you."[2]

Read Verissimo's full article here:

LITERARY EXAMPLE:

Shine On, Luz Véliz by Rebecca Balcárcel

"Yes," I say. "Sí."

Saying it makes me believe it. I *will* be in the Showcase. Even if I'm not a star, or even average.

But I need a program. I say it in Spanish. "Necesito un programa." Again, I'm lucky with the words, remembering "I need a," and stumbling on to a word that's similar in both languages: "program."

"De computadora?" She grabs my arm and does a little jump, squealing a phrase I can't grasp at all. Maybe she thinks I already know how to program.

"But I'm new," I say. "New to all of it."

"New?" Solana asks. "¿Nueva?"

"Nueva," I say.

"Yo también soy nueva," she says.

Wow, yes. Not totally new to programming, but new to school, to English, to Texas. And look at how she's jumping right in and trying everything.

> The author, Balcárcel, has created a scene with a Spanish speaker and an English speaker who are trying to communicate with each other. By not italicizing the Spanish, Balcárcel shows the reader that neither character is better nor lesser than the other because of the language they

speak. The author has effectively removed the "foreignness" that is associated with Spanish when it is italicized, which lessens the chance of othering. Despite the two characters' inability to speak each other's language fluently, they still find ways to communicate.

ACCENTS AND DIALECTS: WHAT'S THE DIFFERENCE?

As we continue our conversation on dialogue, I want to make sure you know the difference between accents and dialects. We tend to use these words interchangeably, but they're quite different.

According to *Merriam-Webster*, an accent is "an individual's distinctive or characteristic inflection, tone, or choice of words."[3]

Alternatively, dialect is a "regional variety of language distinguished by features of vocabulary, grammar, and pronunciation from other regional varieties and constituting together with them a single language."[4]

Let me make it easier for you:

- An accent is how we pronounce words.
- A dialect involves accent, grammar, and words that are common to a specific area.

Here is a very basic example of the two:

- Accent: *I had a tough time understanding him. He spoke so quickly, and his words ran together so that his sentences sounded like the meandering bayous that surrounded New Orleans, the city where he grew up.* (Notice how the narrator is focusing on how the character pronounces his words? The narrator is describing his accent.)
- Dialect: *"I'm fixin' to get a dressed po'boy and a cold drink and eat it by my house," he said in a New Orleans accent.* (As is the case with dialect, I've used grammar and words that are specific to New Orleans, as well as pointed out the character's New Orleans accent. To all the folks from New Orleans, please forgive me for this somewhat odd sentence that does not convey the full beauty of the diverse dialects within your city.)

"PROPER ENGLISH"

In my second book, *Half Outlaw*, there is a character named Linh Loc. She was born in Vietnam and immigrated to Oklahoma City after the Vietnam War.

When I first created Linh, I indicated that she had a thick accent, a by-product of English as her second language. In trying to illustrate her English-speaking capabilities, I wrote certain words phonetically, dropped articles or words, and used fragmented sentences. During the editing phase, I read and reread Linh's dialogue, and I got this bad feeling in my stomach that said, "This is not right, Alex."

Did I really need to write Linh's sentences in a fragmented way? In doing that, would I be othering her? It felt stereotypical, or at least biased.

Help came through a conversation with a literary friend who said, "We all have accents," which blew my mind. I know what you're thinking: obviously, we all have accents. Sometimes you have to hear such an obvious statement to see the fuller picture.

There is no such thing as a person without an accent, and *yet*, in the literary world, we tend to write white characters as being accent-less, unless they're from England, Boston, Australia.

But when it comes to characters of color, especially those from other countries, we run wild with their accents, their diction, their sentences, and their slang, until most of their characterization is wound up in their dialogue.

Some of you may be saying, "People who speak English as a second language, especially those who are newly learning English, don't speak 'proper English.' Their sentences aren't completely correct, they miss certain articles, and they use the wrong tense. Should we not convey that in their dialogue?"

You're right. I get it. You want to be accurate. What I would advise is that if you choose to focus on one character's accent or dialogue so heavily, you should do that for all your characters.

When I'm sitting at a barbecue or family gathering—whether it's among my Mexican American family members or my white family members (all of whom are multigenerational Americans with English as their first language)—not a single person speaks "proper" English. Their sentences are fragmented, they drop articles, they use lots of double negatives (e.g., "there's not nothing to worry about"), their Texan drawls are thick, and half of them pronounce "wash" as "worsh."

Sit among your family and listen to them for about five minutes and you'll realize that most Americans don't speak "proper English." Why then are most white and/or American-born characters not having their dialogue written as they speak, or their accents focused upon heavily? Bias, my friends.

LITERARY EXAMPLE:

Manmade Constellations by Misha Lazzara

She looked out the window toward the bar across the street. "Your accent surprised me. You don't hear many accents around here."

He looked into the garage and nodded slowly. "People have accents. Especially you."

Lo was vaguely aware she had a Minnesota accent but couldn't hear it. She only knew what it sounded like when people made fun of them—long, nasally "o" sounds, particular attention to holding vowels, and an inflection at the end of words that made everything sound like a question—everything sounded just a little more polite that way.

"Yeah, right, well I guess I meant southern accents. The guys working in the garage have accents because English isn't their first language."

He raised his eyebrows at her and scratched his head, staring at her for a minute. She didn't know what to say. Was it rude to say that English wasn't their first language? She realized she didn't even know if that was true. Plus, she only spoke one language, and apparently had a thick accent, at that.

Lazzara does a great job of showcasing her main character's ignorance toward accents in this scene. Lo points out that the man she is speaking with has an accent. In doing this, she inadvertently others him from the locals, whom she perceives as not having accents. The man quickly reminds Lo that everyone in the town, including her, has an accent.

Rather than accepting that, Lo points out that the men who work in the garage (in a previous scene, Lo recognizes them as Latino men) have accents because English isn't their first language. Again, she others these men, and she assumes that English isn't their first language based on their racial/ethnic identity and accents. Lazzara does a good job showing us that Lo mildly recognizes her mistake. She wonders, "Was it rude," and as readers we see that Lo's statements are clear indicators of internalized bias.

HOW TO WRITE ACCENTS

Golden Rule: If you're going to point out one character's accent, point out all your characters' accents.

Accents are affected by many things, from our parents'

accents to our ability to speak multiple languages, and even our education. Location is also a major contributor to our accents. Someone in North Texas does not speak like someone from South Texas. The same can be said for various regions. For instance, New Orleans residents have accents that are different from those in northeast Louisiana or those who live in other Southern states like Mississippi, Alabama, South Carolina, and Georgia.

There are many ways to portray accents in our creative work in respectful ways. Here are a few examples:

1. **Describe how the character's voice sounds:** You can mention how nasally, melodic, throaty, or twangy your character's voice sounds. Pay attention to the associations you make between a character's voice and their identity. Are you describing all women characters as having high-pitched, shrill voices? That would come off as stereotypical and false.

2. **Be direct with accents:** Be straightforward and label the accent for your readers.

   An example: "He had a French accent," or "She was British; her accent pointed to South London."

   For my character Linh, I wrote: "Her accent made me think English was her second language."

   I didn't describe how Linh's accent sounded but kept my character's observation of Linh's accent very generalized. In a later scene, Raqi learns that Linh moved to the U.S. from Vietnam. I left it up to the reader to then picture how Linh might sound. (This line also indicates that Raqi, the main character, assumes that English is Linh's second language, when in fact, she can't know that for sure based on her accent, which exhibits Raqi's own bias.)

3. **Describe accents through exposition:** Certain accents are going to be easier to describe than others. For instance, characters from Southern states may have a "drawl," so you could say, "Her drawl was thick, and she elongated her vowels." Notice that we're describing the accent in exposition surrounding the dialogue—not actually within the dialogue.

   If the character has a localized accent, like those found in Boston, you might write "When he said, 'car,' he dropped the 'r.' If I had to guess, he was a Boston native."

   (I know this is the most stereotypical example of a Boston accent. Do better than me.)

SHOULD I WRITE PHONETICALLY?

In graduate school, I was introduced to Zora Neale Hurston, a Black American author who portrayed the experience of Black people in the South in the early 1900s. The first book I read of hers is the most famous one she has ever written, *Their Eyes Were Watching God*. It stood out to me significantly at the time because it was the first book I'd ever read in which an author wrote the language of all her characters phonetically. Her Southern Black characters' speech was full of slang, dropped letters, and phonetic speech patterns.

Here is a passage:

"You mean, you mad 'cause she didn't stop and tell us all her business. Anyhow, what you ever know her to do so bad as y'all make out? The worst thing Ah ever knowed her to do was taking a few years offa her age and dat ain't ever harmed nobody. Y'all makes me tired. De way you talkin' you'd think de folks in dis town didn't do nothin' in de bed 'cept praise de Lawd. You have to 'scuse me, 'cause Ah'm bound to go take her some supper." Pheoby stood up sharply.[5]

As someone from the South, I had an easy time reading the phonetic words Hurston used in *Their Eyes Were Watching God* because I've listened to language like this my entire life. More importantly, I was able to connect to the characters in the story through their language, which added another level of historical, societal, and cultural insight to the community portrayed in the book.

In her time, Hurston's approach to language was quite contentious. Many literary figures in the Black community, including novelist Richard Wright, were concerned that it would create caricatures of Black people, or further stereotypes that Black people were uneducated. However, as the decades passed, some authors, like Toni Morrison and Alice Walker, found inspiration in Hurston's techniques and her ability to capture a rich dialect of Southern Black people.

What about today? How do we feel about writing the language of characters of diverse backgrounds phonetically? Like many things, it's complicated.

I will start by saying if you want to write the language of a character with a historically marginalized identity phonetically: be careful. Again, in capital letters: BE VERY CAREFUL.

Although I agree that Hurston's stylistic dialogue choice was literary genius, I also understand why authors like Wright were concerned about her decision. I think where I differ from

Wright's argument is the consideration of who the author is and the approach the author takes.

Hurston was a Black author who phonetically captured the language of a community she was a part of. There is a big difference between her doing that and someone like me— a Southerner who is half Mexican, half white—writing the language of Black characters phonetically. I've no doubt that no matter how well I phonetically captured the dialect of a Black character from a specific community or area, I would receive some well-deserved criticism. That's because people from privileged backgrounds have consistently written caricatures of Black characters by writing their language phonetically and not doing the same for every other character in their story.

Does this mean that as a writer you shouldn't use phonetic language for your characters of historically marginalized identities? I don't like to give absolute answers, but I would warn you to do so sparingly or with good reason (see the examples below). In fact, if you're going to write the dialogue of BIPOC characters phonetically, do the exact same thing for your white characters. If you don't, you will have othered, demeaned, and furthered the stereotyping of people of color. Finally, if you do take on this task, be prepared to be comfortable with receiving criticism.

If you still want to write a character's dialogue phonetically, I'll leave you with one last thing to consider: readers shouldn't have to struggle to interpret what you've written.

Most writers and editors agree that if your reader must translate phonetically spelled language, they could become frustrated, get pulled out of the story, or leave the book with incorrect assumptions and biases about people from certain identities. None of these results are particularly positive, which is why most writers don't write phonetically.

If your characters are speaking English—no matter if English isn't their first language or they have a different accent from the part of the country they're in—it's still English. It's best to write out the English conventionally and point out the accent of the character through exposition.

LITERARY EXAMPLE:

"A Few Words about this Book," in *The Immortal Life of Henrietta Lacks* by Rebecca Skloot

I've done my best to capture the language with which each person spoke and wrote: dialogue appears in native dialects; passages from diaries and other personal writings are quoted exactly as written. As one of Henrietta's relatives said to me, "If you pretty up how people spoke and change the things they said, that's dishonest. It's taking away their lives, their experiences, and their selves." In many places I've adopted the words interviewees used to describe their worlds and experiences. In doing so, I've used the language of their times and backgrounds, including words such as *colored*. Members of the Lacks family often referred to Johns Hopkins as "John Hopkin," and I've kept their usage when they're speaking. Anything written in the first person in Deborah Lacks's voice is a quote of her speaking, edited for length, and occasionally clarity.

Since Henrietta Lacks died decades before I began writing this book, I relied on interviews, legal documents, and her medical records to re-create scenes from her life.

In those scenes, dialogue is either deduced from the written record or quoted verbatim as it was recounted to me in an interview.

> *The Immortal Life of Henrietta Lacks*
> is a nonfiction book by a white writer,
> Rebecca Skloot, about Henrietta Lacks,
> a Black woman whose cancer cells have
> been exploited by the medical industry.
> Skloot explains in a small introduction
> section why readers will see words written
> phonetically, as well as certain words that
> are outdated, racist, and discriminatory. By
> referring to Henrietta's relative's opinion
> on these subjects in an author's note,
> Skloot gives credence to her decision and
> prepares readers for what is to come.

LITERARY EXAMPLE:

Girl in Translation by Jean Kwok, page 69

"Don't be afraid," Mrs. Avery said. "I know they can be over woman if you're not used to animals but they *won't hot* you."

Page 16

We saw an older black man sitting on a lawn chair in front of the used-furniture store beside our building. His face was turned up to the sun and his eyes were closed. His hair was a silver poof around his head. I gazed at him thinking that no Chinese person I knew from home would deliberately try to make themselves tanner in the sun, especially if they were already as dark as this man was.

Suddenly, he leaped up in front of us and sprang into a one-legged martial arts pose with his arms outstretched. "Hi-yah!" he yelled.

Ma and I both screamed.

He burst into laughter, then started speaking English. "I got *cha* moves, don't I? I'm sorry *for scaring* you ladies. I just love kung fu. My name is Al."

Ma, who hadn't understood a word he'd said, grabbed my jacket and said to me in Chinese, "This is a crazy person. Don't speak to him, we'll just tiptoe away."

"Hey, that's Chinese, right? You have *anthn* you can teach me?" he asked.

It's important to point out that the narrator is a young Chinese girl who has only recently arrived in the U.S. and is still learning English. Although writing words phonetically can be risky, in these two different scenes, Kwok is trying to convey that the narrator still struggles to understand various pronunciations of English words. Kwok did not limit the phonetic spellings to people of only one racial identity; she does this for persons of varying identities.

In the first instance, we see the young narrator struggle with understanding Mrs. Avery, who is white. In the second scene, we see the same thing happen with Al, a Black man. Phonetic spelling, in this instance, has no relation to the identity of the people speaking, but rather speaks to the main character's language journey.

QUESTIONS TO ASK YOURSELF ABOUT SLANG, COLLOQUIALISMS, AND IDIOMS

I'm a big fan of slang words, colloquialisms, and idioms because they can speak to the setting and the background or interests of your characters. But surprise, surprise—these types of words and phrases are not without their drawbacks.

On one hand, writers of color and queer writers have received unfavorable, racist, homophobic, and classist pushback from editors who are not familiar or comfortable with certain slang words or colloquialisms. Then there are some writers who have used slang or idioms incorrectly in their books, which has furthered stereotypes, exoticized, or othered characters of diverse identities.

Still some writers have used slang in a beautiful way to show how characters of historically marginalized identities "code-switch" like many people historically marginalized identities do in real life. Let's take a moment to look at what code-switching is.

Code-Switch Corner—Language Edition
Code-switching is the process of adjusting your language or behavior depending on the type of people

you are around. In this case, we will be talking about code-switching as it relates to language. For example, we speak differently, usually more casually, among our friends than we do with our boss in a professional setting.

The term "code-switching" is usually used in reference to people of color and/or queer people because no matter if the setting is casual or professional, people of those identities are pressured (and expected) to speak in certain ways, especially if the space is straight, cis, and white (which most spaces are; thank you, institutional discrimination).

How does this look? Take for example a Mixed woman who is half white, half Latina. Her dialogue and the colloquialisms and slang she uses at a family gathering with her extended white family is different from the language she uses around her Mexican extended family members. She adjusts her language to "fit in" and be accepted by her monoracial cousins, aunts, and uncles. At school, she's constantly code-switching with language among various racial communities and feels pressured to "translate" between groups. Among white friends and teachers, she's more reserved and her vocabulary involves slang used by white pop stars of the day. Among Latine students, she's made to feel like a guera because she's half white, so she sprinkles in Spanish— mande and chingon—on occasion to remind them (and herself) she's brown too.

Notice how her language changes depending on whom she's surrounded by or the spaces she's in? She switches her language to fit with the unspoken "code" of each group—i.e., she is code-switching.

Final note: Code-switching occurs with behavior too. As with language, when people adjust their be-

havior based on the environment, it's another form of code-switching.

Slang should not merely be something that you throw into dialogue because you heard your niece use a word and assume that every person in her age range would use the same word. Slang is more complicated than that.

If you want to use slang and colloquialisms authentically for characters of identities other than your own, you're going to have to speak to people from those identities. Listen to the slang or phrases they use or don't use. Then ask yourself: Are they code-switching with you and using different words and phrases than they would with someone else? If you develop an authentic and trusting relationship with this person, there could come a time when you can create a safe space for them to discuss their word and phrase choices with you.

For now, ask yourself these questions while you're working on a creative piece. Hopefully, the answers will help you critically think about your use of slang in dialogue.

1. Are certain characters in my piece using more slang or colloquialisms than other characters? If so, what does it say about those characters versus the others? Am I othering that character and the people who have the same identity?

2. Is that slang, colloquialism, or idiom appropriate for the period or location?

3. Is that slang word used correctly? Are there other definitions of that slang word? If so, have I used it in a way that won't be misconstrued by readers?

4. Who is saying that slang word, colloquialism, or idiom? Would that person say it? If so, why?

5. Is that slang word, colloquialism, or idiom associated with a stereotype of the person who is using it? Should I use it?
6. Am I using that slang word to shock and/or manipulate the emotions of my reader?

LITERARY EXAMPLE:

The Girl Who Fell from the Sky by
Heidi W. Durrow

"Nice to meet y'all," Lakeisha says, grinning and holding in her hand a piece of gum that no one notices but me.

"Go on and get Lakeisha one of your sweaters. She gonna get the death of cold in her," Grandma says, tut-tutting as she puts her arms around Lakeisha, who came up to the house without her coat.

"I'm alright, ma'am. Thank you."

"Next time, tell your mama you need to have a coat with you. This ain't no place to be without a winter coat," Grandma says.

> "She gonna get the death of cold in her" is a colloquialism that speaks to Grandma Dorris's age. The idea of catching the "death of cold" is an old-fashioned one that exemplifies how the medical community once believed that temperature was connected to illness.

Lakeisha follows me to my room. Before I have closed the door, she's run her hand across everything on my dresser top.

"Ooo, you nasty. Your grandma let you wear this?" she asks, holding a red lipstick I took from Aunt Loretta's drawer before Grandma boxed everything else to store or throw away.

Lakeisha talks fast and doesn't let me answer. She has picked up the framed picture of me and Drew and Aunt Loretta in front of the frozen falls.

"Your mom was pretty."

"Aunt Loretta is not my mom."

"Oh?"

"She's my aunt."

"What your mom look like?"

I wish I could say: Just like me, but taller. Like a grown-up me. If I describe what Mor really looks like it will make her seem plain: long blond hair, white skin; she had an accent (and that's important even though it's not something you could tell by looking at her). If I describe her to Lakeisha, it will make Mor seem like any other white person you'd see.

"My mom was light-skinned."

"Light-skinned-ed? For real? That's why you so light?"

When we look at the two different scenes, we see that Lakeisha's dialogue changes dramatically—or code-switches—from when she's speaking to Grandma

Dorris to when she's speaking with Rachel, the narrator of the novel, who is closer to her in age. Lakeisha's dialogue is more formal and polite when she's in the presence of her father and Grandma Dorris. When alone with Rachel, her dialogue relaxes and she uses more slang such as "Ooo, you nasty," "for real," and "light-skinned-ed."

EXERCISE

Write a scene in which two characters who have different identities from your own are having a conversation. They can discuss any topic, but try to write a few pages. (You can also pull a dialogue scene from a piece you've already written that features two characters with different identities.)

Now, examine how you described the characters' dialogue. To help you do that, answer these questions:

- How did I describe the characters' accents or the way they speak? (Look at the exposition around the dialogue.)
- What are the stereotypes associated with each character's identity? (Remember, there are dialogue stereotypes relating to racial/ethnic, gender, disability, nationality, class, sexual orientation, and cultural identities.) Did I unknowingly write those stereotypes into their dialogue?

- Does one character use more slang, cuss words, or sexualized language than the other character? Why?
- Are there phonetics in the dialogue? Why did I use phonetics? Would the dialogue be easier to read without phonetics?
- Is that slang choice authentic, stereotypical, or incorrect? How do I know that?

After writing down your answers, take a day or two to think about them. You don't need to make changes right away. You may want to ask a critique partner for advice, do more research, or give yourself time to get comfortable with the idea of making changes you didn't expect to make. Take all the time you need before reworking the dialogue.

7

IDENTITIES AND GENRE

As a child, fantasy and historical fiction stole my heart. By the time I became a teenager, my interests had expanded to science fiction, and in my young adult years, I explored romance. Later, I'd read other genres like thrillers and horror with a few Westerns and mysteries peppered in. When I look back at the genre novels that I read, I'm aware that most were written by white cis authors, and only a few featured characters of other races, non-heteronormative sexual orientations, or disabilities.

There was a time when I stopped reading genre novels and focused primarily on literary fiction, but in my early thirties I returned to it and was surprised that in some ways things hadn't improved. I spoke with genre writers, read interviews with them, and investigated social media discussions within various genre communities about the lack of diversity and a host of misrepresentations and tropes in some of the most popular books.

I can even recall the first time I taught a class on "Writing an Identity Other Than Your Own," and received a private message before the class from an editor at a publishing house that was having a hard time with one of her romance clients. The romance writer had depicted an interracial relationship between a Black man and a white woman in her novel. The editor was concerned that the relationship felt too idealistic, and lacked certain elements of authenticity that could arise within the relationship's dynamics or from the outside world.

According to the editor, the writer had said, "This is romance, not literary fiction. I'm not going to show any of those 'bad' things." The editor wanted my advice. How might she convey to the writer that her perspective of her characters' interracial relationship not only was hurting the piece but was a disservice to interracial couples?

Unfortunately, I can't recall my exact advice, but each time I teach the class, I remember that editor and her romance author because it speaks to something that I want to address with genre writers: you are just as at risk of writing a trope, stereotype, or misrepresentation as any other type of writer.

I've had people push against this. Fantasy writers have told me, "My story is made-up, not representative of this world, the result of my imagination." We know that isn't entirely true. As writers, we can only build worlds based on the knowledge of our own, and who's to say that our biases about race in our world will not be mirrored among the different races in the fantasy world? Historical fiction writers tend to leave out characters of different sexual orientations, those with disabilities, and those of color from their stories. Some have said that people from these historically marginalized identities would not have been in a specific historical setting like Europe of the past—which isn't true at all. As long as there have been people, there have been people with disabilities, people of different sexual orientations, and yes, even people of color in some of Europe's highest and whitest courts.

So, this chapter is to help genre writers, to point out the tropes, clichés, stereotypes, and pitfalls they may run into when writing. I've separated this chapter by different genres, and while you may not write sci-fi, you might find that some of the tropes I've pointed out in that section could make their way into crime or fantasy. Give the full chapter a read. It can't hurt.

BUT FIRST, SAVIORISM

Before we get into the tropes and stereotypes of different genres, let's talk about saviorism stories, because they can appear in every single genre.

You may have heard about the white savior complex, which showcases a white person "saving" or "helping" a person of color from their plight. There are other savior complexes too. There is the ableist savior "saving" people with disabilities, as well as the straight savior "saving" the LGBTQIA+ community. You could even argue that the damsel-in-distress trope is a sexist savior complex that showcases men needing to save women.

The savior complex presents certain communities as victims in need of saving, but it completely overlooks the fact that privileged communities that place themselves in the role of savior tend to cause the issues that historically marginalized communities face.

A savior story is a tropic storyline. Tropes are not necessarily "bad" things in the context of writing. They can be stylistic devices, especially in genre writing, where tropes are beloved by many readers, and writers use them for a purpose. With that in mind, you could write a saviorism story, but be aware that it comes with a lot of baggage and can send a message you do not intend to send to readers. If you decide to use the tropic saviorism storyline, you'll need to consider the main characters at play. Who is saving whom? What kind of message does that send? Does it perpetuate a stereotype, spread misinformation, or result in a problematic depiction? Does the saviorism story result in inspirational or trauma porn?

ADDITIONAL RESEARCH IS REQUIRED

I can't possibly list every single trope, stereotype, or problematic representation that exists for every genre, and I am aware that new ones may be added after this book is published. You'll need to do some work on your own and look up all the biased and prejudiced tropes and stereotypes that are associated with the genre in which you write. Look at discussions and articles online. If you are connected to other writers and readers within your genre, have conversations with them. What racist stereotypes have they noticed in your genre? Ableist tropes? Through conversation and research, I hope you discover more than I have presented here.

ROMANCE

- **Tokenizing interracial relationships:** Interracial relationships are sometimes tokenized as the ideal relationship in which two people overcome the boundaries of racism and fall in love. The reality is anything but, as I can attest as a child of an interracial relationship. Racism can exist in interracial relationships, as can cultural, racial, and ethnic misunderstandings.
- **Fetishization:** Writers should be conscious of how people of color, disabled people, and people with queer sexual or romantic orientations can be fetishized in the romance genre.
- **Exoticization:** This problem occurs when a writer portrays a romantic element in a romanticized, glamorized, or unusual way. In the romance genre, this can present itself as glamorizing to an excessive extent or without showcasing a balanced perception of certain cultural practices like arranged marriages, or in how a writer portrays a relationship between two people who identify with the LGBTQIA+ community. When something is

glamorized or romanticized, it removes the authenticity and reality of the romantic experience.

- **Sexist stereotypes:** Be it the damsel-in-distress trope or the idea that a man should sweep a woman off her feet, romance stories sometimes present sexist stereotypes that uphold outdated ideas that men are dominant protectors and heads of households, and women should be demure, quiet, and submissive victims.

- **Binary gender romance:** Do not indicate that there is only one kind of romantic experience that occurs between a man and a woman. For example, saying "She was attracted to the opposite sex" indicates there are only two biological sexes—female and male—which is not true. Intersex people exist. To that effect, there are many gender identities beyond woman and man, and to indicate that romance occurs on a binary gender system is being exclusive of queer gender identities and their romantic experiences.

- **Straight characterization of queerness:** One of the biggest complaints I've seen is how straight writers write queer romance by basing the characters on a heterosexual cisgender couple and then replacing their heterosexuality with a queer identity. While many elements of queer relationships are the same as those between straight people, some things are different, and this can be a result of many factors, including queer culture and history, social influences, etc.

- **Tragic queer love story:** This trope occurs when queer characters are not given happy endings in romance or love stories. Whether these couples are given a tragic ending like death or sickness, or if they simply break up, it can send the message that queer characters are not deserving of love, happy endings, and/or a fulfilled romantic life.

SCIENCE FICTION/FANTASY/ SPECULATIVE FICTION

- **Colonialization trope:** Writers may unknowingly depict colonialization from the colonialist perspective—or as something beneficial—and this can result in harm. Even stories told from the colonized perspective can run into issues, especially when the author is from a colonialist culture and doesn't understand the nuances of what it means for a community to experience and be subjected to colonialization.
- **Mad scientist:** The mad scientist trope is ableist and a harmful depiction of people with mental health conditions, as it indicates that people with mental health conditions are evil or villainous.
- **Monocultural races:** In sci-fi, some writers have portrayed other races of beings as having no diversity within their culture, appearance, language, style, music, and beliefs. Depicting a race of beings as having a monoculture is a result of white supremacy in our world and how historically white communities have not seen diversity within other communities and have labeled everyone within them with the same descriptors.
- **Dark vs. light:** Associating people with dark skin as the "bad" people in a story and people with light skin as the good people mirrors the basic trope of good versus evil and indicates that people of color are evil and people

who are light-skinned are good. The dark-light dynamic may also appear in more symbolic ways, such as through the color of clothing or magical powers.

- **Barbarians:** An offensive term that historically refers to Indigenous peoples; it is usually used in fantasy stories as a derogatory term for a group of people who have similar characteristics to Indigenous communities or are people of color. Similarly offensive terms include "heathen" and "savage."

- **Mirroring our history:** It's not easy to come up with a fantastical story in which the author does not build a world without some elements based in our reality. However, when that world's history mirrors our own, writers can find themselves faced with potentially writing trauma porn, minimizing historical moments, or making certain actions by certain groups seem less bad. If you're going to mirror our own history in a fantasy world, you'll need to approach the historical aspect with care, making sure you understand all different aspects of it, and that your depiction is not harmful to the communities who were affected (i.e., does not diminish their pain or trauma, is realistic about the power dynamics that were at play, etc.).

- **Magic and disabilities:** Ableist depictions of people with disabilities can occur in multiple ways such as the "magical healing" of a character with a disability, which can suggest that disabled people are always seeking a cure for their disabilities. At times, fantasy writers have given people with disabilities magical abilities, usually in some way that is connected to their disability, like the blind person who can also see the future. This ableist trope indicates that disabled people have worth or power only if they're magical.

- **Femme fatale and damsel in distress:** Be careful that you don't have sexist depictions of women in your fantasy works whether they are damsels in distress in need of rescuing by a man, or if they are femme fatales, who are generally depicted as seductive women who will bring disaster to the men in their lives.

- **Fantasizing Indigenous, Latine, Asian, African, or Middle Eastern myths, legends, or oral stories:** When fantasy writers take the myths of Indigenous, Latine, Asian, African, or Middle Eastern communities and change, warp, or use them as inspiration for their fantasy stories, this can result in a host of issues, as it may be seen as cultural appropriation (if done by someone not of that identity) or result in exoticism, bias, and stereotypes. In terms of Indigenous oral stories, many Indigenous communities require that their permission be given to share certain oral stories on a larger stage and/or do not like their oral history to be changed for the benefit of a fantasy work. The fantasizing of myths, legends, and oral stories is an ongoing conversation within different communities, and it will be interesting to see what will develop from this conversation in years to come.

- **Associating monsters with ableist and/or racist stereotypes:** Some writers have unintentionally (and at times intentionally) integrated racist and ableist stereotypes into the monsters they create. For example, J.R.R. Tolkien's depiction of orcs exhibits racist stereotypes of Asians and Black people.[1] Pay attention to how you describe your monsters and that you're not unconsciously associating their characteristics with people of color and the stereotypes associated with them.

Monsters have also been consistently described in similar (and offensive) ways to people with physical and intellectual disabilities—dumb, simple, stupid, primitive, twisted, misshapen, disfigured, unnatural, lumbering, limping, hobbling, moronic, insane, crazy, mad, deranged, etc. Sometimes the monsters are even given physical disabilities like blindness, deafness, missing limbs, or diseases that cause physical sores, or growths. Such depictions can indicate that to have a physical or intellectual disability is monstrous.

- **The Magical [enter historically marginalized race/ethnicity] character:** Whether it's the Magical Black character or the Magical Asian trope, we see people of color used in historical fiction as magical or witchy characters who live on the fringes of society and have more insight into the workings of the world—almost as if by magic. This trope generally presents as a magical person of color helping a white character on their journey. Not only does it indicate that their only role in a story is to help a white character, it also implies that a person of color could only be helpful—or understand more than a white person—if they were magical.

- **Centuries-old supernatural man and the teenage girl relationship:** A romantasy trope that occurs when a centuries-old vampire, fairy, werewolf, or other supernatural man "falls in love" and has a romantic relationship with a teenage girl (usually between sixteen and nineteen years old). Romanticizing relationships with large age gaps that involve teenagers is concerning, especially when the creative piece leaves out the harmful power dynamics at play that can cause emotional, mental, and/or physical harm to the teenager who doesn't have a fully developed adult brain, financial security, similar educational levels, or career experience. (Of course, if the teenager is younger than eighteen years old, then it wouldn't be considered a relationship.) Unfortunately, there has been a massive number of fantasy and romantasy books that romanticize large age-gap relationships between teenage girl characters and older man characters who are supernatural beings. Such works do not typically showcase the realistic power dynamic issues that would arise in a relationship between these characters (it doesn't matter if the man character was turned into a supernatural being as a teenager; if they've lived for twenty-five, fifty, or one hundred years, they have far more experience, knowledge, and power than a teenage girl), but instead portray the relationship as normal, healthy, romantic, sexy, and desirable. Just because you are writing fantasy or romantasy does not mean that "anything goes." Let's move on from the Edward Cullen, Damon Salvatore, Angel characters who go after high school girls. It's disturbing.

WESTERNS

- **Lacking diversity:** Western fiction has lacked people of color, those who identify with the LGBTQIA+ community, and people with disabilities, despite the fact that the West was filled with all types of people beyond white, straight, cisgender folks.

- **Damsel in distress:** This is a sexist savior complex that showcases women as victims who are unable to protect themselves. The West was not an easy place to live, and women faced harsh and difficult aspects of that lifestyle every day, but they had to take care of their home, family, land, and business on their own at times.

- **BIPOC speech:** When we look at the speech of BIPOC characters in Western stories, we might see their dialogue crafted in a way that furthers stereotypes of various races and ethnicities. Consider "Tonto Talk"—a trope derived from the character of Tonto from *The Lone Ranger*. This term refers to how the dialogue of Indigenous peoples in Westerns is sometimes depicted as broken, unintelligent, and simple, reflecting colonialist European beliefs about the intellectual and cultural intelligence of Indigenous peoples. We see the same thing happen with Mexican, Black, and Asian characters in Westerns too.

- **Portrayal of Indigenous peoples:** History is written by the conqueror, so it's no surprise that in the U.S., Indigenous peoples have been portrayed as being the aggressors during the era of the West, such as by attacking and being violent toward white settlers. White settlers encroached upon the lands of Indigenous peoples, kicked them out of their ancestral homes, and caused harm to Indigenous peoples through genocide, disease, and attacks. That's not even mentioning how Europeans took advantage of Indigenous people and their kindness time and time again. If you're going to portray Indigenous peoples in Westerns, don't do so with a colonialist perspective, one that portrays settlers as positive and Indigenous people as negative. Equally as important, be mindful of portraying them as "grand," "wise," "regal," "pure," or any other type of stereotype associated with Indigenous people.

HISTORICAL FICTION

- **Complete lack of diversity:** Historical fiction has been incredibly whitewashed. If the story is set in Paris in the 1600s, why are there no people of African descent? They were there. While there are pockets across the world where racial diversity would have been low, that doesn't mean that there wouldn't have been disabled people, queer people (even if they weren't out), or traders from other cultural communities. Sometimes historical fiction is written under the assumption that diversity did not occur throughout the world until the last century, but the reality is that trade routes, war, and many other factors have long brought different people together.
- **Unintelligent person of color:** This promotes the assumption that because a person of color existed before the 1800s, they were uneducated or unintelligent. (Also, education does not equate to intelligence.) This can appear in how the writer depicts their speech, or behavior, and can result in a racist depiction of people of color.
- **Trauma porn:** It is problematic when a writer takes a traumatic moment or event in history related to a certain group or community and showcases that group's pain and trauma excessively to create a sentimental or emotionally wrenching story.

- **The Yellow Peril:** This is a racist trope that suggests that East and South Asian people and their culture are a danger to the West.

Historical Fiction Fallacy

When I teach Writing an Identity Not Your Own, I find that historical fiction writers tend to have the most difficult time with the subject. "It's accurate to the times" is a common excuse for why they want to include problematic portrayals, stereotypes and stereotypical dialogue, misrepresentations, savior stories, and slurs or offensive terms. Here's the thing: "It's accurate to the times" is not going to work in the process of writing an identity not your own.

Just because something is "accurate to the times" does not mean that it is free of bias.

Just because something is "accurate to the times" does not mean you aren't othering characters of a historically marginalized identity or community.

Just because something is "accurate to the times" does not mean that it is the right choice for a fictional piece of creative writing—which, I remind you, is fictional.

Just because something is "accurate to the times" does not mean that it will go over well with your present-day audience.

Just because something is "accurate to the times" does not mean that you won't write the scene in a sentimental way that manipulates the emotions of your reader.

Just because something is "accurate to the times" does not mean that it can't result in trauma or inspirational porn.

I'll sum this up by saying that my second novel is historical fiction and I made certain stylistic choices that could be argued weren't entirely "accurate" to the time in which the story is set. If I had stuck to the "accuracy of the times," it would have resulted in harmful scenes and depictions. Funny thing is, not one reader, editor, reviewer, or person has ever pointed out to me how those scenes aren't exactly "accurate to the times."

HORROR

- **Mental health conditions:** It's a problem when a writer features a character with a mental health condition who then becomes the "bad person," or when a writer attributes the actions of the villain to a mental health condition. Both associate people with mental health conditions as dangerous. Be wary of also depicting mental health conditions as a horrific way to experience life or a simplistic result of a traumatic experience. Mental health conditions are more complicated than that.

- **Disfigured villain:** As with mental health conditions, the disfigurement and disabilities of a villain is a common trope in horror and indicates that there is something horrific about disabilities and/or disabled people are so upset with their disability that they're willing to do something evil.

- **Death to those engaging in sexual activity:** One of horror's most common tropes is showing people who fornicate—have sex—as expected victims. Sometimes this presents itself as characters cheating or teenagers hooking up when they should be in school. If you use characters of the LGBTQIA+ community in this trope, you could unknowingly be sending the message that queer people hooking up is bad or perverse, and thus, their sexual orientation is the reason for their murder. Consider how other historically marginalized communities (like interracial couples) will be perceived if represented in this trope too.

- **The magical BIPOC neighbor or warner:** When a person of color is used as the magical neighbor or the person who warns the (usually white) main character about a dangerous thing, it can be seen as the writer using the person of color as a plot device for the benefit of a white character.

- **The token marginalized character:** When a horror piece features a single character from a historically marginalized community as a way to provide "some diversity," it is a form of tokenization. We generally see it with race, but that's not to say that it doesn't occur with other historically marginalized identities.

- **The Native American burial ground:** This is an offensive trope to explain supernatural hauntings within a specific place. It suggests that Native American cultures are "creepy," "supernatural," or "evil," and that Native American people lack power and thus seek revenge against European colonialization through supernatural means, rather than policy or activism.

- **The ableist asylum trope:** Asylums have generally been showcased as places where abuse happened toward people with disabilities and mental health conditions. Some writers present asylums as something of the far past, when in reality these types of institutions still exist (usually as state-funded group homes or nursing homes) where people with disabilities and mental health conditions are abused or taken advantage of.

If you have a story set in an asylum, be aware of the way your characters with mental health conditions or disabilities are treated within the story. Excessive violence toward these individuals can result in trauma porn. You also risk showcasing these types of people as always being the helpless victim, childlike, dangerous, and/or violent.

Don't forget that asylums were also places where queer people and women, who did not have mental health conditions, were sent. Writers who share these stories of people falsely imprisoned in asylums might suggest through their storytelling that these people are more deserving of the reader's sympathy because they shouldn't be in an asylum. When abled characters are given more sympathetic portrayals than characters with disabilities and/or mental health conditions, it can send the message that the treatment of people with disabilities and/or mental health conditions in an asylum is in some way acceptable, normal, and not deserving of sympathy.

CRIME/MYSTERY/DETECTIVE

- **The othered villain:** Whether the villain is a person of color, has a disability, or has a mental health condition, we tend to see people of historically marginalized backgrounds made into stock villains. By this, I mean that their marginalization has been used as a driving force for them to be "evil" and to do bad things.

- **Elder BIPOC figure or BIPOC gang leader:** This is a tropic figure that law enforcement seeks out for information or assistance on their case. This character tends to be an elderly person of color, often a gang leader, and is presented as having a "mutual respect" for law enforcement. This character and how they're used in the story downplays or incorrectly portrays the real issues that communities of color face with police.

- **Thug and sex worker stereotypes:** There is a tropic tendency to indicate that people who are "thugs," gang members, criminals, or sex workers are people of color. If they die in the story, they are not always given the same sympathy as other characters.

- **A villain with a disfigurement or disability:** Many crime stories feature villains with facial or bodily disfigurements or disabilities. It sends the message that people with disfigurements or disabilities are unhappy, dangerous, evil, villainous, or so enraged about how they look or experience life with a disability that they're willing to commit a crime because of it.

- **Autistic detective:** This paints a picture of autistic detectives as being cold/rude, emotionless, obsessive, incapable of relationships (and therefore more focused on the job), and needing help from others to function in society. Autistic characteristics are given to detectives as a way of explaining why the detective is so good at being able to see into the minds of criminals. In doing this, the writer makes an association between autism and criminality.

Sonya Freeman Loftis said it best in her book *Imagining Autism: Fiction and Stereotypes on the Spectrum*:

Depicted as cold and emotionless machines, imagined as puzzles to solve, these figures perpetuate negative depictions of people with autism. Although the autistic crime fighter may seem to help dispel false perceptions of people on the spectrum as violent, Holmes and other characters like him maintain a lingering liminality between the autistic detective and the villains he pursues, suggesting that there is something inherently criminal about any kind of cognitive difference.[2]

A NOTE ON CREATIVE NONFICTION

After a friend finished her master of fine arts in creative writing, she shared a few of her essays from her thesis, an essay collection, with me. She was a woman of color writing about her childhood, and while the essays mostly had to do with family dynamics, there was one story that focused on her interest in an ethnic identity that was not her own.

I was working on this book when I read her essay, so I was hyperfocused on the subject of writing an identity not your own, and while I had some ideas on how it might appear in creative nonfiction, it wasn't until reading her essay that those ideas became solidified.

There may be this assumption by creative nonfiction writers that they don't have to worry about the concepts of writing an identity not their own. When you're writing about yourself and recounting stories from your past, you're not focusing on other identities, right? Not necessarily.

Unless you're writing in a vacuum about how you never left your house since you were born and have no knowledge about the outside world, there will be times when the practice of writing an identity not your own could come up in your work. Think about your life and all the secondary characters that have played a role in it. You have had experiences with people, possibly with different backgrounds from you, that could be relevant to your creative nonfiction piece.

The most important thing a nonfiction writer needs to do is be aware of their current and past unconscious biases. Such biases could be present in your work, whether that's how you describe people of different identities that you've interacted with, recall notable events in history, comment on pop culture, etc.

You, as a nonfiction writer, are not free of biases and judgments, and I'd wager that you could be less aware of them when you're recounting your real-life experiences. We tend to see our lives, our memories, and our experiences through a certain lens, because we believe we remember exactly how things occurred. Unfortunately, memory is unreliable—even if only a few seconds have passed,[3] which means our memories can form in biased ways.

Discussing your memories of an experience with other people can be helpful, as they can offer their take on what happened and hopefully recognize any of your unrealized biases relating to the situation. You might also have to write your way to discovering the bias. Sometimes you can't recognize all the elements at play until the story is written out.

Nonfiction creative writers can also practice acknowledgment in their work. We have all been lesser-evolved, knowledgeable people who have made mistakes, some of which could be argued were harmful to other communities or offensive in some right. It may have even been part of the culture of our time to use words we would never use today, or we might have been at an age when we did not fully comprehend how our actions impacted others. Whatever it may be, if you as a creative nonfiction writer decide to recount those moments in your past, acknowledge them for what they are: inappropriate, harmful, offensive, problematic—you decide on the exact wording.

When I read my friend's essay, I pointed out two instances in which she recounted some experiences she had as a child that seemed a bit problematic. I admire anyone who can share memories that do not paint themselves or their loved ones in the best light; however, I felt that her approach merely recounted the events, rather than acknowledged them as problematic.

If you don't acknowledge how these moments in your past were problematic or exhibited your lack of knowledge on race, sexual orientation, gender identity, or abilities, it could be perceived as if you're downplaying the situation or ignoring it entirely. Explaining how and why your past thoughts or actions were problematic will allow you to connect with readers in a more personal and authentic way.

It should go without saying that if you do write about real-life people with different identities than your own, you'll need to take care in how you depict them. Nonfiction writers can run the risk of creating stock characters, as well as misrepresenting different cultures and communities. Like fiction writers, nonfiction writers might also use stereotypical dialogue and accents and inappropriate terms too.

8

WRITING HISTORICALLY MARGINALIZED IDENTITIES

This chapter will delve into five major historically marginalized identities: race/ethnicity, gender identity, nationality, disability, and sexual and romantic orientation. Under each section, I'll explain some of the most important things to consider when writing characters of those identities.

PREWRITING RESEARCH

Before you begin writing a character of a historically marginalized identity, do a deep dive into the stereotypes, tropes, and clichés relating to people of that identity. This can be as easy as checking out nonfiction library books related to misrepresentations of people of color in books and media or simply googling "Stereotypes + [identity]."

Make a running list and place each one in different categories like appearance, food, language, clothing style, musical interest, hobbies, and more. The more aware of the stereotypes, tropes, and clichés relating to your character's identity, the less likely you'll be to make the mistake of portraying them incorrectly.

Include a section on intersectional stereotypes, tropes, or clichés that relate to the historically marginalized identity. So, for instance, if the identity you are researching is "South Asian," but you know your character is a South Asian woman, make a list of the stereotypes, tropes, and clichés related specifically to South Asian women in the intersectional row.

Don't throw this list away. You'll need it during the editing phase!

IDENTITY: (race/ ethnicity, sexual orientation, gender identity, disability, nationality, etc.)			
	STEREOTYPES	TROPES	CLICHÉS
Appearance (physical traits, clothing style, hair, skin tone, etc.)			
Food			
Language (dialogue, dialect, words, etc.)			
Interests (hobbies, musical taste, athletics, etc.)			
Intersectional			
Other			

Can You Use Stereotypes Purposefully in Your Work?

Stereotypes can be intentionally used in your creative writing. Here are a few ways to do so:

- Have a character or characters acknowledge the stereotype. This could be a direct acknowledgment or through satire or sarcasm, but it must be called out.
  - Ex: "He understood that a Mexican man who owned a yard business was a stereotype, but

he employed over one hundred people and the business was such a success that he'd put his three children through college and started a scholarship fund for the children of his employees. His business had earned him 'Businessperson of the Year' two years running. If his success was a stereotype, so be it."

- Have one character make a stereotypical assumption about a character of a differing identity. If you do this, have both characters acknowledge the stereotype either through their actions, body language, or internal and external dialogue.
- Satire is a great tool to criticize stereotypes. In a satirical piece, the writer might purposefully include stereotypes throughout the length of the work and use tone, dialogue, and plot to point out what makes the stereotype harmful, incorrect, or ridiculous.

IDENTITY TERMS

In the process of writing a different identity, you will be required to name the identity you are writing about—and it's important to get that name right. In your research, you will find that the name of the community you are writing about has changed many times over the years, decades, and centuries. It wasn't too long ago that a trans person might have been referred to as a "transexual," and many of us were raised to use "slave" to refer to people who were enslaved; now, "enslaved person" is more widely accepted.

In our lifetime, we've seen specific terms intentionally used to refer to certain communities in an effort to create negative connotations toward that community. For instance, "illegals" has been intentionally used over more appropriate terms like "undocumented noncitizen" to dehumanize and demean immigrants, especially immigrants of color.

Naming an identity correctly is therefore not just about accuracy. It's also about ensuring that you don't use a name that others, demeans, misrepresents, or harms your characters and the historically marginalized communities they represent.

As you do your research, make a list of appropriate identity terms relating to the character that you're writing. It's likely that there are multiple appropriate terms for a single identity, each with their own slightly different, nuanced meaning. For instance, a character from an older generation might use a different term than someone from a younger generation who has the same identity. As long as both terms are appropriate, or widely accepted as appropriate and respectful, there is no reason why you can't use both in your creative work.

The question might arise: What if I have a character who would prefer to use an outdated identity term (that is not necessarily a slur) when naming their identity or another identity? Be careful with this. Your reader should be able to tell that you as the author have made a deliberate decision to use the term in such a way that does not misrepresent, harm, or demean the historically marginalized community you're writing about. There should be a clear reason as to why the character would use that term, which is explained to your reader within the text either through dialogue, interior thought, or some action scene.

IS THIS MY PERSPECTIVE OR MY CHARACTER'S?

When writing outside of our identity, we should always question how we've portrayed our character's perspective of themself, their identity, and their community. Ask yourself: Is this my perspective or is it an authentic portrayal of how someone of that identity would view their own body, disabilities, attraction, or nation?

I think it is quite easy for us to assume that our perspective is the same as others', especially when we are not well informed of the mindset of people from other identities. To prevent ourselves from making a mistake, we need to know how society perceives our character's appearance, skin tone, hair type, body type, abilities, attraction, nation, and culture. More importantly, we need to know how people from that character's community would view themselves and work our hardest to ensure that we depict a character who is authentic and not a megaphone for our own perceptions, ideas, or biases.

So again, build relationships with people from the identity you're depicting, for doing so may help you learn about those real-life perspectives and ideas.

RACE/ETHNICITY

In my experience teaching creative writing, I've found that most writers are highly concerned about writing characters of different races and ethnicities—and rightfully so. So many writers of the past did it incorrectly, by creating or perpetuating harmful stereotypes and associations that hurt communities of color. That's not to say that you can't learn how to write characters of other races and ethnicities if you're willing to put in the work.

THE INTERSECTION OF CULTURE AND RACE/ETHNICITY

When thinking about your characters of different races and ethnicities, it's important to keep their culture in mind. How can you include the cultural traditions, language, and pop culture references of a certain racial/ethnic community without seeming cliché or reducing your characters to stereotypes?

Learn about specific traditions, phrases, or references among various cultures and how that might play a role in your character's life. While films and books can be helpful sources, it's unlikely that they'll depict specific references that only people who are in the know would be aware of.

Let's consider the Mexican community. While you may be familiar with mainstream Mexican traditions like Día de los Muertos, the Mexican grito, or references to Selena Quintanilla, have you ever heard of the fuchi face? The fuchi face is a face that children typically make by scrunching up their noses as if something stinks. It has become a cultural phenomenon, not only among Mexicans, but across a variety of Latino cultures. Cara de fuchi, or fuchi face, is still a cultural expression that has not gone mainstream, and therefore its use in a creative writing piece can provide some authenticity to that character of color that other mainstream references wouldn't provide.

If you're going to use mainstream traditions, words, music, or references, use them sparingly—otherwise you could be creating a caricature of your character of color.

WHITE SAVIORISM

I've no doubt that you've heard of white saviorism. It's been called the "White Savior Myth," the "White Savior Complex," and the "White Savior Trope," but they're all the same thing. It is the idea that white people or white culture saves people of color from their undesirable situations. The irony is that the status of people of color in terms of the social and political systems of their society is a direct result of the racist actions by white people and their culture.

In literature, we have seen the White Savior Complex appear as a "well-meaning" white person trying to save or help people of color out of a situation (like a legal one in *To Kill a Mockingbird*) or elevate their voices (like in *The Help*). Other times, it presents itself as an actual "saving of the souls" of people of color.

The most important thing to keep in mind when writing about other races, ethnicities, and cultures is to make sure you don't unknowingly feature white characters "saving" characters of color. We've seen enough of that story in films like *The Blind Side* and *The Last Samurai*.

However, you can critique the White Savior Complex within your work as the television adaptation of *Little Fires Everywhere* did. They depict the white, rich character of Elena trying to "save" the Black artist Mia and her daughter. There is no question that it's a critique of the White Savior Complex. Another great example of this is *The Poisonwood Bible*, in which Barbara Kingsolver critiques the religious and white saviorism of missionaries in Africa.

This may not be an easy task to take on as you begin your journey to writing other identities, but with research and practice, it may have a place in a future story.

DESCRIBING APPEARANCE

You're writing a novel and you're ready to introduce a character with a historically marginalized race or ethnicity. Do you describe the character's appearance as a way of indicating their race/ethnicity or do you name it as such?

In most cases, it's better to say the race/ethnicity of a character from the get-go. There is no reason to tiptoe around their race/ethnicity by giving hints to the reader through your description of their appearance. Be blunt. Be clear. Say they are Arab if they're Arab or Thai if they're Thai.

If you go the other route and try to describe their looks before you name their race/ethnicity (or rather than naming it), you could find yourself describing the character in a stereotypical and harmful way.

Here's a good example. Say a writer was trying to tell the reader that a character was East Asian, but they didn't want to explicitly say the character was East Asian. In the past, many writers described all East Asian characters as having "slanted eyes" as a (lazy and offensive) way to indicate the character is East Asian. The problem was that in doing so, these writers contributed to a harmful and racist stereotype.

So how do you prevent this? Say the race/ethnicity. That way your reader does not have to figure out what you're trying to say or not say, and you don't use stereotypical descriptions.

Again—if you point out a character of color's race or ethnicity, do the same for a white character, lest you run into the issue of othering.

PHYSICAL APPEARANCE STEREOTYPING

We are surrounded by a variety of media that has told us how people of certain races or ethnicities should look. However, many racial and ethnic communities have wide ranges of skin tones, hair types, and facial features. When deciding how your character will look, consider that your character does not have to fit the stereotypical assumptions associated with their race or ethnicity.

Yes, there are Asian women who are tall and have dark skin, as well as Latinos with afros and blue or green eyes. There are Black men with red beards and Arabs with blond hair. Question your preconceived notions about how people from certain racial and ethnic backgrounds should look and it will benefit your characterization.

THE DOS AND DON'TS OF DESCRIBING SKIN TONES

- DON'T compare skin tones to foods or spices (e.g., "his almond skin").

  Comparing skin tones to food or spices can be seen as fetishizing the skin tones of people of color. Not only that, but many people of color were forced—either through slavery, colonialization, forced labor, or oppression—to till and work the fields where certain foods and spices were grown. The comparison and conflation of the character of color's skin tone to that of the things they were forced to produce is harmful, reductive, and insinuates that the character is a thing that can be consumed, fetishized, and/or discarded.

What about using stones, gems, minerals, or woods for skin tone descriptions? I'm not a fan of this. Who wants their skin tone to be described as "limestone," "sand," or "amber"? It's not as bad as foods or spices, so if you decide to go this route, do so sparingly and only if there is no association between the person's race/ethnicity or culture and that item (and you're okay with some readers rolling their eyes upon reading it). Otherwise, it could be seen as problematic and result in a stereotype.

- DO consider describing skin tones simply as brown, tan, or beige.

  If you'd like some other skin tone color options, search Google for a "skin tone graph." These graphs have usually been made in relation to makeup and represent a wide range of skin tones. Be mindful, however, because some graphs describe certain skin tones as food and spices—and as I've mentioned above, we should steer away from those descriptions.

  If I can provide you with one last piece of advice, it's that it is always best to go the simpler route when describing skin tones. Using an obscure color to describe a skin tone can be confusing to readers. Can you confidently say you know what "sienna" looks like, or "umber" for that matter? Yeah, neither can I.

- DO describe the undertones of skin, e.g., "In the summer, the red undertone of her skin is more prominent."

- DO use modifiers like rich, warm, medium, tan, deep, cool, fair, light, or pale, e.g., "The yellow shirt washed out their warm beige skin."
- DON'T use metaphors to describe skin tone without thinking about the associations you're making. Are you making stereotypical or cliché associations? Are you using metaphors to describe darker skin tones in a negative light and lighter skin tones in a positive light?
- DO describe white characters' skin tones with as much detail as you would the skin tones of characters of color.

LET'S TALK ABOUT HAIR

How you describe hair and your character's relationship with their hair is important, especially when that character is from a historically marginalized race or ethnicity.

Start by looking at how different types of hair are categorized through the Andre Walker hair styling system.[1] There are four different hair types—straight, wavy, curly, and coily—which are then broken down by width or diameter of the hair pattern, so wide, medium, and tight. By looking at how Walker has described these hair types, you'll hopefully have a more appropriate way of describing hair. Take the coily hair type, for instance: 4a coils are described as having S-patterns that are considered to be dense and springy.

There are other types of hair typology systems too—like the LOIS System. No matter which hair system you refer to, there are some words we don't want to use to describe hair when writing other identities. "Kinky" or "nappy" should not be used in reference to coily types of hair, and you should never make positive or negative associations to certain hair types. For instance, curly hair is not "difficult" or less attractive compared to straight hair.

Build upon that by describing small details of your character's hair, whether that be flyaways, cowlicks, curly hairs at the base of the neck, or straight hair with a wave that runs around the back of the character's head from one side of their chin to the other.

Consider also how setting will play a role in your character's hairstyle. How will their hair be affected by the humidity of Florida or the dry air of Arizona?

If you're going to describe hair care and styles, it's best to be as specific as possible. Do you know the difference between dreads and box braids? Or a fade and a crew cut? What about the different types of perms for different hair types? A perm for a white person is not the same as a perm for a Black person.

As with skin tone, be careful of the associations you make or the metaphors you use in your character's hair description. It can be helpful to research hair stereotypes and tropes relating to your character's racial and ethnic identity too.

INTERSECTION OF RACE/ ETHNICITY AND BODY TYPES

When it comes to describing the body types of characters of color, we need to be aware of the associations we make and ensure that Black and brown bodies are not being unconsciously described in demeaning, fetishized, or stereotypical ways. It can be a simple cliché like referring to an Asian woman as small or sexualizing a Black man's body. Most importantly, we must not place negative associations on bodies that are different than ours, especially when those body types intersect with race.

For example, if we look at obesity rates, Black and Native Americans have the highest rate of self-reported obesity.[2] (I acknowledge that these statistics have been debated and could be skewed but go with me here for a second.) While science may label certain bodies among these communities as obese, that is not to say that writers should consider their body types as unhealthy, unattractive, or undesirable. Alternatively, there should not be an assumption that all Black and Indigenous characters will have curvy or fat bodies, because there is a range of body types among these populations.

Be mindful when portraying a BIPOC character who sees their body in a negative light, as this could showcase more of the author's bias about body types and race than the character's own. As with hair and skin tone, using metaphor or hyperbole to describe the body types of your BIPOC characters is not the best idea.

Don't forget, if you're going to describe one body type, describe them all or else risk othering, stereotyping, or fetishizing your character of a different identity.

COLORISM

Colorism is a practice among people of the same ethnic or racial group in which the group favors lighter skin and is prejudiced or discriminatory toward those in their community with darker skin.

This presents itself in different ways depending on the racial or ethnic community. In Asia, skin lightening or skin bleaching beauty products are pervasive, and some people will go to great lengths to prevent their skin from tanning in the summer. Among Latino communities, darker skin represents possible connections to Indigenous or African (rather than Spanish) heritage, which is looked upon as being "low status" and unattractive.

One of the most appalling examples of colorism came from a casting call for women actors for the film *Straight Outta Compton*. It called for four different types of women actors described as "A Girls," "B Girls," "C Girls," and "D Girls." Where "A Girls" were noted as needing to "have real hair—no extensions" and were considered "the hottest of the hottest," the "D Girls" were described as "African American girls. Poor, not in good shape. Medium to dark skin tone."[3]

While colorism may occur within a racial or ethnic community, there is no doubt that other racial/ethnic communities adopt such beliefs too. It's why celebrities like Nicole Byer have explained how Hollywood makeup artists, many of whom are white, are not equipped with the correct foundation for darker skin tones. Colorism has been ingrained in the wider consciousness of the American public, so try to be diligent in how you describe characters of color and do not make more positive associations with characters of color who have lighter complexions or appear more racially ambiguous.

You may or may not want your character to have an obvious run-in with colorism within their own community or outside of it, but it's something to keep in mind when writing these characters. If you understand colorism, you'll be better informed of how your character moves in the world and the subtle challenges or privileges they may experience based on their skin tone.

Final Tips for Writing About Your Character of Color's Appearance

There are a few notes that don't quite fit in any of the previous categories, so I've put them below:

- Research the laws, rules, and societal perceptions relating to your character's hair, skin, or body. For instance, we know that there are laws that specifically target the hairstyles of people of Black heritage, a Muslim woman's right to wear hijab, and more.
- Research the cultural appropriation or controversial topics relating to the hair, skin, or body types of different identities. For instance, is it offensive to Indigenous communities if we refer to a specific hairstyle worn by non-Indigenous peoples as a "mohawk"? (The answer is yes.)
- Do research into body care products and how they intersect with your character's race/ethnicity or culture. For instance, Latinos have a strong relationship to Vicks VapoRub, many Caribbean peoples use Jabon de Cuaba, and shea butter has played an important role in Black American skin care.

EXERCISE #1

Find a picture of a person from the racial/ethnic community that you wish to write about. (Use a free image site. Do not use Instagram or any other social media account to source this photo, and do not use a photograph of anyone you know.) Imagine that this is your character. How would you describe their appearance? Write one paragraph describing their skin tone, hair style, body type, and features. Let the paragraph rest and come back to it another day.

Examine what you've written. Is there anything that sticks out? Something that can be better explained? A metaphor that doesn't sit right with you? A subtle stereotype? Negative associations to their facial features or skin tone? Revise your paragraph and then share it with another writer. Ask them for edits, feedback, or suggestions.

EXERCISE #2

Imagine the body of a character you wish to write. Answer the following questions:

- What does the character's body look like?
- What does the character's body feel like?
- How does the character's body move?
- What does the character's voice sound like?
- How do other people perceive this character's body when they walk into a room?
- How does the character perceive their own body?

Now examine your answers. Where do you feel confident in your visualization? Which questions were you unsure of? Did you write anything down that could be considered stereotypical? How? What can you do to better visualize your character?

GENDER IDENTITY

Gender identity is far more complicated than we may think because we're working with an outdated concept of gender. Do you remember being told in biology class or sex education that chromosomes were either XX or XY and that resulted in a child being born either a girl or a boy? That's not the whole story.

The truth is that not everyone is born with either XX or XY chromosomes.[4] People can be born with chromosomes that are XXY or a single X. Some are even born with XY chromosomes and have female-presenting features. Then there are the güevedoces of the Dominican Republic, who are classified as females at birth, but develop male genitalia around the age of twelve.[5]

Gender is not as easy to define, and if we can start from that idea when approaching gender identities in our work, we have a better chance at depicting the complexities of gender in more accurate and inclusive ways.

A CRASH COURSE IN SEX, GENDER, AND GENDER IDENTITY

People sometimes get confused when it comes to understanding sex, gender, and gender identity. Planned Parenthood explains "sex" best when they say that "sex is a label—male or female—that you're assigned by a doctor at birth based on the genitals you're born with and the chromosomes you have."[6] This definition leaves out how some people are labeled as intersex because their anatomy does not seem to "fit" in the categories of male or female. However, even intersex people are given a "male" or "female" sex label on their birth certificate.

The issue with sex is that the medical community only provides two labels, and because of this, it's better to say that someone is "assigned male at birth" or "assigned female at birth" rather than "biological sex." The phrase makes a point of noting that it's a doctor who decides your sex (which may not even be accurate because the doctor usually does not check your chromosomes upon birth). More importantly, one's assigned sex at birth does not always align with how a person feels inside or how they identify in terms of gender.

I like to use "gender identity" rather than "gender" because gender is a social construct, and yet the word itself implies that it is a fixed medical thing, even though it's not.

To understand how gender is a social construct, we can look at how different cultures have different genders. Yes, most societies have two genders, but some communities in places like India, Oman, Samoa, Madagascar, and Siberia recognize three genders. The same occurs in many Native American and Hawaiian cultures. In Indonesia, there are five genders.

Gender can determine your social and legal status. Think of how there were laws that prohibited women from owning land. Gender also comes with a set of norms relating to your behavior and thought process; this is determined by society. Men in our society (and many others), for instance, are expected to be the breadwinners and not show emotions.

Transgender people are legally recognized in the United States. In some cases, the laws favor transgender people and allow them to change their assigned sex on their driver's license. At other times, laws target transgender people and their access to housing and healthcare. Regardless, trans people are recognized in our society because we now have laws—be they oppressive or inclusive—relating to them.

Now let's talk about gender identity, which is "how you feel inside and how you express your gender through clothing, behavior, and personal experiences."[7]

Gender identity, then, is what you choose your gender to be. "Woman" and "man" are gender identities because you do not have to express yourself the way a woman or a man is expected to behave based on the gender expectations that your society has. Other gender identities include non-binary, transgender, agender, bigender, genderqueer, Two-Spirit, and more. Note: Two-Spirit is only to be used for people who are members of an Indigenous community that has a Two-Spirit identity; Indigenous people who have Two-Spirit identity characteristics may or may not define themselves by this term.

In crafting your character, you'll need to know their gender identity. Regardless of what the doctor assigned them at birth in terms of sex, or how society "sees" their gender, what does your character feel like inside? What gender identity do they most align with, and how do they express that?

Thinking of sex, gender, and gender identity in these ways can assist in character development. Answer the questions below and see if they offer more insight into your character.

- **Sex:** What sex did a doctor assign your character at birth?
- **Gender:** What does society believe your character's gender to be? What are the norms—behaviors, appearance, dress, and thoughts—that society expects of your

character's gender? What are the societal benefits and drawbacks of being that gender? What laws affect their gender?

- **Gender identity:** What gender identity does your character feel like inside? How do they like to express their gender identity in terms of their appearance or behavior? When did they recognize their gender identity? Have they had certain positive or negative experiences related to their gender identity?

WHAT ARE YOUR CHARACTERS' PRONOUNS?

When creating a character of a different gender identity, you'll need to ask yourself—what are their pronouns?

It may seem like new pronouns beyond she/her and he/him have popped up in the last ten years, but they've been around a lot longer than we might think. In fact, linguist Dennis Baron, author of *What's Your Pronoun? Beyond He and She,* found that the pronouns e/em/es were being used as far back as 1841.[8] The pronoun tey/ter/tem was coined in 1971 in the preview issue of *Ms. Magazine* by Casey Miller and Kate Swift, who thought of it as the "human pronoun."[9]

> For more insight on the history and politics of pronouns, read Dennis Baron's blog, *The Web of Language.*
>
>

So how do you decide which pronouns are best for your character? The first thing to keep in mind is that your character's gender identity does not necessarily determine the pronouns they use.

For instance, your character may identify as a non-binary person but is comfortable with both he/him/his and they/them pronouns. While people who are non-binary, transgender, or gender nonconforming might use gender-neutral pronouns more often, that's not to say those who identify as women or men may not also use them as well. Pronouns are not fixed and can be changed over a lifetime.

When deciding which pronouns your characters might use, consider who your character is beyond their gender identity. Do their age, bias, or political beliefs make them more inclined to use certain pronouns over others? Are they questioning their gender identity? Does a certain pronoun speak to them for a specific reason, like the pronoun's history or because it's more commonly used in a community they identify with? Is their pronoun determined by the time in which they live?

To get started, here is a list of possible pronouns your character could use.

she	her	her	hers	herself
he	him	his	his	himself
they	them	their	theirs	themself
zie	zim	zir	zis	zieself
sie	sie	hir	hirs	hirself
ey	em	eir	eirs	eirself
ve	ver	vis	vers	verself
tey	ter	tem	ters	terself
e/ey	em	eir	eirs	emself

xe	xem	xyr	xyrs	xemself
ze	hir	hir	hirs	hirself
fae	faer	faer	faers	faerself
ae	aer	aer	aers	aerself
per	per	pers	pers	perself

The chart above might change if some pronouns are replaced by others, expand as more pronouns are created, or shrink as some pronouns go out of use. Language is always evolving.

These pronouns may be relevant for a literary fiction story, but what if you're writing sci-fi, fantasy, or speculative fiction? Make up your own pronouns if you'd like. There is no rule book that says you must use the pronouns that are used in our current time, place, and reality in a world that is inherently different from ours.

Those who are writing in close third person will need to use the character's preferred pronouns throughout the story. It could get confusing switching between pronouns if your character uses multiple pronouns; however, that's not to say that if it's part of the story, it can't be done. For example, if partway through the story, your character concludes that they don't like their previous pronoun and would like to use a different pronoun, you'll need to switch pronoun usage immediately. There are ways to transition smoothly; you'll need to figure out how to best do that so your reader can follow along.

If you are writing in first-person, your protagonist may at times ask other characters about their pronouns. Maybe they're the kind of character who doesn't think about pronouns and so they make assumptions about pronouns for another character and are corrected. There are many ways in which pronouns might appear in your story, and how you choose to approach pronouns can make for a more inclusive, respectful, or authentic piece.

Guess what? Some people prefer not to use any pronouns at all. Yep—zero pronouns! This could be for a number of reasons. A person might still be deciding which pronouns feel right and don't want to use any pronouns until then. Others don't like any of the pronouns available, and still others just don't like the concept of pronouns at all. To be clear, people who don't use any pronouns would not use they/them pronouns.

If you have a character that doesn't use pronouns, how would that look? One of the easiest ways is to replace the spot where the pronoun would be with the character's name (e.g., If Alex does not like that, Alex will voice Alex's opinion, for example). You could also use descriptors like a job title, role, or relationship to another, such as "mother," in place of the person's name (e.g., Bobbie told the manager that it would be a better idea if the manager closed the store that day).

Crafting a character with no pronouns will likely take some practice as most of us are used to writing with pronouns. Be patient with yourself as you find the right rhythm to building sentences without pronouns. You might be surprised by how it'll inspire you to get more creative with your word choices while also remaining true and respectful to people who don't use pronouns.

GENDER-INCLUSIVE LANGUAGE

If you speak another language like Spanish, French, or Italian, you know that gender is deeply integrated into the structure of language. For instance, in Spanish, the "el" article is masculine, while the "la" article is feminine. "La luna," or "the moon," is feminine and "el sol," or "the sun," is masculine.

Gender is not built into the structure of English in the same way, but that's not to say we don't use gender-exclusive language, or language that is biased toward certain genders. Below you'll find a list of tips on how to make your creative writing more gender inclusive:

- Use gender-neutral terms.
  Example: use firefighter instead of fireman, flight attendant instead of stewardess, postal worker instead of postman, police officer instead of policeman, etc.

- Remove any suggestion that gender is a binary.

    Many common phrases indicate that gender is a binary, even though it's not. For instance, many say "the opposite sex," but that phrase infers that there are only two gender identities. Try to use "all gender identities," "all genders," or "another gender" rather than "both sexes" and "both genders."

- Avoid gendered pronouns.

    Many people use the "he" pronoun in a gender-neutral way. For instance, I've seen such things as, "When a student applies for a job, he should . . ." There is no need to use "he" as the gender-neutral pronoun of "student," for students can be people of all gender identities, and yet this is still a common practice. Instead of using "he," use "they/them/theirs," a noun, or second person. Here are some examples:

    - "When a student applies for a job, they should . . ."
    - "When a student applies for a job, the student should . . ."
    - "When you apply for a job as a student, you should . . ."

- Stop using "man" as a catchall.

    "Man" has been used as a neutral term for all gender identities. We see it in phrases like "When man walked on the moon" or "all of mankind" or "man's impact on the environment." By using "man" to refer to all humans, it indicates that men are superior to other gender identities. Therefore, we should replace "man" with "human." For example, we should use "humankind" and "human's impact on the world."

- Don't use gender identity adjectives as nouns.

For instance, you do not want to say "the transgenders" or the "non-binaries," as it takes away the human aspect of those gender identities. Instead, you'll need to write "transgender people" or "non-binary people" or "people who identify as transgender/non-binary."

HOW THE WORLD IMPACTS YOUR CHARACTER'S GENDER IDENTITY

When building a character of a different gender identity, begin your research by looking into how society, politics, history, and institutions affect your character's life.

Let's consider women. It was only recently that women were able to vote, own property, and have a credit card without their husbands' permission. Women's history still impacts women today in institutions like the workplace, where women are paid less than men. Sexism continues to be rampant in politics, particularly in issues such as the overturning of abortion access in many states.

So how does that affect a character who is a woman? Perhaps she lives in a state where there is no abortion access, and while she and her partner want to have children, they're concerned about doing so because it could put her life at risk if a medical issue arises during the pregnancy.

Another example: A transgender woman character lives in a state where she can change her driver's license to reflect her gender identity, but the transphobic clerk does everything in their power to prevent her from obtaining that license.

By researching the history, society, politics, and institutions that affect your character's gender identity, you may discover new motivations for your character or better understand the reasons they would make certain decisions in the story.

GENDERED STEREOTYPES

Meg Vondriska is the mind behind MenWriteWomen, a Twitter (now X) account that exposes the ridiculous ways men write women. She launched the account in 2019 and quickly amassed a huge following by sharing sections about women characters from creative works that were written by men. Typically, these scenes showed how poorly (and stereotypically) men wrote women.

Here's a good example: Back in February 2023, Vondriska shared a photo of a scene in *Rendezvous with Rama* by Arthur C. Clarke. In the first few lines of Chapter 11, Clarke wrote:

> *Some* women, Commander Norton had decided long ago, should not be allowed aboard ship; weightlessness did things to their breasts that were too damn distracting. It was bad enough when they were motionless, but when they started to move, and sympathetic vibrations set in, it was more than any warm-blooded male should be asked to take.[10]

Vondriska's response to this section? "[A]nd some men shouldn't be commanders if they're distracted so easily."[11]

This example is one of many that Vondriska has shared on her account, and it speaks to a large problem: there are so many stereotypes relating to different gender identities, and they are continually published and spread to the masses without a second thought.

Unless the piece you're writing only features a single gender identity, you'll need to inform yourself on the various stereotypes relating to many gender identities and the way they might appear in your genre. I'll share many of these stereotypes in Chapter 11; however, you can research beyond what I've provided, especially as new stereotypes might have been added to the lexicon since this book has been published.

> To learn more about Meg Vondriska's work and how gender identities are incorrectly presented in some creative writing, read her book, *A Tale of Two Titties: A Writer's Guide to Conquering the Most Sexist Tropes in Literary History.*

DEVELOPING VOICE

Can a character "sound" like a transgender woman? A man? A woman? A non-binary person? I've been in critique groups with people who would say, "This character doesn't sound like a 'man.'" While there must be some authenticity to the character's voice, the problem is that we let our stereotypical ideas of how someone of a certain gender identity should sound get in the way.

Let go of the idea that people of certain gender identities speak in a specific way, as it can result in very poor depictions that perpetuate stereotypical ideas we have of certain gender identities.

A single identity will not impact a character's voice. Rather, it's the intersection of their many identities—race/ethnicity, location, age, and culture—that will influence the language they use. If you approach it in an intersectional manner and remove your stereotypical assumptions about gender identities, you will be free to create a more holistic and authentic character with a voice that sounds true to them.

EXERCISE

Get to know your character and their gender identity better by filling out the following. You'll notice that I'm having you build upon an exercise from earlier in this section.

- **Sex:** What sex did a doctor assign your character at birth?
- **Gender:** What does society believe your character's gender to be? What are the norms—behaviors, appearance, dress, and thoughts—that society expects of your character's gender? What are the societal benefits and drawbacks of being that gender? What laws affect their gender?
- **Gender identity:** What gender identity does your character feel like inside? How do they like to express their gender identity in terms of their appearance or behavior? When did they recognize their gender identity? Have they had certain positive or negative experiences related to their gender identity?
- **History, culture, laws:** Write a brief history of your character's gender identity. Do you have a good understanding of how their gender identity has been perceived throughout history? Are there laws that affect their gen-

der identity in positive and negative ways? What are they? Does their gender identity suffer from institutional discrimination? Explain. How is the gender identity perceived in the wider culture? Are they represented in media in certain ways?

- **Pronouns:** What are your character's pronouns? Why have they chosen those specific pronouns? Did they have different pronouns in the past? Does society assume they should use certain pronouns over others? Which ones? Why?

- **Stereotypes and tropes:** Make a list of stereotypes and tropes associated with your character's gender identity. Don't forget to consider specific stereotypes and tropes relating to their gender identity within the genre you write, as well as those stereotypes and tropes that intersect with their other identities. For example, the damsel-in-distress trope is used in relation to women in genre and literary fiction, while the "spicy Latina" stereotype is an intersectional stereotype that involves ethnicity and gender identity.

NATIONALITY

It's not easy to write a character with a differing identity— but it's even harder when that character also has a different nationality from yours. You only have to look up the criticism about *American Dirt* by Jeanine Cummins and *Memoirs of a Geisha* by Arthur Golden to see how poorly it can go.

It's one thing to try to delve into another identity of someone who is from the same country as you. At least you and your character have the same pop cultural references, likely grew up in somewhat similar educational systems, were shaped by the same national laws, and (usually) lived in the same type of society. When you dive into the perspective of a character from another country, you lose all that common ground. Your character will have been formed by a different culture, political system, and society, and may even speak and think in a different language from you. That makes things a lot harder.

THE DANGER OF A SINGLE STORY

At the 2009 TEDGlobal conference, author Chimamanda Ngozi Adichie gave a presentation called "The Danger of a Single Story."[12] In the speech, the Nigerian author speaks of the "single story" or a single perspective about a thing, a place, a culture, or a community. She explains the concept of the single story through a variety of anecdotes, like how when she came to the U.S. at nineteen for college, her American roommate was shocked by her ability to speak English and use a stove, and by the fact that she listened to a wide variety of music.

As Ngozi Adichie said, "My roommate had a single story of Africa: a single story of catastrophe. In this single story, there was no possibility of Africans being similar to her in any way, no possibility of feelings more complex than pity, no possibility of a connection as human equals."

Where did that "single story" come from? Ngozi Adichie believes it started from Western literature, which referred to "Sub-Saharan Africa as a place of negatives, of difference, of darkness, of people who, in the words of the wonderful poet Rudyard Kipling, are 'half devil, half child.'"

Her roommate was not alone in knowing only a single story of Africa. Ngozi Adichie's professor had the same single-story perspective when he said her novel was not "authentically African."

"The professor told me that my characters were too much like him, an educated and middle-class man. My characters drove cars. They were not starving. Therefore, they were not authentically African," she said.

Ngozi Adichie didn't just experience the single story from others; she had internalized it about another culture too. In her speech, she shares how she visited Mexico during a time when discussions about immigration and border policies in the U.S. were heightened and "immigration became synonymous with Mexicans."

I remember walking around on my first day in Guadalajara, watching the people going to work, rolling up tortillas in the marketplace, smoking, laughing. I remember first feeling slight surprise. And then, I was overwhelmed with shame. I realized that I had been so immersed in the media coverage of Mexicans that they had become one thing in my mind, the abject immigrant. I had bought into the single story of Mexicans, and I could not have been more ashamed of myself.

The single story can be applied to any aspect of writing a differing identity, but I like to share it in this section of the book, because it shows how easy it is for writers to fall into the single-story perspective without meaning to when writing a character of a different nationality.

When we depict a people, especially from a different nation, in only one way, it creates a single story, and sometimes contributes to a stereotype. Ngozi Adichie said it best: "The problem with stereotypes is not that they are untrue, but that they are incomplete. They make one story become the only story."

As you begin to develop your character with a different nationality, you must ask yourself, "What is the single story about this person? The nation they come from?" Identify the single story and you have completed the first challenge. Recognizing the single story will likely require diverse research, be it through personal interactions and experience, research and study, or visiting another place. Ngozi Adichie explained that it was through meeting her that her roommate's perception of Africa as a single story was shattered, whereas the writer's own single story of Mexico was realized through a visit to the country.

If you're going to write a character of another nationality, it is best to visit that nation if possible. This cannot involve staying in an American-owned hotel chain in that country. Stay with people who are residents and live there full-time. Speak with as many people who grew up in that community. It is through personal connection that the single story will more easily fall away. To pass through as a tourist once or twice is likely not enough.

I will concede that not everyone is able to travel abroad, whether that is due to financial or personal reasons, so the next best thing you can do is to connect and build a relationship with a person who lives nearby and is of the same nationality as your character. Through conversation, you might be able to break down unconscious single stories you may have about their county or the people from that nation. If this is not enough, decide whether or not to tell this story going forward.

Before I end this section, I want to point out something else Ngozi Adichie said about telling stories.

"How [stories] are told, who tells them, when they're told, how many stories are told, [is] really dependent on power," she said. "Power is the ability not just to tell the story of another person, but to make it the definitive story of that person."

When you tell a story of someone of another nationality or identity, you are picking up a mantle of power and determining how the story of that person, that nation, that community, and that culture will be perceived by others. You can effectively create a single story, whether you mean to or not.

So how do you prevent this? Ngozi Adichie points to Palestinian poet Mourid Barghouti, who "writes that if you want to dispossess a people, the simplest way to do it is to tell their story and to start with 'secondly.' Start the story with the arrows of the Native Americans, and not with the arrival of the British, and you have an entirely different story. Start the story with the failure of the African state, and not with the colonial creation of the African state, and you have an entirely different story."

You can write about a person of another nationality, but to do so through the single story is a disservice and a poor use of the power of a writer.

THE AMERICAN PERSPECTIVE

In addition to being an author, I'm also a travel journalist, published by the likes of *Travel + Leisure, Condé Nast Traveler, National Geographic, Lonely Planet,* and more. In my time as a travel writer, one thing has stood out to me: Americans have a difficult time looking beyond their own nationalistic perspective.

I can't tell you how often I hear Americans complain about the way in which other nations design their cities, how their restaurants work, the rules at different tourist attractions, and so on. Travelers—who choose to visit another country—can't seem to understand that they're in another country. Instead, they expect it to have the same comforts, culture, and systems as the U.S. (Don't even get me started on their behavior in countries that are predominantly populated by people of color.)

I'm not sure why Americans struggle to understand the values, thought processes, and social experiences of other countries. Maybe it is because we are not taught enough history about other countries in schools, or we've been indoctrinated so fully with American Dream patriotism that we believe we are superior to other nations. Whatever it is, I say this now to writers who want to write other nationalities: this mindset, that you may not know you have, is going to make this a difficult process.

American writers creating characters of different nationalities should not craft a character with the assumption that people from other countries have the same values, thought processes, or social experiences as Americans—because they don't. This seems like one of those "Well, obviously" statements, but it's not as obvious to writers as you would think.

Yes, you can do a lot of research on the history of another country, its legal systems, or even how its society works, and that will be helpful. But you'll also have to learn about the values, beliefs, and ideology of people who live or are from that country, while also sloughing off your own American perspective of the world.

For instance, an American may see the slow service at a

restaurant in Italy as poor service or a lazy waitstaff. They're used to their go-go-go restaurants in the U.S., where the food is brought out quickly and servers are on hand at every moment to service their needs. To the Italians, their slow meal service is representative of the servers giving the diners privacy, a chance to enjoy the food and the company of each other without the server hovering. If you're writing from the perspective of an Italian character who is from Italy, you would need to show them appreciating this kind of cultural experience. To them, this type of service is normal, and the American service is not.

That is a very easy example I provided. It will likely be harder for you to inhabit the perspective of your character from a different nationality when it comes to belief systems, ideologies, and values. This may be because you will find it more difficult to research their perspectives on beliefs and values. You might also find that as you try to understand the beliefs and values of other countries, it will challenge your own or be so opposing to the ones you grew up with that it'll be hard to understand them.

Make sure your own bias about the social systems, beliefs, values, political systems, and cultures of other countries do not accidentally appear in your writing. It may present itself in a seemingly inconsequential scene of a character walking down the street. Surely you couldn't get that wrong; don't we all walk down the street the same way? We don't. It may be because our streets, or the buildings that line them, look different, or because we have different laws relating to how people can walk down the street. The differences may lie in the weather, environmental issues, nature, or the type of music blaring from a car radio. This is what we as writers must think about.

When writing about another country or culture, you might be drawn to compare that country or culture to one that is more familiar to your audiences—however, it's probably best if you don't. Comparing two places or cultures that are so vastly different could result in a colonialist description or convey some unrealized bias toward a certain country or culture. It's also a very lazy way of describing another culture or community and can be seen as one country or culture being less than the other.

For instance, you wouldn't want to say that the British Virgin Islands are "a Caribbean version of Great Britain." While locals may speak English and have some British customs, this lazy (and offensive) description erases the colonialization of the British Virgin Islands by the United Kingdom and reduces these islands and their own culture to a knockoff version.

A COLONIALIST PERSPECTIVE

Colonialism is not something of the past. Countries like the U.S., the United Kingdom, the Netherlands, Russia, China, France, Denmark, Israel, and Australia all currently participate in colonialism in one way or another, whether that's governing another territory or country, apartheid regimes, or infringing on the rights of Indigenous peoples who are the rightful custodians and owners of the land.

When we think about colonialism, we usually think about European colonialism between the fifteenth and early twentieth centuries, which essentially affected the entire world. Even though Europeans did not colonize Korea, Japan, and Thailand from the 1500s to the early 1900s, European presence in neighboring places like Hong Kong, Myanmar, Indonesia, and Vietnam affected the culture of Korea, Japan, and Thailand, merely by trade and the introduction of such things like the firearm.

As you develop your character of a different nationality, consider how colonialism affected their country in the past and how it still affects them today, as it may offer a deeper understanding of the racial and ethnic prejudices or the political and social systems of the nation.

Furthermore, we as writers in the United States should think about how colonialism impacted our perspective and how it could influence the way we depict characters from other countries. Although the U.S. is a country that is a result of colonialization, as citizens, we don't all see our country as a colonizer—but it is. The U.S. has colonized such places as Hawaii, Alaska, Guam, Puerto Rico, and many others. We continue to allow the colonialist perspective to exist by subjugating Native American communities, trying to obtain their land resources, and not giving back the land that is owed to them.

You may not think that these things will impact the way you craft your character, but they can, and they unfortunately will likely appear in small, biased ways that are difficult to recognize as you write or during the editing process.

Learn how colonialism affected the country you want to

write about. How did it affect the culture, systems, people, land, and language? Then research how colonialism affected your own country and how it affects the perception we have about other countries.

Lastly, check your superiority at the door: the U.S. is not superior to any other nation and to think so can result in a colonialist perspective of another nation and its people, and result in a very biased, incorrect depiction of a character with a different nationality.

COLONIALIST LANGUAGE AND PHRASES

In an article on *Fodor's Travel* called "Consider Ditching These 11 Words When Talking About Your Travels," seven journalists (Kay Kingsman, Meera Dattani, Jihan McDonald, Marinel M. de Jesus, Johanna Read, Sandra Jackson-Opoku, and myself) discuss how certain words and phrases used in particular situations can, according to Lavanya Sunkara, "connotate otherness and unnecessarily glamorize colonialism. They may perpetuate an 'us versus them' duality, where the entitled and the underprivileged, whites and non-whites, and the haves and the have-nots, continue to remain separated."[13]

While the article speaks about travel writing specifically, when used in the context of creatively writing other nationalities or in the setting we choose, many of these words can contribute to harmful colonialist perspectives. Let's take a look at some of the words the article brings up, as well as a few others:

- **Exotic:** "Their customs were so exotic to Sarah." Exoticizing another country and/or culture is a form of othering.

- **Colonial charm:** "The city center had a colonial charm of centuries past." There was and is nothing "charming" about colonialism. It has resulted in genocide, enslavement, the destruction of rich cultures, environmental disasters, and more. While some architecture is considered colonial architecture, we want to make sure to not downplay the horrors of colonialism by calling anything relating to colonialism "charming," "lovely," or any other similarly positive word.

- **Conquer:** "We conquered the Amazon hike in five hours." World powers have used their militaries to conquer other lands. To use it in a colloquial sense in relation to a colonized country can feel a bit icky.

- **Discover:** "The couple discovered a crumbling temple, long forgotten by civilization." As travel journalist Jihan McDonald said, "Discovery is purely relative . . . Did the one who ventured out 'discover' the sun, or merely come to realize that the sun had always been there and they had been ignorant of it?" In other words, noncitizens or nonmembers of the community or culture cannot "discover" something in a destination as it's always been known by the people who have historically lived there.

- **Explore:** "He hopped in the Jeep, excited to explore the South African wilderness." Colonialism sometimes started as "an exploration" of a place unknown to colonialists, so to use "explore" when writing about a character in a colonized country, you may be unknowingly making a reference to the country's colonialist past and portraying your character as a figure contributing to colonialism (which may not be what you intend to do).

- **Impoverished, poor, underprivileged:** "It was an impoverished country full of poor and underprivileged people." When we make sweeping statements about an entire country's wealth status in our creative writing piece, we tend to leave out nuanced explanations for the wealth disparity. This can lead to stereotyping or othering of an entire nation, culture, or community and result in an unintentional savior story or misrepresentation of the country.

- **Locals:** "We found the locals to be friendly and welcoming of us immediately." In itself, "local" is not necessarily a bad word, but it's often used in relation to people considered "poor" or "uneducated," and can result in othering or infantilizing communities of color. It can be problematic when you use it for certain communities and then use "residents" and "citizens" (which have an air of sophistication and wealth) or specific names (like Canadians or New Yorkers) for others. Pay attention to how you use the word "locals" and if there are any underlying connotations.

- **Paradise:** "The palm trees, ocean breeze, and tropical frozen drink made the Dominican Republic a paradise away from home." Be wary of calling another country a "paradise," whether that is in exposition, through inference, or through the voice of your main character. Oftentimes it's used in reference to countries, states, or territories that have large populations of people of color and whose economies rely heavily on tourists (like Caribbean countries and Hawaii) due to the effects of colonialism. By referring to the destination as a paradise, you essentially exoticize the land and ignore the experiences of people who live there.

The only exception to using these words in a creative piece is to showcase how a character or characters have a colonialist, biased, and/or racist perspective. Make sure that you make it clear through characterization that the biased and colonialist perspective is your character's perspective and not yours. It should be exceptionally clear that you have used these words and phrases with intention and care.

EXERCISE

For this exercise, answer the following questions. Consider how they may inform the way you write a character of a different nationality:

- What is your character's nation?
- Off the top of your head, what do you know about that nation?
- Off the top of your head, how do people live in that nation on a day-to-day basis?
- What is the American perspective about that nation?
- What is your character's perspective of themselves and their nation? Why do you believe that?
- What are the negative and positive aspects you've heard about that nation? Compare your answers. Do you have more answers for the negative aspects versus the positive aspects or vice versa? What do you think that means?

Look at your answers. What do you notice? Determine what you need to research about your character and their nationality. Before and after you do that, ask yourself the following questions and see what you come up with:

- What is the single story of the nation?
- How can I prevent myself from writing that single story? Does the story need to start at a different point? Feature a different plot? Reframe the way I've presented my character?

DISABILITY

While I was working on this book, I attended a poetry reading. During the open-mic section, a man got on stage and read a poem that featured a Deaf main character. The poet depicted the character as a victim who was bullied and ignored, and who suffered over the course of their life because they were deaf. I recall one stanza where the character in the poem even gets lost on a college campus as an adult—not because college campuses are confusing for everyone—but because of his deafness. After throwing out each example of how the character's life was difficult because of their deafness, the poet added another line—one in which he blamed the audience for not seeing, understanding, or being compassionate to the Deaf character.

The poem was a class act in sentimentality, or the act of writing something to elicit an emotional response from the audience. The poet wanted the audience to feel pity for the Deaf character and reflect on how they might hurt, harm, or ignore Deaf people. Additionally, the poet placed the character into the role of a lifelong victim, rather than a capable human being.

While Deaf people may face bullying or be ignored in some cases, the poet never showed the agency that Deaf people have, but rather used their disability as a tool to elicit emotional responses of guilt and pity.

Later, I learned that although the poet was not hard of hearing himself, he graduated from college with a disability studies degree. I was shocked at first—but I shouldn't have been. Just because you know some things about disability history, have studied ASL, or have received a degree in disability studies, does not mean you can creatively write that identity well.

Even though there are one in four adults in the U.S. with disabilities,[14] the representation of disabilities in creative writing is still somewhat lacking (though with some recent publications in the last few years, I'm hopeful that we're seeing a shift). We have had plenty of nationwide conversations about race/ethnicity, gender identity, and sexual orientation, and yet disability continues to be a topic that most people have not ever broached.

In the following sections, I will discuss some of the most important aspects you need to keep in mind when crafting disabled characters and/or discussing the disability community in your work. No matter if you're writing a character with a disability or not, *all* writers will benefit from reading this section.

ABLEISM

Before we dive further, we need to talk about ableism. Ableism is the bias, prejudice, and discrimination that disabled people face on an individual and societal level. It is based on the idea that those with disabilities are less valuable, need to be cured or fixed, and are not "normal." Furthermore, it assumes that people who do not have disabilities are superior, normal, and the standard.

Ableism presents itself in a variety of ways, such as in stereotypes, misconceptions, generalizations, and the language we use. It also appears in our social, political, and cultural systems.

You've likely seen ableism in everyday life, such as how buildings are not ADA-compliant and children with disabilities are typically segregated in schools. It has reared its ugly head in pop culture language ("That's retarded"), in how Trump mocked a reporter with a disability, and in how people who kill family members with disabilities usually get little to no prison sentence.[15] We even see it on-screen with the superfluous number of villains—like Darth Vader and Captain Hook—who have disabilities.

Ableism occurs around us daily, and yet many people are not aware of its presence. If you're going to write characters with disabilities or even a society in which disabilities exist, you need to be aware of how ableism can present.

PERSON-FIRST VS. IDENTITY-FIRST LANGUAGE AND THE DISABILITY COMMUNITY

On July 11, 2006, the Council of the District of Columbia enacted the People First Respectful Language Modernization Act of 2006.[16] It required that respectful and proper terminology be used when referring to people with disabilities. That language was called Person First Language (PFL).

On the website for the Office of Disability Rights, they wrote, "'People First Language' (PFL) puts the person before the disability, and describes what a person has, not who a person is."[17] They have a long list of appropriate terms relating to disabilities, and while I won't list them all here, I will list many of these terms in Chapter 11. Here are a few examples:

- Use "persons with intellectual disabilities" rather than "the mentally retarded" or "mentally disabled."
- Use "person who uses a wheelchair" rather than "wheelchair user," "wheelchair bound," or "the handicapped."
- Use "person with a mental health condition" rather than "the insane."

Not everyone in the disability community likes person-first language. Many in the blind, Deaf, and autism communities prefer identity-first language. In a post titled "Ask a Self-Advocate: The Pros and Cons of Person-First and Identity-First Language" on the Massachusetts Advocates for Children page,[18] Jevon Okundaye defines identity-first language as a "language that leads with a person's diagnosis, such as being a disabled person."

For many, identity-first language represents a person that sees their disability as a positive and fundamental part of their identity. In a post on Medium called "How Person-First Language Isolates Disabled People,"[19] written by the elysian collective in 2019, they said, "Using person-first language implies that any disabled individual would be the same without their disability. Our life histories shape who we are, so this is not and cannot be true." They added later in the piece, "I don't want to be a 'person with autism' or a 'person with a disability' just as I don't want to be a 'person with a non-binary gender' or a 'person with queerness.'"

So how do creative writers choose the right terms? Is person-first or identity-first language better? There are a lot of pros and cons for both. Okundaye wrote, "Since society tends to view the disability community as inferior, person-first language helps ensure that people with disabilities are treated with the same respect as people without disabilities."

He added, "There are also some negative things about using person-first language. For instance, this type of language treats having a disability like having a disease or illness."

On the other hand, Okundaye says that there are benefits to identity-first language: "For example, this type of language conveys a disability as being a permanent and important part of a person's identity. The blind, Deaf, and autistic communities see their disabilities as being fundamental parts of who they are," he explains.

"There are also some drawbacks to using identify-first language. For instance, this type of language may cause people to think that a person's disability completely defines who they are," he adds. "This is especially problematic when some people's views on disabilities are based solely on negative stereotypes, such as that autistic people lack empathy."

Shannon Wooldridge, a public affairs specialist for the National Institute of Health's Office of Communications and Public Liaison[20] offered this advice:

> The goal of person-first language—to avoid language that dehumanizes or stigmatizes people—is a worthy one. Person-first language is still best practice when

writing about people who have defined diseases, such as "children with epilepsy" or "men with diabetes." It is also best when writing about people with mental health disorders, such as "people with schizophrenia" or "women with bipolar disorder." Communities that prefer identity-first language tend to be those centered on different ways of perceiving or interacting with the world. These communities have often developed a culture and sense of pride around their disability identity and don't view it as an impairment.

She also added, "You don't always need to use a single word or term. For example, you can switch back and forth between 'people on the autism spectrum' and 'autistic Americans.'"

There are many different perspectives about the right terminology to use. For writers, this means that you'll need to do as much research as you can into the specific disability community that is featured in your creative writing, which should include speaking to people in that community about their thoughts on person-first and identity-first language. Likely, you will receive different perspectives and feedback and will have to determine the best path forward in your work.

Within this book, I have decided to showcase both identity-first and person-first language as a way of recognizing both schools of thought. I believe there are benefits to both, and no matter how we utilize them in our work, they are by no means the only thing that we need to consider when portraying the disability community in general or within a specific character. It is just one of many things we need to keep in mind.

TYPES OF DISABILITIES

Disabled people are not a monolith, and if you're going to write a character who has a disability, you must understand this.

The CDC points out nine ways[21] in which a person may experience a disability:

- Vision
- Movement
- Thinking
- Remembering
- Learning
- Communicating
- Hearing
- Mental health
- Social relationships

While some disabilities are present at birth, others are a result of injury or occur with age. Disabilities can be physical, intellectual, and psychological. A physical disability is the "impairment in a person's body structure or function,"[22] which can affect how someone sees, hears, or moves. Intellectual disabilities, on the other hand, are "when there are limits to a person's ability to learn at an expected level and function in daily life."[23]

Under the Americans with Disabilities Act, people with mental health conditions are protected, especially as it relates to the workplace. Additionally, there are eleven mental health conditions that qualify under the Social Security Administration for disability assistance.[24]

Some people may experience only one type of disability,

while others experience different kinds of disabilities at the same time. Think about Alzheimer's. In the U.S., early-onset Alzheimer's is considered a disability.[25] Alzheimer's not only affects cognitive thinking and memories, but can also contribute to loss of speech, affect social behavior and psychological health, and result in physical disabilities.

One of the biggest misconceptions about the disability community is that those who have physical or intellectual disabilities also have a mental health condition. This is not always the case, and perpetuating that association as inherently true is harmful and should be prevented in your creative writing.

ABLEIST LINGUISTIC MICROAGGRESSIONS

No matter what kind of writing you do, you may find that you have unintentionally included ableist linguistic microaggressions in your work. These are everyday words and phrases that imply disabilities are something negative.

Sometimes this presents itself as full statements, like if a person without a disability said to someone with a disability, "I don't even think of you as having a disability," or "I'm going to pray you are healed." It also presents itself in words that are widely used, like "moron," "lunatic," or "crazy." Historically, these words were used to describe disabled people, but we use them without thought to describe people or events in negative ways, and in doing so, we are making negative associations to disabilities.

Again, I will share a more extensive list in Chapter 11, but I do want to provide some common ableist language examples that you can easily remove from your work:

- "That's insane."
- "So dumb."
- "She's crazy."
- "The blind leading the blind."
- "His ideas fell on deaf ears."
- "That's retarded."
- "I swear he has ADHD."
- "He can be so OCD sometimes."
- "So lame."

> Let's look at these two examples: "I swear he has ADHD" and "He can be so OCD sometimes." When we casually self-diagnose others or ourselves as having a learning, intellectual, or psychological disability, we are being ableist. It diminishes the real experience that people with ADHD or OCD go through.

VALUING THE LIVES OF CHARACTERS WITH DISABILITIES

In my eighth-grade history class, we were discussing how people with intellectual disabilities were treated horrifically in the U.S. in the eighteenth and nineteenth centuries, when my teacher said, "Perhaps we should have killed them all." Without thinking, I stood up and yelled at him for his discriminatory and ableist statement. As someone who has a sister with intellectual disabilities, I was appalled and furious that he suggested that as a society we should have killed people like my sister in days past. I knew what he said was wrong, but at the time, I was not old enough to realize that his belief that the lives of disabled people were not as important or valuable was widespread and is still something that people believe today. The idea that people with disabilities are less worthy to live (and live well) has become such an ingrained concept in our minds that many people are not even aware of it, which is why it appears in a lot of creative writing.

We can't begin to write about characters with disabilities without facing the biases that many of us have about disabilities. There is a widely held assumption that to have a disability is "bad" or "negative," and this in turn causes us to see disabled people as something to pity or be fixed, or not valuable.

We must face this bias, or it will likely find its way into our work as a stereotype, trope, or cliché; in the form of ableist language; or in a stock characterization. More specifically, it can appear in the following ways:

- Characters with disabilities are typically placed in the margins of a story.
- Disabled characters are used to elicit an emotional reaction from the reader.
- Characters with disabilities are used as a plot device.
- Disabled characters are sometimes used for the benefit of a character without disabilities—like showing how that character becomes a better person after having an interaction with a character who has disabilities.
- Characters with disabilities are used as inspiration to other characters or to rally everyone toward disability advocacy.

In 2014, an Australian disability activist named Stella Young used the term "inspirational porn" in a TED Talk called "Inspiration Porn and the Objectification of Disability."[26] The term referred to how the media use disabilities to provoke pity or sentimentality and create an uplifting message for people who do not have disabilities. In other words, it's the act of using disabled people as an inspiration for those who do not have disabilities.

Inspiration porn absolutely makes its way into literature, especially in relation to writing about disabilities. (It has been used in relation to other identities too.)

TROPES AND STEREOTYPES

As with any identity presented in this book, you'll need to research all the tropes and stereotypes related to people with disabilities, as well as the specific stereotypes and tropes related to your character's specific disability and how it intersects with their other identities and the genre in which you're writing.

While you may find some helpful information relating to this in Chapter 11, it is by far not an exhaustive list. Additional research will need to be done, and you will need to connect with people who have the same disability as your character. In building those relationships, you will gain a better understanding of their experience.

SEXUALITY, ANIMALITY, AND VIOLENCE

I'd like to focus on three common associations that are made about disabled people: sexuality, animality, and violence.

SEXUALITY

There is a common practice of depicting people with disabilities as not having sexual feelings or experiences, as asexual, or as sexual deviants.

For example, there is the trope of the autistic detective who has no interest in relationships, romance, or sex, and is only obsessed with solving the case. This trope and others like it are a result of disability stereotypes as well as discomfort in society with the idea that disabled people have sexual urges or experiences. This is because of the biased idea that disabilities are "abnormal" or an obstacle to a happy life full of romantic relationships. Because of this, characters with disabilities may be depicted as not engaging in their sexuality and thus be seen as "pure" and "virginal."

We also see depictions of disabled people, especially those with intellectual disabilities, as being incapable of controlling their "sexual urges." The assumption is that their intellectual level prevents them from understanding consent. This biased idea has resulted in a trope that associates those with intellectual disabilities as being sexually deviant or a danger to others.

ANIMALITY

People with disabilities, especially intellectual disabilities, have long been associated with animality or having an animalistic nature. This misplaced way of thinking argues that people with intellectual disabilities are no smarter than animals and thus have behaviors that are animalistic. Make sure you do not make associations between characters with disabilities and animals.

VIOLENCE

Violence against disabled people is a real issue in our society, so we should be extremely mindful of how we depict people with disabilities experiencing violence or engaging in it. For instance, there is a common practice of making disabled people the villains who perpetuate violence against others. The reason? A stereotypical assumption that people with disabilities are bitter that they have a disability or an association between mental health conditions and disabilities, and the idea that mental health conditions result in violence. None are true.

On the other hand, when characters with disabilities are depicted as victims of violence, it can become problematic when the violence against a character with a disability is for the purpose of a plot device or to push the story forward. Other times, violence against characters with disabilities is used to "inspire" or "teach" a character without disabilities about empathy, activism, or some other thing. The most concerning aspect of these kinds of scenes is the messages they can send to readers, such as the idea that disabled people are always victims and/or are more deserving of violence than people without disabilities.

DISABILITY AND DIALOGUE

There is a common practice of infantilizing the language of people with disabilities—no matter if they have a physical or intellectual disability—which furthers the stereotype of disabled people being unintelligent, emotionally immature, or childlike.

You'll also need to pay attention to specific words and topics that you have characters with disabilities use. For instance, we know that TV and film writers have given Latina characters more sexualized language. While we could not find a similar study relating to characters with disabilities, it's still best to question yourself about the matter. Are you having your characters with disabilities use certain words or speak in a certain style that connects back to a stereotype relating to people with disabilities? You'll likely discover these patterns in the editing phase, but it's something to keep in mind when writing.

Equally as important is how you present the dialogue between disabled people and people who do not have disabilities. As Sonya Freeman Loftis explains in *Imagining Autism*: "*Extremely Loud and Incredibly Close* uses disabled characters to suggest a world in which truly reciprocal conversations are impossible (for neurotypical and autistic alike)."[27]

By this, Loftis means that characters with disabilities, especially those with intellectual or learning disabilities, are portrayed as being unable to have meaningful conversations with others.

EXERCISE

Create a scene in which a character with a disability meets a character without a disability. Write in third-person perspective. For the purpose of this exercise, it might be a good idea to have a character that only experiences one type of disability (yes, people can have multiple disabilities at one time, but start with one for now).

Write the scene first and then examine it for the following:

- How did you physically describe the disabled character? And the character without a disability?
- Did you hyperfocus on the character's disability? In what way?
- Look at both characters' dialogue. Do you notice any difference?
- Did you imply that the character's disability is something that they "suffer from" or that it is a "negative" thing?
- Do you make any associations about the character with the disability that you did not make toward the character without a disability? What are they? Are they negative? Inspirational porn?
- Is there any ableist language in the scene?
- Do you notice any stereotypes that you did not intend to write?

Now challenge yourself to rewrite the scene two more times in first-person—once from the perspective of the disabled character and another from the perspective of the character who does not have a disability. How does that affect the story?

Did you feel comfortable writing from a character with a disability's perspective? Does your depiction showcase an ableist perspective that a character with a disability would not have?

SEXUAL AND ROMANTIC ORIENTATIONS

Back in 2021, I taught a creative writing class called "Crafting Your Character" in a rural town about twenty-five minutes from my hometown of Wichita Falls, Texas. The very first exercise I had the small class do was the same exercise that is listed at the end of Chapter 4. I asked each writer to take their character and fill out a list of personal information that included everything from their name, age, and familial history to their hopes, dreams, fears, hobbies, and quirks.

One of the items on the list was "sexual orientation." I gave the class about five minutes to fill out the list and most writers got to work immediately—except for one. A white cisgender man in his late sixties crossed his arms and stared at the PowerPoint that listed all the character traits and background information.

When the five minutes was up, I asked the class what they learned from the exercise. Did anything interesting come up? The man who hadn't engaged in the exercise raised his hand and asked, "Yes, I want to know why you're pushing sexual orientation on us?"

I saw the faces of the event organizer and another author who was teaching a session after me drop. I didn't think before responding firmly, "Everyone has a sexual orientation. You have one, I have one, whether you like what that sexual orientation is or not, we all have one. And your character does too. It may not play a role in the story, but you should know what it is."

I'm still amazed by how uncomfortable many writers are with sexual orientation. I have a sexual orientation. You have a sexual orientation. Your character has one too. While you may not have a single romantic scene in your work, you need to know what your character's sexual orientation is, because it's a big part of the human experience, no matter if you're comfortable with the subject or not.

SEXUALITY IS A SPECTRUM

In 1948, Dr. Alfred Kinsey and his partners published a study on sexual orientation called "Sexual Behavior in the Human Male,"[28] which showcased that people don't fit in a binary category system of homosexual or heterosexual. Rather, attraction is far more complicated than we think. It's a spectrum, not two columns.

Dr. Kinsey wasn't the last to examine sexual orientation. A study by the University of Sydney that was published in 2021 found that people can change their sexual orientation after reading one-page informational articles on sexual orientation.[29] It suggested that the more information that people have about sexual orientation, the better they are able to interpret their own.

Today, sexual orientation is not exclusive to sexual attractiveness but has also expanded to include romantic orientations, which has been very helpful for asexual and aromantic peoples to explain their sexual and romantic attractions.

By understanding that sexuality is a spectrum, you may be able to craft more authentic characters. It's okay for your character to not fully know their own sexuality, to want to explore it, to do things that may seem contradictory to what they recognize as their sexual orientation, or to not acknowledge it at all.

Sexuality is not the only driving force in our lives, and it will not be for your character. However, by understanding how sexuality and romantic attraction can impact how your character sees themselves or engages in relationships (or not), you'll be better prepared to write characters of differing sexual orientations.

DEFINING SEXUAL ORIENTATION AND ROMANTIC ORIENTATION

Before we go further, we need to address the differences between sexual orientation and romantic orientation, because they're not the same for every person, and thus may not be the same for your characters. We generally work off the assumption that sexual orientation explains who we are sexually and romantically attracted to, but for some people it does not.

The Split Attraction Model (SAM) was created by the asexual community because "the model can help explain individuals who are asexual yet still experience romantic attraction."[30]

Pay close attention to the definitions and how they differ depending on whether you're asexual, aromantic, or not.

Sexual orientation (for people who are NOT asexual or aromantic) refers to the gender identity that you're *romantically and sexually attracted to.*

Sexual orientation (for people who are asexual or aromantic) refers to the gender identity that you're *physically attracted to.*[31]

People who are asexual or aromantic may find that who they

are physically attracted to is not always who they are romantically attracted to. This is where romantic orientation comes in.

Romantic orientation is typically referenced by asexual and aromantic individuals and is easily defined as the gender identity they are romantically attracted to. Romantic orientation does not always match an individual's sexual orientation. It includes heteroromantic (romantically attracted to people of a different gender identity), homoromantic (romantically attracted to the same gender identity), biromantic and panromantic (romantically attracted to more than one gender identity), and aromantic (not romantically attracted to any gender identity).

This may not relate to your character at all, but it can expand your concept of how your character can be sexually, romantically, and physically attracted to different gender identities—and how that's entirely normal.

If you're going to write asexual or aromantic characters, I hope that this inspires you to learn even more than I can share here.

I may not reference romantic orientation throughout the rest of this section but know that I acknowledge it is a real orientation and one that should absolutely be considered for certain characters.

Lila Shapiro wrote an article called "Who Gave You the Right to Tell That Story?" for *Vulture* in 2019 in which she interviewed ten famous writers about the times they wrote outside their identities. Renowned author N. K. Jemisin pointed out how her representation of the asexual identity was not as informed as she wished it had been. See what she said below:

> Ehiru, a character from *The Killing Moon*, is asexual, and I don't think I explored that well. If I were writing it now, I would have made him more clearly ace. I figured this out by reading Tumblr. I am on Tumblr quietly—I have a pseudonym, and nobody knows who I am. Because lots of young people hang out there and talk about identity and the way our society works, it's basically a media-criticism lab. It's an interesting place to talk about identity, and I did not understand until I saw these conversations that asexuality was an identity. I thought about it as a broken sexuality. My story reflected my lack of understanding of how that worked.[32]

I am so impressed with how honest and open Jemisin was about her past characterization of the asexual identity. I encourage you to read this entire article, as it showcases not only how writing other identities is no easy feat, but that it is okay to take responsibility for our past mistakes.

THE LGBTQIA+/QUEER COMMUNITY

We can't talk about sexual orientation without referencing the LGBTQIA+ community, as they have long been marginalized for who they are physically, sexually, and romantically attracted to.

Before we continue, I do need to acknowledge that the transgender and intersex communities, which are represented by the "T" and the "I" in "LGBTQIA+," are gender identities, not sexual orientations. They've been discussed in previous sections. So why are they grouped with sexual orientations like lesbian, gay, bisexual, queer, and asexual? And what does the plus sign stand for?

LGBTQIA+ is representative of a community that is not straight and not cisgender. The acronym stands for lesbian, gay, bisexual, transgender, queer or questioning, intersex, and asexual. The plus sign refers to any other non-straight and non-cisgender identities, of which there are many.

If you're going to write about the sexual and romantic orientations of a character within the LGBTQIA+ community, you might want to start with learning all the different sexual orientation identity terms. You might know what lesbian, bisexual, and gay mean, but are you familiar with demisexual, ace, queer platonic, gray-A, bisexual, pansexual, polyamorous, biromantic, or asexual? You'd be surprised by how a simple definition can help you to understand your character better.

Once you've determined what your character's sexual orientation is, do some deep research on the historical, cultural, and political experiences of that sexual orientation. History has not been kind to the queer community, and that's been made exceptionally clear with how laws have prevented people with queer sexual orientations from marrying, having access to healthcare, or having protected rights as renters. If you can better understand how people who are lesbian, bisexual, gay, asexual, or pansexual (and plus!) have been affected by laws, social norms, and the broader culture of their society, you'll better understand your queer character and how society impacts their lives in numerous ways.

> If you believe queer sexual orientations are a "lifestyle" or a "choice," I implore you to not feature characters with such sexual orientations in your work. Stick with heterosexual orientations, as your bias toward queer people will likely result in misrepresentation and more harm to queer communities.

QUEER TROPES AND MISINFORMATION

Most writers are aware of the gay best friend trope, but it's not the only one that exists for the LGBTQIA+ community. There is the trope that all lesbians are "manly" and that bisexuals are massive cheaters. Equally as problematic is the array of misinformation that continues to be spread about queer folks, like the false idea that all queer people were abused as children or all gay men have AIDS.

If you're going to write characters who are bisexual, gay, lesbian, queer, demisexual, or pansexual, you'll need to know all the tropes and false ideas relating to that sexual orientation. Not only will it help you on your journey toward breaking down false biases relating to these sexual orientations, it'll help you to prevent or catch any of them from appearing in your writing.

Illustrating violence against people with queer sexual orientation identities can be problematic too. Yes, the queer community has been subjected to violence in the past, and in many places in the U.S. and the world, they still are! However, depicting them as victims of violence, if not done well, can be triggering to readers or exploitative of the queer community, and it can result in trauma porn. It also limits the very diverse and real experiences that queer folks have—which have nothing to do with violence.

As is the case for many identities, the writer should not use queer folks as plot points to help straight characters learn to be open-minded or to further some agenda.

If aspects like the AIDS crisis come into play in your story, be careful not to write trauma porn. The better informed you are about major issues relating to the queer community, like the AIDS crisis, the better you can write about them. We should do everything in our power to not cause further damage to a generation of people who are still trying to process the lack of care or commitment they received from their governments and society during the AIDS crisis and the grief they experienced from those they lost.

LGBTQReads.com is a great resource for novels, poetry, and nonfiction that feature LGBTQIAP+ identities. Run by author Dahlia Adler, the site features LGBTQIAP+ literature that's broken down by different reading categories (children's, middle grade, young adult, and adult), genres (romance, sci-fi, etc.), poetry, accessibility (books in braille, translations, audio, large print, etc.), and even intersecting identities (body types, race, religious beliefs, etc.). If you're interested in writing about the queer community, it's a fantastic place to start your prewriting research.

HOW DO YOU DEPICT SEXUALITY?

How people engage with their sexuality differs from person to person, which can make representing sexual orientation a bit tricky.

People within the queer community are sometimes depicted as being hyper or oversexualized persons simply because they are gay, bisexual, or lesbian. This is a result of false narratives that like to paint queer individuals as perverse or consumed by their sexuality, simply because they're not heterosexual. It's just not true.

This is not to say that heterosexual identities are perfectly depicted in literature either. Women of color tend to be hypersexualized, while elderly people, especially elderly women, are depicted as having no sexuality at all.

Sexuality and sexual orientation aren't always about sex. They intersect with physical attraction, emotional connection, and society's expectations and pressures. If you want to depict sexuality as accurately as possible, you'll need to connect with people who have that sexual orientation (and other intersecting identities). Ask questions.

Kinks and Fetishes

If you have a character that has kinks, fetishes, or is into BDSM (bondage, dominance or discipline, sadism, and masochism), ground the character in other aspects of their identity. Yes, these aspects of their sexual identity may be important to your character, but they are not representative of their entire identity and who they are as a person.

If you hyperfocus on these aspects of your character's sexual identity, you could be missing out on a chance to create a holistic and authentic character that has hopes, joys, dreams, goals, fears, traumas, and happiness that have nothing to do with their kinks.

Lastly, if you're writing about these sexual interests, make sure that you've worked through your biases relating to them and that you write these characters with the mindset of sex positivity, and the full knowledge of these sexual identities and how they present in real life.

EXERCISE

For this exercise, you will be writing two different scenes. They can be in first or third person.

Here's the premise: A couple has just arrived at their vacation destination. Write a romantic scene between the couple.

For the first scene, the couple should have the same sexual and/or romantic orientation as your own. In the second scene, the couple should have a different sexual and/or romantic orientation than the one you identify with.

You are free to decide the vacation destination and the activity or activities the couple engages in (it does not have to be sex but can be). Romance, for the sake of this exercise, can be presented in any way—from one character unpacking another character's suitcase to a couple taking a bath together. In terms of other identities (beyond sexual orientation or romantic orientation) the couple can have the same or different identities from each other, and/or be similar or different from you in terms of identity.

Write the two scenes and then let them sit for at least an hour. Reread the scenes and ask yourself the following questions.

For the couple who has the same sexual and/or romantic orientation as you:

- Where did the couple go? Why did you choose that destination?
- What romantic activity did the couple engage in? Why did you choose that activity?

- How did you portray romance between the couple?
- What do you think the romance you portrayed says about the couple?
- Was there anything about the scene you felt the most confident writing? The least confident?
- Was it easier to write this scene? Why or why not?

For the couple who has a different sexual and/or romantic orientation from you:

- Where did the couple go? Why did you choose that destination?
- What romantic activity did the couple engage in? Why did you choose that activity?
- How did you portray romance between the couple?
- What do you think your portrayal of the romance says about the couple?
- Was there anything about the scene you felt the most confident writing? The least confident?
- Why did you choose this specific sexual and/or romantic orientation? Do you know anyone with that sexual and/or romantic orientation? What did you draw upon—for example, personal experience, TV, books, podcasts—to try to write this scene?
- Did you find anything in the scene that could be considered a stereotype, trope, negative association, or misinformation?
- Was it harder to write this scene? Why or why not?

Consider your answers. They may tell you that you need to do more research into different sexual and romantic orientations before you write them. Or they might have shown you an unconscious bias that you weren't aware you have. The more open and honest you are with yourself, the better able you'll be to move forward with a plan to write characters with different sexual and/or romantic orientations from your own.

EDITING IDENTITIES OTHER THAN YOUR OWN

9

THE EDITING PROCESS

QUICK CHAPTER NAVIGATION

While we would like to mindfully write our stories and novels without any stereotypes, tropes, or misrepresentations, unfortunately, some unrealized bias may weasel its way into the dialogue, a description, or the storyline. That's what makes the editing process the most important step in writing an identity not your own.

YOUR EDITS

Be prepared to go through multiple rounds of editing your manuscript. Start by editing your draft as you normally would, by focusing on the main story elements like setting, plot, character development, and language. Only when you've polished those aspects of your draft should you begin focusing on editing for tropes, stereotypes, storyline, and the characterization of your characters with differing identities.

While the editing checklist in the next chapter will be helpful, I want to point out some important things to keep in mind when editing characters of a different identity.

LOOK AT EVERY SCENE

When you're ready to start editing a character of a different identity from your own, be prepared to read every single scene in which they are mentioned. You'll need to examine how they're described by other characters, the narrator, and themself, and study every piece of dialogue they have.

IF YOU'RE NOT SURE, WRITE AN ALTERNATIVE SCENE

There may be times when you come across a scene or a characterization that is difficult to interpret as discriminatory or a trope. Maybe you're not sure if you should use a certain slur or bad word in a scene or you have a feeling in your gut that the scene in question isn't quite offensive, but there is something off about it that you can't put your finger on.

Whatever the case may be, if you're not entirely confident in that scene, characterization, storyline, or word, write an alternative scene in which that trope, description, word, or characterization is entirely different. If you need to write a few alternate scenes, do so. Let the scene rest for a few hours or days and then come back to it. Do you like the other scenes better? Do you get the same bad feeling in your gut when you read those scenes? Do the alternate scenes add something beneficial to the storyline or the characterization?

Listen to your gut and don't be afraid (or too stubborn) to choose a different scene.

DESCRIBE PRIVILEGED CHARACTERS TO THE EXTENT YOU WOULD CHARACTERS OF HISTORICALLY MARGINALIZED IDENTITIES

One of the easiest things you can do during the editing process is examine how you've described characters of privilege—straight, cisgender, white, abled, and/or a man. Do you describe their accent, skin tone, hair type, style, or voice as extensively as you do characters from historically marginalized identities? If not, you need to do so. Otherwise, you could be unknowingly sending the message that white, cis, abled, and straight characters are the standard and historically marginalized characters are not. This could lead to othering and a host of other issues.

DON'T FORGET THE BIG STORYLINE

The Seven Husbands of Evelyn Hugo by Taylor Jenkins Reid is about a Cuban American woman named Evelyn Hugo who was an actress in Old Hollywood. Little is known about Evelyn except that she had seven husbands. For instance, most people are unaware that Evelyn is bisexual. Monique is a half-Black, half-white journalist at a magazine who has been chosen to interview Evelyn Hugo when she's seventy-nine. Upon meeting Evelyn, Monique learns that Evelyn wants the journalist to write her life story. Monique agrees, not realizing that Evelyn's life intersects with her own.

Published in 2017, the novel was a huge hit, and it's gained more popularity over the years since. In 2022, book blogger Jesse Morales-Small of *Bowties and Books* discussed *The Seven Husbands of Evelyn Hugo* in a video on their YouTube channel—specifically how Taylor Jenkins Reid, a white straight woman, wrote characters with historically marginalized identities including queer people, people of color, and queer people of color. Jesse's main critique? The novel's problematic plot.

At the end of *The Seven Husbands of Evelyn Hugo*, there are two gay men driving in a car. Evelyn's best friend, Harry, who is white and drunk, is driving the car, while his partner, a Black man named James Grant, sits in the passenger seat. Eventually, Harry crashes the car and James dies. Before taking her best friend to the hospital, Evelyn puts the recently deceased James in the driver seat. Because of Evelyn's actions, everyone believed that James crashed the car and died while driving drunk.

"Why is this concerning? Off rip, it might not seem that concerning, right?" Jesse says in the YouTube video. "A lot of people would argue, 'Hey, the Black dude was already dead and there was no need for both lives to be ruined. She was protecting her best friend,' and so on and so forth. However, we have to put that into context with how race was handled throughout the novel, which was catastrophic, if I'm honest."

Jesse explains how Monique, the biracial Black journalist interviewing Evelyn Hugo, was not given a lot of characterization in comparison to other characters. They also point out that in choosing to have James die at the end, his death becomes a plot device for the novel's big twist—Monique is James's daughter. While Jenkins Reid may have done well in showing the nuances of a queer Cuban actress passing as white and straight in Old Hollywood, she did not recognize how she used the two main Black characters in the story, James and Monique, as plot devices.

"There is a long history of white authors and white writers using Blackness and Black characters as vehicles for trauma and to be easily discarded from the narrative," Jesse says.

For the purpose of the novel, Jesse argues that Monique and James could have been any other race—they didn't need to be Black. There was nothing in the story that made that necessary. So why did Jenkins Reid make them so? Jesse believes it was "to add diversity to the story."

In watching Jesse's video, I had to agree with them. If you decide to write a character with an identity not your own, it shouldn't be because you need their historically marginalized identity for the benefit of a plot twist. That's called a problematic storyline.

Taylor Jenkins Reid is not the first to write a novel with a problematic storyline, but this begs the question: How can writers catch these storylines before they go to print?

To examine the overarching storyline or plot, create an outline *after* you've written your creative writing piece. You could create the outline in numerous ways—chapter by chapter or plot element by plot element—but make sure that it offers plenty of details as to what happens to the characters in the story, especially those with historically marginalized identities. If you can see where those characters are placed in the storyline, you can analyze their role in the plot.

By condensing a larger piece into a small outline, you might be able to examine the story in a new light. From there you (and your critique partners) can analyze the plot for exoticism, trauma or inspirational porn, bias, othering, stereotypes, and harmful tropes.

Watch the full video by Jesse of *Bowties and Books*:

LOOK AT YOUR DRAFT FROM A NEW ANGLE

Catching a stereotype, misrepresentation, or trope in your text isn't going to be easy. If you have a bias block, you might not be able to see your bias in the text. To better recognize these mistakes, look at your draft from a new angle. After finishing the first draft, let your creative piece "sit" for a while—a few days, weeks, or a month—before you start editing. Giving yourself some space from the story can help you see it in a new light.

Additionally, edit the draft in different ways: print it out and edit by hand, read scenes aloud, get others to read it aloud to you, or read it backwards. A new angle can bring a new perspective, and you need that in the editing process to recognize problematic larger portrayals and storylines.

DO YOU FEEL COMFORTABLE READING YOUR PIECE ALOUD?

I was listening to a podcast episode of *SmartLess*, in which Jason Bateman, Sean Hayes, and Will Arnett were interviewing award-winning actress Octavia Spencer. During the episode, Hayes asked Spencer about her experience going on a book tour with author Kathryn Stockett of *The Help*. According to Spencer, Stockett wasn't comfortable reading aloud the sections of her book that featured Black characters' dialogue (Spencer said, "Kathryn knew it would have been kind of weird to do the dialect") and so Spencer was hired to join her on the tour and read those sections aloud for Stockett.[1]

I'm not commenting on Spencer's choice to go on this tour with Stockett. It was a gig, she got paid, and it seems she had a positive experience doing that tour and acting in the film. Keep doing you, Octavia. However, I think this story brings to light something important to think about in the editing process:

If you are not comfortable reading your creative work aloud to an audience, maybe there is a reason for that.

The Help has been criticized widely for its white savior narrative and decentering Black voices of the South. After the film came out, Viola Davis said it's the one film she regrets making. Ablene Cooper, the woman who inspired the real-life role that Davis played—sued the author for using her likeness without her permission, as well as the "embarrassing" portrayal of her character. (The suit was eventually thrown out.)[2]

According to Spencer's story about touring with Stockett, it seems that the author believed that her portrayal of Black characters, or at least their dialogue, would not come off well if read aloud by a white author. Why? Was the author slightly (or seriously) concerned that the dialogue was stereotypical, created a caricature, was offensive, and/or committed othering? If so, hiring a person from that identity to read aloud from the scene seems icky to say the least.

I've never heard of an author doing this, because it's not a normal thing for any author to do. Men haven't hired women actors to read aloud novel scenes with women characters, or vice versa. I know many authors who have written outside their racial and ethnic identities, and I've never heard of them asking someone of that racial or ethnic identity to read that character's dialogue for them. If you didn't write their dialogue in a stereotypical, caricature-like, or misrepresentative way—you won't need to.

I wanted to include this story because it brings up a good point for those who are editing their creative work. As you edit, ask yourself: "Would I be comfortable reading this aloud to an audience that was filled with people of the same identity that I'm portraying in my work? Why or why not?"

If you're uncomfortable with the idea of reading your work aloud to an audience of people with historically marginalized identities, you need to examine why. Is that because your piece has a problematic storyline? Stereotypical dialogue? Offensive tropes? If so, how do you fix that?

It might not hurt to find a small private audience from the identity in which you are writing as well as others to whom you can read sections of your piece aloud. Examine how you feel as you read your draft. What reactions and feedback do you get from your audience? How can you utilize that feedback to improve your piece?

If you conclude that you're not comfortable reading your work aloud simply because you do not have the same identities or historically marginalized identities as your characters, then you might want to rethink putting this work out in the world. It may mean that you need to do more investing in the community that you are portraying or that you cannot handle the possible feedback that comes with writing an identity not your own. There is nothing wrong with that.

What doesn't feel right is the idea of moving forward with a piece that you can't even read aloud, whether that's because of a problematic portrayal or some unrealized sense of guilt.

CRITICAL FEEDBACK

When you've gone through multiple rounds of editing your manuscript and feel fairly confident with your choices, it's time to get feedback.

If you hire an editor, it's likely they'll focus on editing the main elements of the story. Depending on the editor, they may point out misrepresentations, stereotypes, or tropes, especially if you ask them to. However, I would not rely solely on an editor to catch elements of misrepresentation in your draft. Rather, seek out two different types of critical feedback: from beta readers and sensitivity readers.

BETA READERS

Beta readers are test readers who give feedback from the point of view of an average reader. They provide feedback on everything from grammar to content, characters, plot, and setting.

It's a good idea to seek the assistance of more than one beta reader. At least one beta reader should be a writer.

Some tips when looking for beta readers:

- Have at least two, ideally three, different beta readers from various identity backgrounds.
- Look for beta readers who have the same identity as the character you are portraying in the book, as they can offer personal insight on certain scenes, the characterization, dialogue, slurs and bad words, and more.
- When asking beta readers to read your manuscript, you might want to offer an in-kind exchange. If the person is a writer, offer your services as a beta reader in the future. If the person is not a writer, consider what skills or gifts you can offer them, like advice on their social media strategy, helping them move from an apartment to a house, or buying them a drink, dinner, or coffee. A bookstore gift card is always a great idea!

So how do you find beta readers?

Join online and in-person writing critique groups, which can be found through an online search or your local bookstores, libraries, writing organizations, writing nonprofits, creative writing programs, coffee shops, and community centers. Getting involved in your local literary community, such as by attending literary readings, festivals, and events, can lead to a network of beta readers (and literary friends!) too. If you have a literary agent, you might ask them if they have another client who would be a good fit.

Remember how I encouraged you throughout the book to build relationships with people from the community you are representing in your creative writing? If you've done that, it will undoubtedly come in handy during the editing process when you're looking for beta readers.

If you've built an open and honest two-way relationship with people in the community, you will find that the feedback you receive on your manuscript will be more thorough and helpful. As I mentioned above, when it comes to beta readers, an in-kind exchange can be helpful, and that is especially true when you're asking someone from the same community as your character to read your work. Beta reading is emotional labor, so be prepared to show your appreciation for it.

Lastly, not everyone is equipped to provide helpful, insightful, or engaged feedback or critiques. A simple "You did great" or "Fix this" is not going to cut it. A great beta reader will explain *why* your creative choices work or don't work. Finding a beta reader who knows how to provide in-depth insight to your work (and isn't afraid to do so), especially in relation to depicting identities not your own, is necessary for this entire process and will give you the greatest chance to improve the piece.

SENSITIVITY READERS

Sensitivity readers are paid editors who help authors who have written identities not their own to avoid portraying the character in an inauthentic or uninformed manner based off their lack of firsthand experience. The editing process of a sensitivity reader will involve examining the creative writing piece for one-dimensional or stock characterizations, tropes, clichés, stereotypes, and harmful overall storylines.

As I mentioned, you will have to pay sensitivity readers.

Their rates will vary and could be dependent on the length of the piece or the number of words. It may even be a flat rate.

Finding a sensitivity reader can be a bit tricky. Seek out referrals from other writers, writing organizations, or writing programs. You can also find directories of sensitivity readers through the likes of Writing Diversely, Editors of Color, Dot and Dash, the Binders Full of Sensitivity Readers Facebook group, Sensitivity Reviews, and Firefly Creative Writing.

A few tips for hiring sensitivity readers:

- It might be helpful to hire a sensitivity reader who has the same background as your character, but that's not to say that a sensitivity reader from a different background would not do an equally amazing job.
- Make sure you sign a contract that spells out the payment for the service and how the payment will be provided. A contract is as much for the sensitivity reader's protection as it is yours. Contracts should be signed before the sensitivity reader begins reading.
- If a publisher has acquired your creative work, request that they hire a sensitivity reader. Small publishers or literary magazines may not have the funds to do this, but it doesn't hurt to ask. It should be the standard for medium and large publishers, and if it's not, it's up to writers and their literary agents to request it and include it in contracts.

GUIDE YOUR BETA AND SENSITIVITY READERS

Sometimes it can be helpful to beta readers, sensitivity readers, and editors if you provide them with specific things that you'd like them to focus on when reading your creative piece. Is there a specific scene that you don't feel very confident about? Do you want a second opinion on a scene that exhibits discrimination? Are you worried about a specific personality trait of a character who has a historically marginalized identity? Do you have concerns about a tropic storyline?

To make what and where you need help as clear as possible to the beta reader, sensitivity reader, and editor, do the following:

- Make a list of everything in your creative piece that you would like your beta readers, editors, and sensitivity readers to focus and provide feedback on.
- If you can, provide page numbers next to each request so that the reader knows exactly what you are talking about and where they might be able to find it in the text.
- You could also make notes in the margins of a Word document with the Comments feature or highlight things in the text.

WHAT TO DO WITH FEEDBACK

As a writer, it can be difficult to get feedback of any sort, but I have found that it is especially challenging for writers to receive critical feedback on their portrayal of a character of a different identity. Why? Because people have a hard time accepting that they have biases and bias blocks. I'll say it again: accept this as fact. We all have biases, and when you accept that, the critique process will be a lot easier.

When receiving critical feedback, ask the reader to write down their thoughts within the manuscript and in a separate summary. Doing so will allow you to read the feedback and then let it sit for a few days before rereading it again. I find that in doing this, you are a bit more open the subsequent times you read the criticism.

You may not agree with all the suggested edits, but you need to determine why you feel that way. Is it because you can't accept that you made a mistake? Or is it a suggestion that wouldn't benefit the piece? If not, why? No matter how you answer these questions, if there is a suggestion that you don't agree with, do your due diligence, and ask the editor to explain their suggestion aloud.

Sometimes hearing it explained by a person aloud, rather than in written form, will give you a better understanding of what the editor meant. They may explain something better on a call or provide more insight than they gave in their written summary. You could even ask permission to record the conversation so that you can refer to their explanations later when you're ready to start editing.

Be open-minded during the conversation and control your natural inclination to be defensive. No one is attacking you. They're trying to help you.

If you have asked someone from the same identity as your character to read the draft, work hard to really listen to what they have to say. Of course, they do not speak for their entire identity, but their lived experience can offer some incredible insight to your piece. They will likely be more invested in making sure that a misrepresentation or stereotype is not released to the world. Don't be like a white woman I once had as a student who complained heatedly about her beta reader, a Black man who tried to point out issues with the slurs she used in her novel. She went on to change her mind when a large group of white women writers gave her the same advice as the Black beta reader. (Eye roll.)

If someone points out something in your draft, it's likely that something is missing or isn't being fully conveyed to the reader. What harm does it do to rework the scene and see if that makes the draft better?

EXERCISE

Do you recall the Circle of Trust exercise at the beginning of this book? We're going to do a version of that exercise to analyze the beta readers you have in mind.

On a piece of paper, list four to seven people whom you typically use as beta readers. If you have never used a beta reader, think of four to seven people whom you would trust to read your creative piece. List them vertically (on the y-axis) on the left side of the paper. At the top of the paper (on the x-axis), horizontally list the following categories: gender identity, sexual/romantic orientation, race/ethnicity, disabilities, nationality, age group, class, religion, political views, and education level.

Your paper should look like this:

Next to each name, place a check mark if they have the

	GENDER IDENTITY	SEXUAL/ROMANTIC ORIENTATION	RACE/ ETHNICITY	DISABILITIES	NATIONALITY	AGE GROUP	CLASS	RELIGION	POLITICAL VIEWS	EDUCATION LEVEL
Person #1										
Person #2										
Person #3										
Person #4										
Person #5										
Person #6										
Person #7										

same gender identity, sexual orientation, race/ethnicity, disabilities, nationality, age group, class, religion, political views, and education level as you. For instance, if you are a queer person, you will place a check mark next to all the individuals who are also queer.

Now look at the chart and ask yourself these questions:

- How diverse are these beta readers? Or do they all have a similar background?
- Do you think these beta readers are the best people to read your creative piece and edit a historically marginalized identity? Why or why not?
- Will some beta readers do better than others? On what specific topics?

Once you've done this exercise, you may realize that you need to find other beta readers who might have better insight into editing characters from historically marginalized backgrounds. Make a list of potential beta readers. Next to each name, explain what makes them a great candidate to edit your piece.

10

THE EDITING CHECKLIST

You've received so much information in the previous chapters about writing an identity not your own and it can be overwhelming to remember it all, especially in the editing process. Below, you'll find an editing checklist that will guide you through an editing process that is specifically designed to catch stereotypes, misrepresentations, clichés, tropes, inappropriate depictions, and so much more. I encourage you to use this checklist each and every time you finish a draft of a creative writing piece that features an identity not your own.

☐ Finish the manuscript and edit the storyline, setting, character development, and plot. If you notice anything related to identity that needs to be fixed, make a note of it and return to it later. Focus mostly on editing the main story elements.

☐ Search for all identity terms within the text and examine how they're used. Are they accurate and up to date? Are races and ethnicities capitalized? What approach did you take with person-first and identity-first language?

> The search function in Microsoft Word can be a very helpful tool during editing. Windows users can type Ctrl + F and Mac users can type Command + F to open the navigation window. From there, type in the word you want to search for and hit Enter. Microsoft Word will then take you to those words within the manuscript.
> Here is a good example of how to use the search navigation tool:
> If I want to make sure that I have not used an inappropriate identity term like "Indians" in reference to Indigenous people, I will type "Indians" into the search window. If it appears in the text, I remove and exchange it with a more appropriate identity term.

❏ Search the text for slurs or bad words. Consider if they're necessary, there for shock value, or result in a sentimental scene. If need be, replace these words or rewrite the scene so that it features a subtler form of discrimination.
❏ Search the text for ableist language, gender-exclusive language, and language that suggests only two types of sexual/romantic orientations. Make changes where necessary. Optional (but highly suggested): search the text for language that is demeaning to different classes, ages, people with substance use disorders, those experiencing

houselessness, immigrants, different religions, and differing body types.

- ❏ Remove italicization of other languages unless there is a specific reason for keeping words italicized.
- ❏ Is there anything in the text that promotes harmful colonialist perspectives or could send the message that other countries and cultures are not equal to the U.S.? Did you use colonialist words or phrases that exoticize, other, or demean another country, community, or culture?
- ❏ Choose a character who has a different identity from your own. You will focus only on their presence within the manuscript for the following steps.
  - ❏ Search the text for appropriate and inappropriate terminology related to your character's identity and make changes where necessary.
  - ❏ Read every scene with that character. Look for stereotypes, tropes, and clichés relating to their identity or identities.
  - ❏ Read every scene again with the character and examine how you've described their appearance, personality, and style.
  - ❏ Assess the character's dialogue and dialogue tags for how you describe their accent and dialect, as well as the types of words they use (and if those words are related to stereotypes), how often they cuss, appropriate slang and colloquialisms, their topics of conversation (and if they are stereotypical), if they code-switch, the use of phonetics, the "broken English" trope, etc.
  - ❏ Inspect scenes that feature discrimination. Do they commit sentimentality? Are they nuanced? Should you have used a subtler form of discrimination rather

than an overt one, or vice versa? What purpose do they have in the story? Are these discriminatory scenes resulting in trauma or inspirational porn?

❑ If your character is from another country, analyze their perspective, opinions, and behaviors. Do their values and beliefs sound similar to your own nation's rather than the kind of values and beliefs a person from their own country would have? How do you know?

❑ Re-examine every scene with your character for stereotypes, tropes, clichés, problematic associations, and false information that you may have missed.

❑ If you have multiple characters with different identities from your own, do the previous step for them as well.

❑ Examine your characters of privilege—especially white, straight, cis, abled, and/or men characters.

❑ Read every scene with that character. Are there stereotypes, tropes, or clichés in those scenes that paint them in a more positive light because of their privileged identity?

❑ Read every scene relating to their appearance, personality, and style. Did you use more positive associations in the description of their looks, personality, or style? Did you describe them equally to how you described characters from historically marginalized backgrounds? For instance, if you described every character of color's skin tone, do the same for a white character's skin tone.

❑ Analyze the character's dialogue and dialogue tags. Did you describe their accent? Is their speech more posh than the speech of characters with historically marginalized identities? Why?

❑ Re-examine every scene with the character of privilege for anything you may have missed.

❑ Assess the text for genre-specific tropes and stereotypes and make changes where necessary. Example: If you are writing Western fiction, you'll need to look for stereotypical and tropic depictions of Indigenous nations that are common in Westerns (e.g., "Tonto Talk," the violent band of warriors, etc.).

❑ Create a reverse outline to determine if the overall storyline commits exoticism, has a stereotypical trope, is a problematic savior story, mirrors colonialism, is inspiration or trauma porn, or exhibits some other problematic plot.

   ❑ Have someone else read the reverse storyline and get their feedback.

   ❑ Make changes to the storyline based off the feedback and your own analysis.

❑ Read the entire manuscript from start to finish and make any additional changes.

❑ Get at least two or three beta readers to read the manuscript.

   ❑ After receiving the beta reader feedback, make any necessary edits. You may want to do another editing run-through for your characters with different identities.

❑ Hire a sensitivity reader. Make any edits suggested by the sensitivity reader. This is especially important for self-publishing writers or writers who go through a process where there is little oversight from editors, literary magazines, an organization, a company, or a publisher. Those who are traditionally publishing can speak to their editor about the sensitivity reading process at that particular publishing house. While I believe that all medium-to-large publishers should make this a part of their internal process (to protect themselves and their authors), it is not yet an established industry-wide practice. Therefore, you'll need to speak to your editor about whether or not they can obtain a sensitivity read for you. Remember, small publishers and literary magazines likely don't have the budget to do so.

❑ Read through the piece one last time from start to finish, flagging anything that needs to be changed—and then fix it. You should be able to read through the piece with confidence in your depiction of identities not your own.

❑ Self-publishing writers (or writers with no extra layer of oversight) should do one more beta reading and/or sensitivity reading session to ensure everything is in tip-top shape before uploading or posting their work online or printing their work for dissemination, etc.

❑ Writers who are publishing traditionally can share the manuscript with their agent, editor, publisher, literary magazines, etc.

11

TERMS, STEREOTYPES, AND TROPES

QUICK CHAPTER NAVIGATION

To make the editing process as easy as possible, I've broken down the different identities into sections—race/ethnicity, gender identity, disabilities, sexual and romantic orientations, and a final section of "other identities." Feel free to read this chapter before you start your next creative writing piece, as it can inform you on the stereotypes, tropes, and terms not to use.

In addition to laying out some of the most notable stereotypes and tropes of a specific identity, I'll provide certain identity terms and quick insights and notes about writing different identities.

There may be some terms, stereotypes, and tropes not listed in this section. It is likely that I have missed some, or that in the years following the publication of this book, a new term, stereotype, or trope will become more prevalent. You are responsible for being aware of the tropes and stereotypes related to your character—this section is a starter, not an end-all.

DEFINING STEREOTYPES AND TROPES

Before we jump in, let's define a stereotype and a trope as it relates to writing and, specifically, writing an identity other than your own.

Stereotype: This is a widely held idea, belief, image, or misconception about a particular community, identity, or type of person. It is usually an oversimplified perspective, idea, belief, or characterization that can present itself in the traits of a stock character, a one-dimensional characterization of a group of people, or an assumption or misconception about a type of culture, community, identity, or person.

Tropes: These are recurring images, motifs, words, symbols, language, clichés, style, plots, storylines, settings, and characterizations across creative works. While tropes are not inherently negative, when they incorporate stereotypes, misconceptions, assumptions, exoticism, tokenism, or discrimination of any kind, they can be problematic.

SHOULD YOU REMOVE STEREOTYPES AND TROPES COMPLETELY FROM YOUR WORK?

There is nothing that says you can't have stereotypes and tropes in your creative piece, as long as you are aware of them and you handle them in a way that subverts the stereotype or trope.

What do I mean by that?

I once had a student who was writing about a successful businesswoman. The businesswoman was Vietnamese, and she had a chain of nail salons where she employed other people of Asian descent. Even though the businesswoman was clearly successful, the problem was that Asian people, especially Vietnamese people, working in nail salons is a stereotype. Should she change the character's business to something else?

By definition, stereotypes are oversimplified perspectives about a group of people or type of person. The key word is oversimplified. What the definition leaves out is that there can be some truth to the stereotype—but that truth becomes oversimplified, over sensationalized, the butt of a joke, or merely the only characteristic of a particular type of person.

The student could have an Asian woman character who owns nail salon businesses, but only if the character wasn't completely characterized by that aspect. The character has to be three-dimensional, full of other noteworthy characteristics, interests, hobbies, ideas, positive and negative traits.

That's how you subvert a stereotype or a trope.

There are other ways to subvert stereotypes and tropes too. You could write a satirical piece to ridicule and expose a trope or stereotype. One of my favorite methods is to acknowledge the stereotype or trope. Here is an example I've made up: "She could feel like a stereotype—another Asian woman working in a nail salon—but she knew who she was. She owned the place and ten others like it. They could call her a stereotype all they wanted, but this job had given her a life, cleared her of debt, and given her a beautiful house and an immense retirement fund. She was proud of what she'd done."

I should also mention that some stereotypes and tropes are themselves so triggering, harmful, and offensive to readers that it might not matter how they're presented. This, of course, can be hard to determine, so you'll have to speak with the communities you're writing about when it comes to those tropes and stereotypes.

If at any point you don't feel confident about subverting the stereotype or trope, go in a different direction. Just because you imagined your characters or story in one way doesn't mean it can't be changed. Kill those darlings and create some new ones.

RACE/ETHNICITY

CAPITALIZATION OF RACES AND ETHNICITIES

Always capitalize races and ethnicities. The only race in which this is called into question is when we discuss whether to capitalize white/White. There is some debate on this. Let's look at two different perspectives.

The *Seattle Times* style guide provides definitions for Black and white that explain why they do not capitalize white.

> **Black (adj.):** Belonging to people who are part of the African diaspora. Capitalize Black because it is a reflection of shared cultures and experiences (foods, languages, music, religious traditions, etc.).

> **White (adj.):** Belonging to people with light-colored skin, especially those of European descent. Unlike Black, it is lowercase, as its use is a physical description of people whose backgrounds may spring from many different cultures.[1]

As they point out, white is not to be capitalized, because it is a physical description rather than an indication of a specific racial culture.

However, the Center for the Study of Social Policy has a different perspective. In a statement made by two non-white staff members, the Center says that they will capitalize "White" and this is why they believe others should too:

> To not name "White" as a race is, in fact, an anti-Black act which frames Whiteness as both neutral and the standard. We believe that it is important to call attention to White as a race as a way to understand and give voice to how Whiteness functions in our social and political institutions and our communities. Moreover, the detachment of "White" as a proper noun allows White people to sit out of conversations about race and removes accountability from White people's and White institutions' involvement in racism.[2]

So, what do you do? We currently do not have a society-wide decision on this matter, and it's even more complicated the further we dive into arguments from both sides.

Some point out that by not capitalizing "white," we are distancing ourselves from white supremacists who consistently capitalize "white." As *AP News*'s vice president for standards, John Daniszewski, said, "We agree that white people's skin color plays into systemic inequalities and injustices, and we want our journalism to robustly explore these problems. But capitalizing the term white, as is done by white supremacists, risks subtly conveying legitimacy to such beliefs."[3]

In an essay in *The Atlantic* in 2020, New York University philosophy professor Kwame Anthony Appiah disagreed, saying that by capitalizing "white," it would take power away from racists, many of whom capitalize it as a "provocative defiance of the norm."[4]

Then there is Dr. Jenn M. Jackson, a Black queer abolitionist and professor and the author of *Black Women Taught Us*, who said in a Twitter thread (now X) in 2020 that "Capitalizing the 'w' is only a performative act for white people. The rest of us are already aware that whiteness is *not* invisible. Not capitalizing the 'w' in white is decolonizing work. We don't need any more mechanisms to make whiteness more visible."

They added, "Not capitalizing the 'w' in white is a systemic disruption which decenters whiteness with respect to other groups. That should be the purpose of capitalization. . . . Whiteness sets itself as the norm. Thus capitalizing, to me, esp when done alongside capitalizing oppressed groups, normalizes because it implies sameness."[5]

As you can see, this is a very complicated topic with legitimate arguments on both sides. For now, I'm going to leave "white" lowercased as I continue to explore this topic. This may be a mistake. I could be wrong in this choice.

Moving forward, you will have to make up your own mind on whether or not to capitalize "white." Keep in mind that a literary magazine or publishing house will have their own stylistic guidelines and rules, though they generally defer to a writer's preference and/or work with the writer on such subjects by sharing resources and having conversations.

If, for some reason, your publishing house does not capitalize Black, Indigenous, Mixed, Latine, or some other racial or ethnic identity term, fight for it to be capitalized.

> Did you know that the United States doesn't just identify people of European ancestry (British, Scottish, German, Polish, etc.) as white? They also label people who are Latine, Middle Eastern, and North African as white.
>
> Latinos, Middle Eastern people, and North Africans are people of color—which makes labeling them racially "white" very confusing (and incorrect, if you ask me). The reason why these three groups are told to tick the "white" racial box on census forms has more to do with politics and history than anything else.
>
> Latinos are labeled as white because of the Treaty of Guadalupe Hidalgo, which ended the Mexican-American War.[6] Per the treaty, the U.S. had to

give Mexican citizens living in areas that were turned over to the U.S. full citizenship, and the only people who had full citizenship at the time were white people. Thus, these Mexican-turned-American citizens were labeled as white, and subsequently all Latinos were too from then on.[7]

The root reason as to why Middle Easterners and North Africans are classified as white on the census has to do with a court case in 1909 that involved a man named George Shishim, who was born in Lebanon and wanted to be naturalized as an American citizen. At the time, Lebanon was considered part of Asia, and per the Chinese Exclusion Act, Asians could not become American citizens.[8] Therefore, Shishim had to prove that to be Lebanese was to be white. He eventually won, and a California court granted U.S. citizenship to all Middle Easterners.[9] This eventually led to the Office of Management and Budget listing all Middle Easterners and North Africans as white in the late 1970s.[10]

Latinos, Middle Easterners, and North Africans have all suffered under white supremacy. Not only do they experience socioeconomic disparities, but they have been dealing with systematic racism before and since being labeled as "white." (Latinos were subjected to segregation in the South, while Middle Eastern people and North Africans have been targets of Islamophobic questioning and security checks in airports, etc.) They do not have the same experience or privilege of white individuals of European descent in the U.S.

For the purpose of this book, and when writing identities not your own, you should not consider these groups white by any means. While there are some within these ethnic identities who may have skin tones that make them white passing, in terms of socioeconomic disparities and institutional racism, these groups are still considered people of color.

CHOOSING A RACIAL/ETHNIC TERM FOR YOUR CHARACTER

How do you choose between "Indigenous" or "Native American"? Are there differences between the two identity terms? The answer is yes.

Because this is a writing guide and not an anthropological guide, I did not write definitions for the different identity terms lest I make this book much longer than it already is. I do want to say that there are subtle differences between Hispanic and

Latino or Black and African American. Before choosing a term to identify a racial/ethnic group or character in your story, do a deep dive into the different terms and learn more about the social and political discussions surrounding each one.

Would your character be more likely to identify themselves as biracial or Mixed? Is there some nuance to Arab versus Middle Eastern that you should know about? Is your character more connected to their ethnicity than their race? Would one character call a racial group one thing and would a character from that group identify as something different? These are the kinds of questions you must ask yourself when choosing racial/ethnic terms for your characters.

HISTORICAL FICTION IDENTITY TERMS

Certain racial and ethnic terms were more widely used in the past but are considered offensive today. Historical fiction writers may struggle with the question: Do I include such a term to be historically accurate or do I leave it out so as not to offend readers of today?

This is a tough one and not something that I can give you a straight answer on. However, I would say that if you can avoid using an offensive, outdated term relating to race/ethnicity in your historical fiction, do so. Your work is fiction and therefore is not beholden to the same standards as historical nonfiction. I doubt any reader would stop reading your novel because you used an identity term that is less offensive.

If you decide to use an outdated term, one that would have been used in the era in which your work is set, I suggest including a note at the beginning of the piece to inform readers as to why it is included. The argument of "historical accuracy" is not good enough and will not win over most readers, especially those who come from the same racial/ethnic group that is related to the outdated term.

> New identity terms may arise a year after this book is published or an outdated term comes back into use. I can't predict what identity terms will become outdated, so I've tried my hardest here to include those that seem as if they will have a longer shelf life than others.

TERMS, STEREOTYPES, AND TROPES: RACE/ETHNICITY

INDIGENOUS
Indigenous
Native American
First Nations

Alaska Natives
Hawaiians, Native Hawaiians, Kānaka Maoli, Kānaka ʻŌiwi
Pacific Islanders, Pasifika

Aboriginal Australians
Torres Strait Islanders

Indigenous peoples of Africa

Be specific, e.g., Cherokee, Zulu, Sioux, Athabascans

Terms to avoid in relation to Indigenous peoples
While some of these terms are used by Indigenous peoples or may still be present in educational settings, textbooks, and museums, there is quite a lot of discussion around each of them and how they have been used in negative contexts toward Indigenous people. You might want to avoid these terms in most cases, as it's clear that they have caused considerable harm to various communities or are at the least being used less and less in comparison to other terms. Not only that, but it could come off poorly when used by a writer writing outside of their identity.

- Indians
- American Indian
- Bushmen
- Eskimo

Is "Tribe" an Appropriate Term?

There is a common practice of referring to Indigenous communities as "tribes." The term was placed upon Indigenous peoples around the world by colonialists and not something they used themselves.

Today, there is a lot of discussion around this term. It tends to have offensive associations with stereotypes such as Indigenous primitivism and violence. Some Indigenous communities use the term "tribe" (on their websites or in conversation, for example) even with all of its implications. Usually, you'll see a mix of perspectives and opinions on this word within the same community. Among Alaska Natives, "tribe" is the most widely accepted term above all others, and that has a lot to do with their history forming into corporations under the Alaska Native Claims Settlement Act rather than reservations (except for one, the Metlakatla Indian Community).

As a writer writing outside of your identity, it might be best to use other terms, such as:

- nations
- societies
- communities
- peoples
- chiefdom (more often used in Africa)
- village
- pueblo (used among some Indigenous nations of the southwestern United States)
- clan
- mob (used among Aboriginal and Torres Strait Islander peoples)
- identifying the Indigenous group without any additional identifier; examples: "the Cherokee" or "the Tlingit"

You'll need to do your research into the community you're writing about and speak to a variety of people in the community, ideally those who are representatives of the nation, community, society, or peoples. This is just one of those terms that is very difficult to give you a clear answer on, as much as I wish I could.

The words "tribe," "nomad," or "native" *should not* be used in a colloquial way. Here are some examples of what not to do:

"She found her tribe of stay-at-home mothers,"

or "He lived like a nomad, moving from London to Paris and then to Berlin all within a year," or "The natives are restless."

To use these terms in such casual, colloquial ways comes off as disingenuous and offensive, and it erases the real experiences that Indigenous people have had since colonialization.

Stereotypes

- **The stoic Native American:** Someone who is stoic is a person who endures pain or hardship without showing their emotions or complaining. Native Americans have experienced hardships and pain, and to depict them as stoic is to indicate that they have risen above that pain and hardship, and hold in their feelings. Such portrayals allow non-Indigenous audiences to feel comfortable with the hardships that Native Americans face and insinuate that Native Americans should repress their feelings.

- **Pacific Islander body types:** The stereotype is that all Pacific Islanders have larger bodies, and are stocky and/or short. Such depictions can intersect with other stereotypes that infer that Pacific Islanders are lazy, more prone to alcohol use disorders, or should have certain jobs like that of a football player or security guard.

- **Primitivism:** Indigenous peoples have been associated with the idea of primitivism, or incorrectly presenting certain Indigenous nations as living primitive lifestyles and having no connection to modern technology, or education. While some Indigenous communities around the world live a more traditional lifestyle, this doesn't negate the experience of many Indigenous peoples who live modern lives, go to college, and work in different sectors.

- **Alcohol use disorder:** It is stereotypical to make alcohol use disorder the most prevalent feature of the Indigenous community you are portraying.
- **Stereotypical items:** A writer might use stereotypical items, food, and clothing to describe an Indigenous character. Examples include fry bread, headdresses, igloos, teepees, moccasins, war paint, leis, and dreamcatchers. This surface-level description usually results in a stock character.
- **Indigenous magic and spirit guides:** Indigenous spiritual beliefs have long been associated with magic by outsiders. Sometimes this idea of Indigenous magic is presented through the depiction of spirit guides who are either people or animals. It becomes problematic when these spiritual beliefs are generalized and not particular to a specific Indigenous society, are for the benefit of a non-Indigenous character (usually a white character), or are romanticized and exoticized.
- **The noble warrior:** This stereotype involves portraying Indigenous men as noble, righteous, virtuous, and worthy warriors.
- **The wise elder:** A tropic character that is a wise elder—often, though not always, an official leader or a wise woman—who has all the right answers to the question or concern at hand. They can also be depicted as having magical or spiritual powers, like a shaman.
- **Happy and relaxed Native Hawaiians welcoming tourists:** This stereotype occurs when Native Hawaiians are

portrayed as laid-back, excessively happy, and/or eager to welcome tourists to their traditional homelands with leis and hula dances. This is a false representation of Native Hawaiians that centers the tourist, who is often white, as the main character, while the Native Hawaiian is there to serve their travel needs and experiences.

I included Pacific Islanders in the Indigenous section, because many Pacific Islanders are Indigenous peoples of their original lands and are recognized as such by various organizations and governments.

AAPI is commonly used to refer to Asian American and Pacific Islanders. It's also been shorthanded to API (Asian Pacific Islander) and APA (Asian Pacific American). This acronym is hotly debated because many feel that Asian Americans and Pacific Islanders should not be grouped under the same umbrella, while others believe that in doing so, it helps raise issues that both groups face.[11]

Be mindful of how closely you associate Pacific Islanders with Asians, as many would argue that the connections between the two are flimsy at best and that Pacific Islanders are not Asian. For instance, stereotypes about Asians, like the "model minority" stereotype, are usually not even considered in relation to Pacific Islanders, and they tend to experience higher health and socioeconomic disparities compared to Asian communities. If you feature Pacific Islanders in your work, it is best to do a deep dive into how Pacific Islanders identify themselves and how the world perceives them.

Tropes

- **A pure primitive society:** Indigenous nations, especially in pre-European times, are sometimes depicted as pure societies because of the colonialist perspective that they were "primitive" societies. This can also present itself in fantasy and sci-fi narratives that feature Indigenous or nomadic types of people in the same trope-y and stereotypical way.

- **The captivity narrative:** The Western genre has a habit of presenting the captivity narrative, usually when a white person is taken by Indigenous peoples in a raid and imprisoned in their camp. It is usually done from the perspective of the captive and highlights the Indigenous nation in a negative way as the aggressor, evil, and violent, while also leaving out the atrocities that settlers and colonizing military bands committed.

- **The loyal sidekick:** Often an Indigenous person is put in the role of a sidekick to a non-Indigenous person, usually a cowboy, sheriff, lawman, or bandit who is white. Tonto is the most popular example of the loyal Indigenous sidekick. This trope presents the Indigenous person as not having agency in their own story and there to help the (usually) white character to succeed.

- **The violent Native American:** Indigenous peoples, especially in historical fiction and Westerns, have been showcased as uncouth, violent, uneducated, primitive, and animalistic.

- **The chief's daughter/Native American princess:** Pocahontas's story has become so romanticized and exoticized that it has resulted in an Indigenous princess or chief's daughter trope. This woman or girl is usually the savior of a white person, typically a man, and is the catalyst of harmony and communication between two different communities of peoples.

- **Native American burial ground:** The Native American burial ground trope has made its way into folklore, gothic fiction, and horror stories. It insinuates that Indigenous peoples are resentful of what happened to them during colonialism and are looking for ways to enact revenge, generally on white people, through spiritual hauntings.

- **Cannibalism and human sacrifice:** These are storylines that depict Indigenous peoples, often Pacific Islanders, Africans, and Mesoamerican nations, as being violent and engaging in human sacrifice and cannibalism. These actions are often depicted in contrast to European explorers, which results in the villainizing of these cultures and communities.

- **Fantasy interpretations of Indigenous stories:** When a non-Indigenous person takes an Indigenous oral history and uses it in a fantasy story, it may be considered cultural appropriation. Many different nations have rules about not sharing certain stories on a large public stage, so doing that through a fantasy genre may be going against the nation's laws or customs. In changing up the Indigenous oral story for your fantasy story, you could be creating an offensive, biased, or stereotypical perspective that the nation would not like.

- **Homogenizing Indigenous communities:** Indigenous societies are incredibly diverse from one another, and yet there is a practice of homogenizing these communities within literature. For instance, although "Alaska Natives" may be used to refer to the Indigenous communities within Alaska, writers should remember that there are 229 federally recognized Alaska Native tribes that are different from each other in terms of language, beliefs, culture, and practices. When writing about Indigenous communities within a specific region, state, or country, it is imperative that we showcase how distinct and diverse they are from each other and do not mesh, meld, or reduce their vastly different experiences as Indigenous peoples into a singular experience or identity. We can do this by being specific and detailed when describing different nations, and societies.

- **Using Indigenous ancestry in a disrespectful way:** When an author gives a character, no matter their racial background, a tiny amount of Indigenous heritage to make their character seem more "exotic," culturally rich, or less associated to "whiteness." An example of this would be an author writing a white character who then claims that their great-grandfather was half-Cherokee at some point in the text. Some writers do this to explain why Indigenous-specific magical realism—like the appearance of spirit guides—occurs or why the character has a good relationship with Indigenous communities. Others think that it will make the character seem more connected to the land or the legitimate owner of the land they own and seem less like a colonizer. Whatever the case may be, it's a disingenuous and offensive way to build a character because it showcases how the writer does not want to put in the effort or the time to create an Indigenous character, but rather sees Indigenous ancestry as something they can piecemeal to manipulate the perspective of the reader. It's disrespectful to Indigenous people and their culture and ignores the real history of genocide, oppression, and systematic discrimination (like blood quantum systems) that they've faced from other races.

BIPOC + POC

BIPOC stands for Black, Indigenous, and people of color, while POC stands for people/person of color. These acronyms are generally used to discuss a group of historically marginalized races and ethnicities; however, they are impersonal and are frankly controversial among the communities in which they represent. Be sure to research the current status of these terms and question if they are really necessary to include in your work.

BLACK

Black

African American

Afro-[enter ethnicity or race], e.g., Afro Latina or Afro Asian

Be specific, e.g., Nigerian American or Jamaican

Stereotypes

- **Angry Black woman:** Black women are depicted as angry, sassy, and/or aggressive.
- **Food stereotypes:** Certain foods and drinks have been associated with Black people so much that they've become stereotypes. These stereotypical food items include watermelons, fried chicken, 40s, Kool-Aid, etc.
- **The gangbanger/thug:** Black people have long been considered violent and/or criminals labeled as thugs or involved in gangs. The gangbanger and thug stereotype is generally associated with Black men.
- **Hypersexualizion:** Black people have been depicted as more sexual, sometimes with an animalistic overtone, in their speech or behavior. This also relates to how Black women's bodies are oversexualized and Black men have been stereotyped as dangerous sexual predators.
- **African American Vernacular English (AAVE)/ African American English (AAE) and cussing:** When the language of Black characters includes more cuss words than characters of other identities, it is stereotypical. African American Vernacular English/African American English has sometimes been used by non-Black writers in such a way that it creates a caricature of a Black character.

If you're going to write a character with a Black identity, you should read Black literature. Your first stop? The African American Literature Book Club (aalbc .com), which is known as the "largest site celebrating Black writers since 1998."[12] On the site, you'll find book reviews, a large author database, and other resources like articles on Black literature, lists of Black-owned bookstores and websites, discussion forums, and an events page.

Tropes

- **The Black best friend:** The Black best friend trope arose when writers wanted to add some diversity to their work but didn't feel comfortable making their main character a Black person. It has sometimes resulted in a stock Black best friend character and sent the message that Black characters couldn't be the focus of the story and were there to benefit the usually white protagonist.
- **The magical Black character:** This trope features a magical Black stock character whose purpose is to help a non-Black character in their quest or journey.
- **Single Black mother and absent dad:** The single Black mother and absent father trope is an overused and over-simplified perspective of Black families.

- **Enslavement and pre–Civil Rights narrative:** This is a historical fiction storyline in which white characters "help," "save," or emotionally connect with Black characters who are enslaved people and/or in domestic roles during the pre–Civil Rights era.
- **Once-upon-a-gangbanger:** This trope is an extension of the gang member stereotype and presents itself as a Black character who has undergone some change that makes them want to be good and stay out of trouble. This journey is usually fraught with their past violent life tempting them back or ruining their current situation.
- **Violent, crime-infested neighborhoods:** Black people are generally depicted as living in violent, low-income, and crime-infested neighborhoods.

LATINE

Latino/Latina
Latine/Latinx
Hispanic
Chicano/Chicanx
Combination, e.g., Afro Latina or Asian Latino
Ethnicity, e.g., Mexican American or Chilean

Stereotypes

- **Feisty Latina:** Latinas are showcased as being feisty, passionate, or sassy in a stock character way.
- **Unauthorized immigrants:** Latinos in the U.S. are perceived as being immigrants or first-generation Americans, despite the reality that Latinos have been in the U.S. since the 1500s. Today's border politics have turned into the idea that all Latinos are undocumented or unauthorized

noncitizens. There is also a perception that Latinos from other countries want to move to the U.S. and will do so by any means.

- **The poor Latino:** Latinos are stereotyped as poor and uneducated, even though many of them are well-off business owners, middle class, or wealthy.
- **English as a second language:** It is assumed that all Latinos speak Spanish as a first language and English as a second language. Some Latinos speak Spanish and others do not or have a varying degree of fluency. Many speak Indigenous languages or languages that combine a mix of Spanish, Indigenous, African, Portuguese, and/or French.
- **Machismo:** While machismo, or a toxic form of masculinity, is a real issue in the Latino community, it can become stereotypical when men of Latino heritage are depicted as having only machismo characteristics.

Tropes

- **Maids and yard workers:** Latinos tend to be depicted in certain occupations such as maids, yard workers, nannies, or field hands, even though they hold a variety of positions in the real world like business owner, congressperson, dentist, and more.
- **The Latino immigrant or first-generation story:** The first-generation or immigrant Latino story is starting to become a trope in literature. It contributes to the misconception that all Latinos are from other countries. Many Latinos are multigeneration Americans with families that have been living within the U.S. borders since before the American Revolution.

- **Fleeing the cartel:** The trope of Latinos fleeing their countries because of the cartel or some other violence is a common one. While this does happen, it is not the story of all Latinos and can result in the U.S. looking like the "promised land" and Latin American countries as dens of hell. It leaves out the nuances that the U.S. is responsible for some of the violence in Latin America.

- **Cartel and crime connections:** Cartels, gangs, crime, and violence dominate Latino stories and/or are sensationalized for a thriller, crime novel, mystery, literary fiction novel, and neo Western stories.

- **Homogenous people:** Although we might use an over-encompassing word like "Latino," Latinos are not a homogenous group of people. The Dominican culture is so different from the Argentinian and Guatemalan cultures. We must represent that in our literature and not default to the overarching signifier of "Latinos/as/xs/es."

- **The Latin lover:** The suave, handsome, romantic Latin lover is not a new trope by any means. It exoticizes the Latino culture and turns Latino men into a stock character of romantic and sexual behavior.

- **Fantasizing Mesoamerican myths:** When a non-Latino uses a Mesoamerican myth in their fantasy novel, it can be considered cultural appropriation. It's been done incorrectly many times before, showing the author's lack of knowledge on the Mesoamerican community or myth or legend they're portraying, which has resulted in bias, stereotypes, misrepresentations, exoticism, and othering.

- **Evil Mexican bandit:** If a Latino appears in a Western, it tends to be as an evil Mexican bandit or gang of bandits.

ASIAN
Asian
South Asian
Desi
East Asian
Ethnicity, e.g., Chinese American or Bangladeshi

Stereotypes
- **The smartest overachiever:** Reducing Asians to the nerdy, smart, overachieving student is a harmful stereotype that doesn't always speak to the nuance of the cultural expectations in Asian households. This contributes to the "model minority" stereotype, which aligns Asians to whiteness by saying that Asians behave more like white people.
- **Quiet/shyness:** Presenting Asian people as shy and quiet can result in stories that don't showcase Asian people as having agency in their own lives.
- **Petite, submissive Asian woman:** This stereotype removes strength, power, and independence from Asian women and places them in the role of a victim or makes them seem childlike, small, petite, submissive, innocent, or in need of men.
- **Unmanly, weak, feminine-looking, emasculated Asian man:** Characterizing Asian men as feminine, weak, or unmanly is a common and harmful stereotype.
- **Accents:** This is the assumption that all Asians are im-

migrants or first-generation Americans and thus have accents. "Your English is so good" is a microaggressive stereotype that many Asians experience.

- **Job stereotypes:** Asians are associated with certain jobs, like nail salon workers, doctors, engineers, convenience store owners, or tech professionals, which has resulted in stereotypical depictions.

- **Tiger Moms:** The Tiger Mom is a stereotypical representation of Asian moms. It presents them as overbearing, harsh, controlling, strict disciplinarians. This stereotype can be used to devalue the achievements of Asian children and credit their achievements to "overbearing" mothers.

- **Arranged or assisted marriages:** It is a false assumption that all South Asians are in arranged marriages. There are also many xenophobic perceptions about arranged marriages, insinuating they are *forced* marriages.

> Referring to Asian people as "Orientals" or Asia as "the Orient" is offensive and inappropriate.

Tropes

- **The magical Asian:** This occurs when an Asian person with magical powers is meant to assist a non-Asian character in their journey.

- **Yellow:** Associating Asian people with the color yellow, especially as it relates to their skin tone, is a harmful trope that is a result of the Yellow Peril/Terror, a xenophobic and racist mindset in the U.S. It perceives Asians in a negative light, sometimes in relation to communism, and other times as immigrants intent on taking white jobs.

- **Slanted eyes:** Like yellow skin, focusing on the eye shape of Asian people is a harmful and reductive trope that contributes to stereotypes.
- **Tropic figures:** Samurai, geisha, dragon ladies, and South Asian gurus have become tropic figures. Reducing Asian cultures to these tropic figures minimizes the diversity of Asian cultures and exoticizes certain Asian cultural elements.
- **The homogeneity of Asians:** Asians as a race are a diverse group of people, but as writers we run the risk of homogenizing Asian cultures rather than showcasing how vastly different they are to each other. Not all South Asians are from India; Vietnamese people have a different culture, history, religion, and society from people from Thailand or Pakistan, and so on.
- **The unique eye color:** In fantasy, sci-fi, and literary fiction, a single Asian character is sometimes given a unique eye color—blue, green, gray, or hazel—to separate the character from other Asians in a physical way and align the character with whiteness usually for the benefit of white readers. (Yes, some Asian people do have blue, green, or hazel eyes. However, within this trope, these eye colors are presented as not existing among Asians as a way to exoticize the character who does have them.)
- **Poverty in South Asia:** The "rags to riches" trope can also intersect with the South Asian trope of heavily focusing on poverty such as presented in movies like *Slumdog Millionaire*.

- **Fantasizing Asian myths:** When a non-Asian person uses an Asian myth or legend in their fantasy novel, it may be considered cultural appropriation. Through the changing of the myth or legend, it may result in an incorrect portrayal, stereotypes, bias, or exoticism, by someone who is not aware of the nuances of the myth and the culture.

> ### Associations with dragons, tigers, kung fu, saris, or chopsticks
>
> When writing Asian characters, we should aim to not use certain stereotypical foods, drinks, items, or music to represent their culture. For instance, imagery relating to dragons or tigers can come off as stereotypical. The same occurs with mentions of kung fu, chopsticks, Buddha, Bollywood, etc. When these stereotypical things appear in a creative writing piece, it tells the reader that the writer did not do extensive enough research to learn about the specific Asian culture they're writing about and is instead throwing in kung pao chicken or saris to seem "authentic."

MIDDLE EASTERN
Middle Eastern
North African
Arab

Kurd
Persian
Turk
Azerbaijani
Armenian
Assyrian
Ethnicity, e.g., Iranian American, Palestinian, or Jordanian

There is some discussion around the term "Middle Eastern" and whether it is an appropriate term to use. We typically see Middle Eastern and North African (MENA) people categorized under the same umbrella, even though it's such a vast region (on two continents) with very diverse cultures, communities, and histories. Some people from this region have started using "West Asian" rather than "Middle Eastern" to create some distance from the term "Middle Eastern," which was invented by white Europeans and white Westerners and is so wrapped up in negative stereotypes. In the U.S., the term "Middle Eastern" is still very much in use and is still seen as an appropriate term among many. That being said, it's always best to be specific when creating characters from this region. For instance, if your character is Persian, use the term "Persian" rather

than "Middle Easterner." By doing
so, you're providing a more specific
reference for your reader and
character.

Stereotypes

- **All are Muslim:** The assumption that everyone who lives in the Middle East or is of Middle Eastern heritage is Muslim. The reality is anything but. There are Jews, Christians, Buddhists, Hindus, and smaller religions like Yazdânism or the Bahá'í faith that are present in the Middle East.
- **The terrorist/barbaric Arab:** When we depict people of Middle Eastern or Arabic heritage as barbaric, violent, or terrorists, we contribute to the wave of xenophobia that has been incredibly prevalent since 9/11 and even the more recent Palestinian genocide.
- **All are desert nomads:** Despite many parts of the Middle East being modern and urbanized, there is still this stereotypical perception that it's full of nomadic peoples.
- **The submissive woman:** There is an assumption that women of Middle Eastern heritage are submissive victims of a strict and conservative society.

Have you heard of the acronym
AMEMSA? It stands for Arab, Middle
Eastern, Muslim, and South Asian. While
these identities are incredibly different
from one another, the term arose to

272 · ALEX TEMBLADOR

explain how people from these identities
tend to be racially profiled and under
government surveillance as a result of
the Islamophobia and xenophobia that
arose from the events of 9/11.[13]

I am only mentioning this here because
it's something to keep in mind when
writing people from these identities.
Yes, South Asians are Asian, and some
are Hindu and not Muslim, but they get
racially profiled in airport security lines,
experience scrutiny from government
institutions, and deal with xenophobia
and/or Islamophobia from society in the
same way that Middle Eastern and Arab
people (no matter their religion) do.

Tropes

- **The sheikh billionaire:** The rich sheikh is a trope character that pops up in stories set in the Middle East, generally
  in a romanticized or exoticized way. This trope sometimes
  appears as an evil man who holds people hostage or is involved in illegal activities.
- **Tropic symbols:** Veils, hijabs, belly dancers, hummus,
  oil, and turbans, among other things, have become
  tropic symbols of Middle Eastern culture.
- **A homogenous peoples:** The cultures of the Middle
  East are not always shown as being distinctive and very
  different from one another. For that matter, people of

Middle Eastern heritage do not all look the same, and yet there is a common trope of depicting all of them as having dark brown skin, hair, and eyes. Middle Eastern people can have red or blond hair; some have green eyes and others have blue eyes.

- **The violent Middle East:** The Middle East is rarely mentioned in literature except to bring up the violence that occurs there. While there may be violence in some parts of the Middle East, it is not present everywhere and paints the region in a negative light through stereotypical and tropic representations.

- **Fantasizing Middle Eastern myths and legends:** When a non–Middle Eastern person uses myths or legends from the Middle East as inspiration in their fantasy work, it can be seen as cultural appropriation. Changing the myth or legend might result in exoticism, bias, stereotypes, and misrepresentations, especially by someone who is not aware of the nuances of the myth and the culture.

JEWISH

Stereotypes

- **The Jewish body:** The appearance of Jewish people has been stereotyped horrifically, resulting in antisemitic characterizations. Whether it be describing Jewish people as having large or hooked noses, red hair, gold teeth, or only having light skin, these stereotypes cause considerable harm and contribute to antisemitism.

- **The greedy Jew:** Depicting Jews as greedy or obsessed with money has been a constant antisemitic stereotype for centuries.
- **Overbearing Jewish mother:** Jewish mothers have been reduced to a stock character, that of the overbearing, strict, and controlling helicopter parent.
- **The nice Jewish boy:** The "nice Jewish boy" stereotype is harmful in that it infantilizes Jewish men—making them seem like innocent, good, pure boys. Not only that, it creates a false narrative of the ideal type of man that women, particularly Jewish women, should aim to date.
- **Jews influencing banks, politics, and media:** There is a false idea that Jewish people dominate the banks, politics, and media and are an all-powerful group that are doing nefarious things "behind the scenes." Such stereotypical ideas have resulted in conspiracy theories and antisemitism.

Tropes

- **The Christian enemy:** Depicting Jews (either specifically and/or collectively) as being responsible for the death of Jesus, thus making them the "enemies" of Christianity. This harmful trope contributes to antisemitism because it usually results in stock characterization of Jewish characters, especially in retellings of Jesus' life and death. Other times, it is used as an argument for characterizing Jews as villains in modern fiction (be it Christian fiction or otherwise) or used as a false argument to justify violence toward Jewish people.
- **The Holocaust:** Writing a story that focuses on the Jewish experience of the Holocaust and/or Jewish Holocaust

survivors, if not done well, can result in trauma porn, inaccurate depictions, and stereotypes of Jewish people. It should go without saying that your creative writing should not distort the reality of the Holocaust, infer the denial of the Holocaust, or how the Jewish people suffered during it.

- **Homogenization of Jewish people:** Jewish people are often thought of and treated as a monolithic group in terms of race and ethnicity when the reality is anything but. On their website, Jewish Voice for Peace notes: "Antisemitism does not impact all of us who identify as Jewish in the same way. The experiences and histories of Jews of color and/or Sephardi/Mizrahi Jews are distinct from those of white, Ashkenazi Jews."[14] For instance, Mizrahi and Ethiopian Jews have faced considerable government-sanctioned racial prejudice in Israel from mass immigration to medical experimentation and sterilization. Understanding the diversity among Jews and the experiences that different Jews have had in the U.S. and abroad can contribute to more realistic and accurate depictions of the Jewish people in literature.

- **Conflating antisemitism and criticism of Zionism and Israel:** When a writer depicts criticism of Zionism or the actions of the Israeli government as antisemitism. This is inaccurate and harmful, especially to Jewish people. As the Jewish Voice for Peace writes, "The majority of Jews are not Israeli, and not all citizens of Israel are Jewish. Israel is a state; Zionism is a political ideology; Judaism and Jewish identity encompass a diversity of religious and secular expressions and a robust, varied set of traditions, cultures, and lived experiences."[15] To conflate the two in your creative work "dilutes the understanding of antisemitism and makes it ever more difficult to fight," the Jewish Voice for Peace explains. Work to understand the definition of antisemitism and how it presents if you wish to portray it in your piece.

- **Perpetual victims:** As with many different racial and ethnic identities, it can be easy to position a Jewish character or the Jewish people as perpetual victims, whether in need of saving by a non-Jewish character or community or always in the role of being harmed. In doing this, you may be crafting trauma porn or committing sentimentality in your scenes. It also contributes to a single story of Jewish people, one that homogenizes them as a group of victims and removes the diversity of the experiences of different Jews within the community, such as how Jews of color have less privilege and power than European-descended Ashkenazi Jews who tend to benefit from whiteness and white privilege.

MIXED

Mixed
Biracial
Multiracial/Multi-ethnic
Race and ethnicity, e.g., "Half Mexican, half white"

Stereotypes

- **Exotic and beautiful:** Mixed people are exoticized for their physical appearance. They tend to also be thought of as beautiful simply because they're Mixed.
- **Sexualized Mixed person:** Mixed people are stereotyped as hypersexual or promiscuous.

- **Align with one race over the other:** There is a misconception that all Mixed people identify with one of their races or ethnicities over the other. While this may occur with some, many Mixed people do not strongly identify with a single race or ethnicity, but more aptly with their biracial, Mixed, or multiracial identity.

Tropes

- **Only Black-white Mixed identity:** Despite the fact that they are not the largest multiracial group in the U.S., the Black-white Mixed identity is presented as the default or the only type of Mixed identity that exists.
- **Unhappy and confused:** There is a misconception that Mixed people are unhappy and confused because they have two or more racial or ethnic identities. It is sometimes shown as Mixed people feeling "pulled between" their identities. This trope contributes to racist ideas, like interracial relationships will result in "damaged" Mixed children. Ironically, it is not Mixed people who are unhappy or confused, but other people who feel the need to create a racial society that is comprised of clean, separate boxes of which the Mixed person does not fit in.
- **The Mixed person who passes:** The Mixed person who passes—usually as white—is a common trope in fiction and is an extension of the "unhappy and confused" trope.
- **The Mixed person who doesn't belong:** This is the idea that Mixed people don't belong or feel out of place while around monoracial people who inhabit one of their racial or ethnic identities.
- **Beyond racism in interracial families:** There is a misconception that interracial families are "beyond racism"

278 • ALEX TEMBLADOR

simply because the family represents two or more races/ethnicities. This is not the case for many interracial families.

- **The answer to racial harmony:** When we present the idea that interracial families are "beyond racism," we tend to suggest that Mixed people are the answer to racial harmony. Mixed people are not symbols for any such thing, and to make that connection is demeaning to them and removes the real experience that Mixed people also have bias when it comes to race.

The Roma or Romany people are said to have moved outside of India prior to the eleventh century, going to areas like Persia before making their way to southern and western Europe. They are considered nomadic itinerants.[16] Roma, or groups of people based on the Roma, appear in literature in exoticized and romanticized ways, usually without the full complexities of their culture explained. They are sometimes given magical or psychic powers or are stereotyped as criminals, lazy, poor, seeking pleasure, and flighty.

If you wish to include Roma in your work, they should not be referred to as "gypsies," as this is an offensive term. The term should also not be used in any genre fiction (I'm looking at you, fantasy and historical fiction writers), whether it be in reference to the Roma or a fictionalized community with a similar history and culture. For that matter, it is best to refrain from using the words "gypsy" or "nomad" in colloquial ways like "He lived a nomadic lifestyle" or "She was a gypsy at heart," as it is demeaning to the Roma culture and reduces the experiences of nomadic peoples.

WHITE

Caucasian
White
Ethnicity, e.g., "Irish American" or "Polish"

Stereotypes

I am not going to include any stereotypes for persons of Caucasian descent here. We know that stereotypes are oversimplified ideas about a group of people, and while there are stereotypes about white people, these stereotypes are not to their detriment.

Stereotypes harm historically marginalized races and add to the status quo, one in which white people have the power and the privilege. To include stereotypes about white people here does not seem like a good use of our time. If you wish to write a parody of stereotypes relating to white people, it would likely not be hard to do (as it has been done before).

Tropes

- **White savior:** This is a trope that depicts a white person saving someone of lesser privilege, generally a person of color.
- **White is right:** This trope connects the color white or lighter skin tones to something that is right, correct, and positive. It can present itself through symbolism or thematic literary choices.

GENDER IDENTITY

TERMS, STEREOTYPES, AND TROPES: GENDER IDENTITY

WOMEN

Woman

Cisgender woman

Transgender woman

> Note: Transgender women are women. Differentiating between cisgender women and transgender women is only meant to signify that some women's gender identity matches the sex they were assigned at birth, which ultimately has resulted in cisgender women having more privilege than transgender women.

Stereotypes

- **Too emotional:** The idea that women are "emotional creatures" or ruled by their emotions. This is a long-standing stereotype that has been informed by things like past medical diagnoses such as "hysteria" and it presents women as hysterical, or more apt to let emotions like anger, frustration, and sadness control their behavior and make them illogical.

- **Demure, shy, soft, submissive, weak:** When women are depicted as soft, demure, shy, or submissive in a stock character sort of way, it furthers the idea that women are weak, victims, or in need of protection.

- **Natural nurturers:** Women tend to be associated with children and childcare, which has resulted in a stereotype that women are natural nurturers and better at childcare.

- **All want kids:** Even though many women do not want children, there is a widespread assumption that women want children, especially if they find the right partner. This stereotype is an extension of the "natural nurturers" stereotype and assumes that women are ruled by their horomones and romantic relationships and would only say they don't want children if they were single and alone.

- **Love obsessed:** When women are depicted as being interested primarily in finding love, a long-term partner, and getting married. This stereotype places a woman's worth on being able to find a partner, rather than the woman's morals, behaviors, beliefs, skills, and talent.

- **Conniving, "crazy":** This stereotypical characterization presents women as manipulative and conniving, sometimes to the extent of being "crazy." In this instance, "crazy" is not used to refer to an actual mental health condition (which makes it an ableist statement) but is more closely associated to the stereotype of women being too emotional, to the point that their emotional state becomes excessive, violent, immoral, or dangerous.

- **Saint or a whore:** There is this dichotomic characterization of women as either a saint or a whore. Women who are not very sexually active—or perceived as not sexually active, like mothers and grandmothers—are placed in the saint role, while women who are sexually active, are successful in their careers, travel the globe on their own, and have strong and vociferous personalities are depicted as whores.

- **Single and lonely:** Depicting a single woman as lonely is a stereotype that reinforces the idea that a woman's worth is only found in relationships.

- **Transgender women are confused:** The false idea that transgender women are unsure of their gender identity. This stereotype seeks to undermine transgender women and convey that they are not really women but "momentarily confused" and will soon identify with the sex they were assigned at birth.

- **Transgender women are dangerous:** Transgender women have been portrayed as tricking others into believing that they are women and are donning a woman gender identity for some nefarious purpose. This stereotype aims to present transgender women as dangerous because they were assigned the sex of male at birth. Again, this is all false, as we know that transgender people are four times more likely than cisgender people to be victims of crime.[17]

"Masculinity" and "femininity" are two descriptors that came from the binary gender system, and yet we still defer to them when describing men, women, and even genderqueer identities (e.g., "masculine of center" or "feminine of center" or "masculine-presenting" or "feminine-presenting."

As a creative writer, be mindful of how you use terms like "masculine" and "feminine" in your work, as it can result in stereotypical and tropic depictions. This is not to say that they do not have a place in your work, but in certain situations they can be gender exclusive or have a negative connotation.

Tropes

- **Damsel in distress:** This is a trope that depicts a woman who needs to be saved by a man. It can appear as her needing saving because she was kidnapped, imprisoned, or is in peril. It also presents itself in more subtle ways, like if she needs a man to save her from financial ruin or for an emotional experience.
- **Femme fatale:** A sexy, sultry woman who lures men into dangerous traps, or causes them some form of distress.
- **The black widow:** An unhinged serial killer who is a woman who seduces people into relationships, usually including marriage, and then kills them, typically for their money.

- **Evil stepmother:** A stepmother is often depicted as cruel, evil, unkind, and unloving to her stepdaughter.
- **Sheltered princess:** This is a trope that presents a woman as an actual princess who has been sheltered in her castle by her family and is naïve and in need of help when she enters the world. This trope has evolved into more modern storytelling by characterizing a young woman as innocent and naïve (sometimes wealthy), who enters a harsh world that shatters her fairy-tale sensibilities.
- **Love-obsessed BFF:** The love-obsessed woman best friend is a stock character trope that elevates the main woman character as smart and worldly, while the best friend is ditzy and obsessed with love, relationships, and sex.
- **Ice queen:** The ice queen is typically a strong, self-assured, confident, and successful career woman who doesn't show "feminine" emotions, so she seems "icy," "aloof," or "haughty." This trope seeks to put down successful women and portray them as hard or "man-like," an unvirtuous trait for women.
- **Devious ex-girlfriend:** This trope presents an ex-girlfriend as being manipulative, dangerous, and willing to do anything to get her partner back and/or harm the new person her ex is in a relationship with. While I called this trope "devious ex-girlfriend," it is usually referred to as the "psycho or crazy ex-girlfriend" trope. This trope is ableist because it attributes the actions of the ex-girlfriend to mental health conditions and paints people with mental health conditions as dangerous.
- **The girl next door:** A woman character is depicted as

the ideal love interest for a protagonist. She is sweet, approachable, and generally unassuming in her looks, the ideal of "femininity."

MEN
Men
Cisgender men
Transgender men

Stereotypes

- **The provider:** The idea that a man's role in a family is to be the financial provider. This stereotype precludes men from providing any other assistance to their partners, whether it be in terms of childcare, meal prep, emotional care, or housework.

- **Machismo/hypermasculine:** The hypermasculine man or machismo depiction of men is a harmful stereotype, and yet it continues to have a huge presence in literature, especially in genres like romance, fantasy, Westerns, and sci-fi. It's the idea that men should be strong, aggressive, and virile, and proud of it. The stereotype tends to emphasize certain interests for men like sports, cars, action movies, boxing, and beer, as well as ideas that men should make more money than women, are the dominant partners, alphas, shouldn't cry or behave in any way considered "feminine" or "weak."

- **Men are slobs:** A stereotype that presents all men as slobs, dirty, messy, or gross. It infantilizes men and conveys the idea that they are more put together when they have a partner who expects it of them, like a parent would.

- **Men lack emotions:** The stoic man who doesn't show

his emotions is a harmful stereotype. Not only does it continue to convey to men that they should push down their emotions and not express them, it's a foil to the stereotype of women being ruled by their emotions.

- **Men are the strong ones:** This is the stereotypical idea that men are stronger than other gender identities, are responsible for being the protector of the relationship, and should take on certain duties like yard work and mechanical maintenance.
- **Not as engaged in parenting duties:** Men are characterized as not being nurturing or as involved with their children. This can be presented as the father who misses parent-teacher meetings, has a strained, awkward relationship with their kids, or is too tired after a day of work to give the kids a bath.
- **Hypersexual:** Assumes that all men have high sex drives, which makes them focus on only one thing: sex. This stereotype presents sex as something that all men need, rather than want, and so their behavior, whether that's cheating, sexual assault, rape, gaslighting, or abuse, should be excused.

> Although men have the most power in society, we do find that stereotypes and tropes about men cause equal amounts of harm to men as they do to other gender identities. It's important to point them out here because if we can subvert these stereotypes and tropes relating to men, this could affect how other gender identities are represented in literature.

Tropes

- **The bad boy:** This is a tropic man who is silent, mysterious, and is either a troublemaker or appears to be one. Usually, the protagonist discovers that he has a heart of gold and is worthy of their love, despite the bad boy's serious misgivings, risky behavior, or toxic masculine attitudes.

- **All-American guy:** A type of character that is deemed to be a good ol' American boy whose style, language, and personality traits align with white, Christian, and conservative qualities (the character may not actually be white, Christian, or politically conservative, but he typically comes off as such). He is not too stylish but is mindful of his appearance and dresses nicely. He is involved in activities that are deemed "American," like football, 4-H, or debate. He is known for his manners, like being respectful of the elderly, and is the head of organizations like a fraternity.

- **Knight in shining armor/Prince Charming:** The knight in shining armor and Prince Charming tropes are very similar. The knight in shining armor is a man who seems larger than life, exceptionally skilled, super successful, incredibly strong, or handsome, and swoops in to rescue a love interest. Prince Charming is a version of the knight in shining armor. He's a stock character who is dashing, strong, brave, gallant, and charming, symbolizing the perfect love interest.

- **The pathetic, nerdy best friend:** This trope presents itself as a nerdy, goofy, or fat best friend who is a man, and the main character, usually a woman, does not see as a potential love interest. Despite all these things, he is finally seen for his worth by the end of the story.

- **Alpha man:** This trope takes toxic masculinity and re-imagines it as a personality trait that some men are born with. The alpha man is a leader who is strong, brave, and confident, who rules his group of friends, motorcycle club, wolf pack, or some other men-dominated group because he has what is perceived as the most masculine energy among the men.
- **Mr. Darcy:** The Mr. Darcy trope (which gets its name from Jane Austen's *Pride and Prejudice*) is one that exists within the enemies-to-lovers trope. He is a man who is stubborn, prideful, and antagonistic toward a potential love interest for seemingly no reason. By the end of the enemies-to-lovers trope, Mr. Darcy finally opens up and shares his emotions to the love interest and they fall in love.
- **Tall, dark, and handsome *or* dad bod:** Men are portrayed as either being the tall, dark, and handsome character or the goofy, wholesome, kind guy with a dad bod. There is little variety or nuance in between.

GENDERQUEER

Intersex
Transgender
Non-binary
Enby
Gender nonconforming
Genderqueer
Gender fluid
Gender expansive
Gender void
Agender

Aporagender
Bigender
Masculine of center/Feminine of center
Omnigender
Polygender/Pangender
Two-Spirit

> Gender is not a binary—meaning there are not only two gender identities, so remove any indication of that notion from your creative work. Example: "She was attracted to the opposite sex." The phrase "opposite sex" infers that "sex" is the same as gender identity, which it is not. "Sex" is what a doctor assigns people at birth (and it has no bearing on a person's gender identity). "Attracted to the opposite sex" suggests that there are two gender identities, which is not true. There are many.

Stereotypes

- **They're confused:** The idea is that genderqueer people are confused and haven't decided whether they want to be a man or woman. This harmful stereotype reduces gender identity to a binary and takes away the agency of people who have genderqueer identities.
- **This is a fad:** This is a stereotypical idea that genderqueer identities, whether they be non-binary, transgender, or polygender, are a fad or a trend that will pass. It

insinuates that genderqueer people are following trends rather than truly knowing themselves.

- **Lonely, single, or unattractive:** Presents people who are genderqueer as not being sexually attractive, not in relationships, or unmarried, and are thus lonely, single, and unattractive. It insinuates that their gender identity precludes them from love and/or sex.

- **Sex reassignment surgery:** The stereotypical idea that some genderqueer identities, particularly transgender people, must have sex reassignment surgery to be transgender. This is not true.

- **They have a mental health condition:** This very harmful idea that people who identify as gender fluid, gender void, transgender, or some other genderqueer identity must have a mental health condition because they do not identify within a binary system of gender.

Sexual and romantic orientations and genderqueer identities

A person's gender identity does not determine their sexual orientation. For example, do not assume that a transgender man is gay and only attracted to men. They may identify as poly, asexual, or straight. Mixing up sexual orientation and gender identity, especially as they relate to genderqueer identities, would be a big mistake in your creative writing.

Tropes

- **The genderqueer best friend:** This trope has become such a common occurrence in literature that it sends the message that genderqueer people are unable to be the protagonists because of their gender identity.
- **The genderqueer outcast:** Presented as a genderqueer person who is not accepted by their peers, community, or family because they have a gender identity that doesn't fit within the cisgender binary.
- **The genderqueer victim:** Someone with a genderqueer identity is showcased as being the victim of a hate crime, sexual assault, discrimination, or verbal and physical abuse simply as a means for a cisgender character to save them, help them, or learn to be a better person.
- **Parents didn't support them:** This storyline says that people who have genderqueer identities must come from homes in which their parents do not accept them. It places these characters into the role of an unloved, unaccepted, and tragic victim.
- **Bury your queer characters:** A literary trope in which the (usually) only queer character in the story killed off through some tragic means such as suicide or murder. Oftentimes, their death is excessive in its grisliness, though not always. This trope indicates that queer characters don't deserve to make it to the end of the story.

DISABILITIES

A NOTE ABOUT IDENTITY TERMS

Deciding on the proper terminology for a character with disabilities is no easy task, because you have two competing thoughts on the subject: person-first and identity-first language.

Person-first language: This puts the person first, followed by the characteristic.

Here's a good example of PFL: "person with intellectual disabilities."

Here is a bad example of PFL: "intellectually disabled person."

"Intellectually disabled person" puts the characteristic or the disability first, which insinuates that the person's identity is solely focused on their disability.

The goal of person-first language was to end the stigmatization of disabilities and the people who had them. By adjusting the structure of disability terminology, there was this hope that it would stop abled people from seeing people with disabilities in stereotypical ways and thus dehumanize them. There are many who would say that person-first language is especially a great way to talk about people with mental health disorders or who have certain diseases like epilepsy and diabetes. Some critics, however, argue that person-first language is designed to make abled people feel better and still paints disabilities as a negative thing. The consensus on person-first language changes from individual to individual and even among different disability communities.

Identity-first language: This places the identity or characteristic first, followed by the person. Identity-first language is usually, though not always, used in relation to the blind, Deaf, and autism communities.

Here is a good example of IFL: "the blind person."

Here is a bad example of IFL: "the person with blindness."

The blind, Deaf, and autism communities like identity-first language because it denotes how their disability is a lifelong experience that is an important part of their identity. They compare it to how you would more often say "an Asian person" or "a non-binary person" rather than "a person of the Asian race" or "a person with a non-binary gender identity." Identity-first language is not exclusive to the blind, Deaf, or autism communities, but may be preferred by those who experience other types of disabilities.

After doing a lot of research and speaking with people from the disability community that you're portraying, you may decide to use one or both of these types of terminology systems in your creative piece. Identity-first and person-first language aside, there are certain terms that, no matter the case, would not be appropriate to use in relation to the disability community. This includes slurs and outdated terms.

Admittedly, some disabled people may choose to identify with a term that seems outdated or not necessarily in line with either person-first or identity-first language. For instance, a person who has dwarfism may call themselves a dwarf rather than "a little person" or "a person of short stature."

When thinking about whether this is appropriate to do within your creative piece, you'll need to get as much feedback from the specific community of people you will be representing. It is likely that you'll get many different kinds of advice, and from there, you'll have to make the decision on which identity term is appropriate for your character.

Remember, it may not be easy to change the terminology in your creative piece in the future—so are you okay with that term being read in five years? Will it be outdated within a year? Will it make people feel uncomfortable reading your work? Should you use a term that is widely accepted rather than one that is only acceptable to a few? Are you only using terms that make you feel comfortable but would feel ableist and dismissive of the disability community you're portraying? How would the disability community perceive a person who doesn't have a disability using certain terms over others? These are questions to ask yourself.

> Unlike with race/ethnicity, we don't typically capitalize disability types. However, it is a common practice to capitalize "Deaf" when talking about the Deaf community.

APPROPRIATE TERMS

Take notice that there are identity-first and person-first terms in this list. Not all are appropriate for all disability communities or would even be preferred by certain disabled individuals.

- Accessible bathroom/building/office, etc. or bathrooms/buildings/offices, etc. that are accessible to people with disabilities
- Adults/children/people with disabilities
- Deaf/blind/autism community
- Deaf/blind/autistic person
- Deaf or hard of hearing
- Disabled person
- Has a cognitive/intellectual/physical/learning disability
- Has a disability
- People with limited mobility
- People with mental health conditions
- Person of short stature or little person
- Person who uses a wheelchair

OUTDATED TERMS

- An insane person
- Brain-damaged
- Crippled
- Deaf and dumb
- Differently abled
- Dwarf/midget
- Emotionally disturbed
- Feebleminded
- The handicapped
- Handicapped bathroom, bus, etc.
- Imbecile
- The insane
- Invalid
- Learning disabled
- Lunatic
- Maimed
- Mentally disabled
- The mentally ill
- Mentally ill person/adult
- Mobility issues
- Mongoloid
- Moron
- Mute
- Physically challenged
- Physically, cognitively, or learning-challenged
- Retarded
- Slow (i.e., describing someone as "slow" in terms of their intellect)
- "Special" (e.g., He is "special.")

- Special needs
- Special ed
- Wheelchair user or wheelchair-bound

> Disabled people, with regard to their disability, should not be described as suffering from, afflicted by, stricken with, surviving with, or as victims of disabilities. For example, you wouldn't want to say, "They suffered from a disability their whole life" or "He was afflicted with a disability at the age of seventeen." Such phrasing conveys that disabilities are negative or bad.

ABLEIST TERMS AND PHRASES

We may use ableist terms in our everyday lives and in our creative writing. While we don't mean to be ableist when using these terms, it doesn't negate the fact that we are using phrases and terms in a way that makes negative associations with disabilities. Here are some ableist terms that you can easily remove from your creative writing piece.

- Blind as a bat
- Crazy
- Crippled by/a crippling degree of ____
- Dumb
- Falls on deaf ears
- Hypersensitive

- Idiot
- I'm so ADHD/OCD/etc.
- Insane
- Lame
- Nuts
- Psycho
- Spaz/Spastic
- That's retarded
- Turn a blind eye
- Wacko
- You're acting bipolar/schizo/etc.

Stereotypes

- **Childlike or innocent:** This is the suggestion that people with intellectual or physical disabilities are childlike and innocent. By infantilizing disabled people, it makes them appear less knowledgeable and less intelligent, paints them in an overwhelmingly positive light, and makes them less human than those without disabilities. It is used as a device to make people without disabilities "feel good."
- **Victim:** This stereotype occurs when people with disabilities are portrayed as victims who have little agency, must always be protected by people who don't have disabilities, and are never at fault for their decisions or behavior.
- **Angry or unhappy:** This is the idea that disabled people are angry, upset, unhappy, or bitter because they have a disability.
- **Single, alone, lacks relationships:** This suggests that people with disabilities are incapable of love or friendships, or are too awkward or "odd" to have relationships.

- **A burden to others:** An idea that disabled people are a burden to their families, friends, and society.
- **Connection between disabilities and mental health conditions:** No matter if they have physical or intellectual disabilities, people with disabilities are seen as more likely to have a mental health condition, which is just not true.

> Characters with disabilities are not inherently an inspiration, courageous, or brave because of their disability.
> They *should not* be used to inspire other characters (or audiences) who do not have disabilities.

Tropes

- **The mystical disability:** This presents in a variety of ways, from the blind person who can see visions that others cannot to the person with a mental health condition or intellectual disability whose ramblings are a prophecy. This suggests that a person with a disability is only useful to the plot or protagonist if they have magical powers.
- **Autistic detective:** Generally, this trope appears in mysteries, crime fiction, thrillers, and detective novels. This indicates that those on the autism spectrum have a special ability to think like criminals and are thus better detectives. They are usually depicted as obsessive, ruthless, unable to form connections, and one step away from being as "mentally unhinged" as the people they put away.
- **Autistic savant:** This enforces the false idea that people

on the spectrum are geniuses, extremely intelligent, or have special abilities.

- **Overcoming the disability:** When a character is willing to do anything to "cure" their disability.
- **Villain with a disability:** People with disabilities or disfigurements are associated with criminals. This assumes that such people are so angry or upset about their disability that they'd be willing to commit crimes. Sometimes the writer connects their disability and bitterness to a weakening of the mind, mental health conditions, or "madness," which results in evil behaviors and actions. This is an ableist mindset.
- **Weaponized prosthetic limbs:** These are seen mostly in sci-fi or spy genres. By making the prosthetic limb robotic or a weapon, it seeks to give people with physical disabilities a power that is implied to have been lost.
- **Inspirational narrative:** This occurs when using a person with a disability as a plot device to create an "inspirational" story with a happy ending. It can also appear when a character without a disability "grows" after having an experience with a character who has a disability.

SEXUAL AND ROMANTIC ORIENTATIONS

TERMS, STEREOTYPES, AND TROPES

Heterosexual

Heterosexual
Straight

Stereotypes

- **Dominant man, submissive woman:** This is a stereotypical type of relationship where men are expected to be dominant, strong, protectors, and providers, and women are weak and submissive, must follow a man's guidance, and need protection or provision from a man.
- **Unhappy, abusive arranged marriages:** This is a harmful stereotype that all arranged or assisted marriages were made without the consent of the woman and/or always result in an unhappy and abusive marriage.
- **Super-persistent men are romantic:** This romantic stereotype depicts a man's persistence toward a woman who has shown no romantic interest. It reinforces the idea that women are not capable of knowing what they want and overlooks the hard rule of "no means no."
- **Centuries-old supernatural man and the teenage girl:** Occurs when a centuries-old vampire, fairy, werewolf, or other supernatural type of man "falls in love" and has a romantic relationship with a teenage girl (usually between sixteen and nineteen years old). Does not showcase the realistic power dynamic issues that would arise in a relationship between a teenage character and a centuries-old supernatural man. Rather the relationship is portrayed as normal, healthy, romantic, sexy, and desirable.

QUEER
Homosexual
Gay
Lesbian
Bisexual
Asexual/Ace

Apothisexual
Demisexual
Cupiosexual
Non-libidoist asexual
Sex-averse/Sex-favorable/Sex-indifferent/Sex-repulsed
Graysexual
Pansexual
Allosexual
Androsexual/Androphilic
Gynesexual/Gynephilic
Skoliosexual
Autosexual
Polysexual
Sapiosexual
Spectrasexual
Demiromantic
Aromantic
Autoromantic
Grayromantic
Panromantic

LGBTQIA+ refers to a community of people who are not exclusively heterosexual or cisgender. The acronym stands for "lesbian, gay, bisexual, transgender, queer, intersex, asexual," with the plus sign indicating that the community is comprised of more identities. If you include "LGBTQIA+" in your writing, it should only be in reference to the community. For instance, a character might say, "I'm part of the LGBTQIA+ community." They wouldn't usually say, "I'm LGBTQIA+" because the acronym itself is not really an identity; it is representative of many queer identities.

Stereotypes

- **The sassy, feminine gay man:** This is a stereotype that feminizes gay men and usually gives them a sassy or sarcastic personality.
- **The fashionable queer person:** This is the idea that all queer people, especially gay men, are super fashionable and well dressed.
- **Manly lesbians:** This idea stereotypes all lesbians as being butch or having manly, masculine traits in terms of physical appearance and personality.
- **The hypersexual, cheating gay man or bisexual:** This stereotypes bisexual people and/or gay men as being hypersexual, promiscuous, and constantly cheating.
- **Ace, the broken sexuality:** Asexual people are depicted as having a "broken" sexuality. This insinuates that asexual people have a trauma, mental health condition, or some other aspect about them that makes them not want to have sexual or romantic relations with others. This is just not true.
- **Asexual people hate sex, are lonely, single, or celibate, and can't be married:** Asexual people are stereotyped as not liking sex and/or people who choose to be celibate. They are also depicted as being single, lonely, and unmarried.

- **Asexual people don't have romantic feelings:** This is a stereotypical misconception that insinuates that all asexual people lack romantic feelings.
- **Only a top or bottom:** The sexuality of queer people is hyperfocused on the idea of a person being either a top or bottom. Sexuality is more complicated than one person being a top and one person a bottom, and to insinuate otherwise reduces the complexity of sexual experiences to something that feels more palatable to non-queer audiences.
- **The depressed queer person:** This is the idea that because someone is queer, they experience or have experienced depression.
- **All gay men have HIV or AIDS:** A false assumption that all gay men have HIV or AIDS. It reinforces the incorrect idea that gay men are promiscuous, dirty, unclean, irresponsible, and hypersexual. It also insinuates that straight people do not have HIV or AIDS or are not at risk for them.
- **Bisexuality occurs before someone comes out as gay:** This is the idea that bisexuality is something that gay people claim as they grow more comfortable with their sexual orientation. While people can change their sexual orientation over time, this stereotype is harmful because it assumes that bisexuality is not a real sexual orientation.
- **You aren't bi if you are in a heteronormative relationship:** This occurs when someone's bisexuality is disregarded because they're in a heteronormative relationship. For instance, if a bi woman gets in a relationship with a man (or vice versa) and others determine that she is really not bisexual. This stereotype can also be used in reference to other sexual orientations like pansexual.

304 • ALEX TEMBLADOR

- **Sexual abuse:** This is the harmful idea that people who are queer are such because they were sexually abused as children or adults and are so traumatized that it has made them like people of the same gender identity.

Tired Romance/Dating/Marriage Tropes

Below are some romance/dating/marriage tropes that can be present in the depiction of any kind of relationship in your creative writing. They're self-explanatory and don't need any defining. If you want to use these tropes in a new way, consider changing the type of characters involved or the way the trope plays out in the end.

- Happily ever after
- Love triangle
- Love at first sight
- Enemies to lovers
- Soulmates
- Forbidden love

Tropes

- **The gay best friend:** This is a common trope that makes the best friend of the protagonist gay or queer as a means of adding diversity to the text. It can sometimes result in a stock character representation of a queer person.
- **HIV/AIDs storyline:** The HIV/AIDs storyline as it relates to gay men is a common trope in literature.
- **Parents who don't accept them:** Queer people are consistently portrayed as having parents who don't accept their sexual orientation.
- **Asexual character who has autism:** Asexual charac-

ters are sometimes associated with autism to explain why an asexual person is not sexually or romantically active. This trope is harmful to autistic people and asexual people in different ways. It assumes that asexual people have a cognitive disability that makes them not want to have social, sexual, or romantic contact. The trope also incorrectly assumes that autistic people do not have or should not have sexual or romantic lives.

- **Jealous, murderous, depraved lesbian/bisexual woman:** Lesbian and bisexual women are depicted as being jealous and murderous, especially toward their partners. They tend to be labeled as "psycho" or "crazy," both of which are ableist terms.

- **The tragic queer love story:** This love story trope doesn't allow queer people to have happy endings. Through some way or another, the queer couple can't be together whether that's because of a breakup or cheating, or because someone dies, goes to jail, or gets sick. It pushes the idea that queer people don't deserve happy endings simply because of their sexual orientation.

OTHER IDENTITIES

AGE

Stereotypes

- **Older adults don't engage in sex:** Whether it is through inference or characterization, older adults are depicted as being celibate, not having sex, and not being sexy or attractive.

- **Old, grumpy, and cranky:** Older adults above the age of fifty are characterized as being cranky and grumpy simply because of their age. This suggests that older adults do not have anything to be happy or joyous about because they are not considered "young" by society's standards.
- **Lonely older person/cat lady:** This trope portrays a single adult who is older as lonely and sad. This usually differs depending on the gender identity of the adult. For instance, women over the age of forty who are not married are considered sad, sometimes characterized as "cat ladies," or people who are only kept company by animals.
- **Lazy Millennials and Gen Z:** Millennials and Gen Z are perceived by older generations as being lazy and unwilling to put in hard work.
- **All teens engage in risky behavior:** This stereotype considers teens to be spontaneous, risky, and up to no good. This may present itself in behaviors such as sex, drug and alcohol use, or partying.

Tropes
- **The wise elder:** This trope portrays older adults as being wise simply because of their age.
- **More religious older person:** Adults are shown becoming more religious and conservative the older they get.
- **Unhinged old person:** This is a character who is an older person and is perceived by others as having a mental health condition, being unstable, or experiencing dementia or Alzheimer's. It removes the agency of an older adult.

- **Midlife crisis:** The midlife crisis storyline is a common one for adult characters who are in their forties, fifties, and sixties. The adult may start to behave abnormally according to their family and friends, and take risks in their career or relationships.
- **The moody, troubled teen:** The quiet, moody, troubled teen appears in many forms of literature. The teen may be presented as dressing like a goth, getting in trouble in class, disappearing in their room, or having emotional outbursts at home or in school.
- **The old hag, shrew, or old maid:** The old hag, shrew, and maid are three different types of tropes, but all make the argument that to be an older adult woman who is single is bad. The old hag is generally described as ugly, elderly, and nasty in demeanor. The shrew is unpleasant, nagging, and aggressive, while the maid is a lonely older woman who may be depicted as sad and pathetic or not appealing because of her looks and personality. All three are generally perceived as sexless, sad spinsters.
- **Dirty old man:** He is an older man who makes other characters, generally women, uncomfortable by his use of sexual innuendos, inappropriate sexual behavior, or in his dating of women who are much younger than he is.
- **Love-obsessed teen or young adult:** Many YA novels showcase teens or young adults as being entirely focused on one thing: love. Such characters will do anything to be with their crush, ignoring other major aspects of the teenage experience, including school/college, friends, family, and extracurricular activities.
- **Growing older is depressing:** This storyline presents growing older as a sad, depressing thing.

CLASS

Stereotypes

- **People with low incomes scam the government:** This stereotype depicts people with lower incomes as criminals who scam the government through government assistance programs like food stamps or housing care.
- **People with low incomes are uneducated:** This is an incorrect idea that people with low incomes are less educated than those with higher incomes. It assumes that they make less money because they are not educated enough to get a higher-paying job.
- **People with low incomes are lazy:** A false assumption that people with lower incomes are lazy and have no work ethic.
- **People with low incomes use drugs:** A stereotype that assumes that people with lower incomes are more likely to use illegal drugs and/or abuse legal drugs. The idea is that by using drugs they are unable to make a higher income.
- **People with low incomes do not speak properly:** People with low incomes are depicted as being so uneducated that they do not speak proper English (in terms of grammar), have low levels of vocabulary, use a lot of slang, speak African American Vernacular English (AAVE), etc.
- **People with low incomes are bad parents:** It is assumed that because people with low incomes do not make higher incomes, they must be bad parents or are not present for their children.
- **All people with low income are people of color:** This stereotype assumes that most people with lower incomes

are people of color. Alternatively, there is a stereotype that says there are not wealthy or upper-middle-class people of color or that all people of color lack generational wealth.

> As you will notice, I did not include people with higher incomes in the stereotypes section, as the stereotypes related to them do not cause irrevocable harm to their societal (or financial) standing. However, they have been included in the tropes section because the tropes relating to people with higher incomes are problematic.

Tropes

- **The American Dream:** This storyline trope showcases someone who has a lower income reaching wealth, success, and status through sheer determination and hard work. It reinforces harmful ideas that anyone living in the U.S. can achieve success despite the systems in place that are designed to make it harder for certain historically marginalized communities to achieve "the dream."
- **Rags to riches:** A person with low income is shown gaining riches very quickly, usually by luck (like winning the lottery), through marriage, or because of a unique skill like singing, athleticism, or some other talent.
- **Rich people work hard; people with low incomes do not:** This harmful trope presents rich people as hard-working and people with lower incomes as lazy, uneducated, or criminal.

- **The unhappy rich person:** This trope depicts wealthy or rich people as being unhappy or depressed. This trope tries to diminish the wealth, privilege, and abilities that rich people have to make them more palatable to people with low to middle incomes.

IMMIGRATION STATUS

Appropriate immigration terms
- Immigrants
- People who immigrated to the U.S.
- Emigrant
- Person in immigration detention
- Undocumented noncitizen
- Undocumented immigrant
- Unauthorized immigrant
- Migrant/vulnerable migrants
- Refugee

To Use the Term "Immigrant" or Not?

Immigration is a charged topic, and because of that, it is no easy feat to firmly say which terms are most appropriate when referring to people who have immigrated to the U.S. So let me start by saying that we know the inappropriate terms for people who have immigrated to the U.S. (They are listed below.)

The term "immigrant" is a hotly debated term. It is the same with refugee, migrant, and undocumented or unauthorized immigrant. Some people like these terms, but a lot of people do not because they have negative connotations. Not to mention "immigrant" removes the human from the experience.

I cannot go as deep into this conversation as I'd like, but I will say this—if you are going to write about people who are immigrants, speak with a variety of people who have immigrated to the U.S. Ask them what terms they prefer and if they prefer certain terms in specific contexts. Do more research into each term that I've presented and see what the negative and positive connotations are. At the end of the day, it is going to be up to you to choose the one that fits your story and prevents othering as it relates to your character.

You might have to get creative with this. That might mean not even using the word "immigrant" in the story (or a similar word) but providing enough contextual clues in the storyline that indicate immigration is part of your character's background and identity.

I wish I could provide a more concrete answer here, but unfortunately, I have found that in this line of work, there are not always hard and fast rules.

Inappropriate immigration terms

- Illegals/illegal immigrant/illegal worker
- Alien/illegal alien
- Detainee
- Foreigner

Stereotypes

- **Can't speak English:** This stereotype assumes that people who have immigrated to the U.S. can't speak English, have an accent, or speak "broken English." This stereotype seeks to other people who are immigrants.

- **All are undocumented:** This is the assumption that people who have immigrated to the U.S. from another country are undocumented. This stereotype is typically associated with immigrants of color, such as those from Latin America, the Caribbean, and Africa. It is usually not associated with immigrants from European countries or from places like Canada.
- **All want citizenship:** This is the idea that people who have immigrated to the U.S. want U.S. citizenship and will do anything to achieve it, even by deceiving the government, such as through an arranged type of marriage with the intent of becoming a citizen or receiving a green card.
- **Criminals, rapists, drug dealers:** This stereotype associates people who have immigrated to the U.S. with criminals, rapists, and drug dealers.
- **Uneducated, poor:** This stereotype indicates immigrants are uneducated and had low incomes prior to coming to the U.S.

Tropes
- **Only people of color are undocumented noncitizens:** This tropic storyline depicts only people of color as undocumented noncitizens.
- **Patriotic and grateful immigrant:** A common depiction of a person who immigrated to the U.S. is someone who is overwhelmingly grateful and patriotic, and does not criticize the U.S. government in any way.
- **White immigrants are better:** White immigrants are depicted as favorable compared to people of color who have immigrated to the U.S. For instance, the white

British and French people living in the U.S. are portrayed as being suave, charming, attractive, and well off. People of color who immigrated to the U.S., generally those who are Latine, Middle Eastern, Black, or Asian, are seen as criminals, shady, or violent.

- **Escaping the cartel:** This is a storyline that is typically associated with Latin American immigrants as an explanation of why they're "escaping" to the U.S.
- **Positive views of emigration:** Despite judgmental depictions of people immigrating to the U.S., many stories depict emigration, or Americans going to live elsewhere across the world, as a positive thing. The character who is emigrating is typically portrayed as going on a romantic or idolized journey of self-discovery, or to help others in nations where there is war, strife, or poverty, or moving somewhere to live with the love of their life.

RELIGIOUS BELIEFS

Stereotypes
- **The fanatical, jihadist Muslim:** Muslims are depicted as being fanatical, conservative, and willing to be violent or create chaos in the name of their religion.
- **Submissive Muslim woman:** Muslim women are presented as being submissive, quiet, demure, or subjugated by the men in their family. This stereotype typically harps on apparel like the hijab or burka, or customs like arranged marriages.
- **Kind, pure, good Christian:** Christians are showcased in an overwhelmingly positive light—as being kind, pure, good, and helpful to all.

- **Hindu guru:** The Hindu religion is typically romanticized and exoticized through a guru character who is wise, insightful, charming, and sometimes magical.
- **Zen Buddhist:** Buddhists are depicted as super zen, calm, relaxed, wise, and insightful.

Tropes
- **Christianity is good; other religions are bad:** Christianity is showcased as being a better or more positive religion than others, especially in comparison to Islam, Judaism, Hinduism, and Buddhism. This trope can also present as monotheistic religions being written in a more positive way and polytheistic religions written as evil, bad, or primitive.
- **Magical religious leader:** A spiritual or religious leader is given magical powers. It usually appears in religions that are mostly dominated by people of color like Native American shamanism, Hinduism, voodoo, and brujeria.

EXPERIENCING HOUSELESSNESS

It's likely you've referred to people who do not have a permanent residence as "the homeless." This moniker is harmful because it removes the person from the experience. Instead, we should be using the terms "person experiencing houselessness" or "people who are unhoused." It infers that houselessness is not necessarily a permanent experience and a lack of a home is not the defining aspect of the person who is unhoused. They are more than where they live or don't live. It should be noted that the terms "houselessness" and "unhoused" have only recently become more widespread. The idea behind these terms is that "homelessness" is not accurate. People who are unhoused are without a physical housing structure that is safe and sound for human habitation. Someone who is experiencing houselessness could still have a home, as a home could be something beyond a physical structure like a community, a general area, a group of people, a place of worship, or a feeling.

Inappropriate terms
- bum
- hobo
- the homeless
- transients
- street people
- homeless woman/man/child/person

Stereotypes
- **Lazy, scammers:** This is the idea that people experiencing houselessness are too lazy to get a job and would rather scam people out of their money through begging.
- **Substance use:** This is the false assumption that people experiencing houselessness have a substance use disorder and the money they receive from strangers will go toward drugs or alcohol.
- **Mental health condition:** This is the stereotypical idea that everyone who experiences houselessness has a mental health condition.
- **Living on the streets:** All people who are unhoused are depicted as living on the streets, be it under a bridge, on a highway, or in a camp. There are many different ways

that people experience houselessness, and they do not all include living on the street.

SUBSTANCE USE

Appropriate substance use terms
- Person with substance use or alcohol use disorder
- Person with opioid addiction
- Person in active use
- Person who misuses alcohol
- Person in recovery
- Person who previously used drugs
- Substance use
- Tested positive/negative for drugs
- Substance use disorder

Harmful/inappropriate substance use terms
- Addict/former addict/reformed addict
- Alcoholic
- Junkie
- Use/user
- Drug or substance abuser
- Drunk
- Former addict
- Substance abuse
- Clean/dirty
- Drug habit

Stereotypes
- **Criminals:** People who have substance use disorders are depicted as criminals, usually because they use or have

used illegal drugs. However, this criminal stereotype can extend to other behaviors and stereotypes like theft and homicide.

- **Violent:** This harmful stereotype depicts people who use drugs as being violent and unable to control their emotions or behavior while using drugs.

- **Experiencing houselessness:** This suggests that people who use drugs or have a substance use disorder experience houselessness or are at a higher risk for being unhoused.

- **Uneducated and lower income:** This is a false stereotype that assumes that people who use drugs or have a substance use disorder are uneducated and have lower incomes.

- **Not able to function in society:** This misconception suggests that people who use drugs or have a substance use disorder are not able to function in society whether that's in terms of having a job or successful career, taking care of their families, paying bills, etc.

- **Identify with marginalized communities:** This is a stereotype that assumes that most people who use drugs or have a substance use disorder are from historically marginalized communities, especially those who are people of color, have lower incomes, have a disability, or have mental health conditions.

Tropes

- **Descent into addiction:** This is a storyline that shows a "normal" person whose good life drastically changes because of their use of drugs or alcohol. It typically shows their life devolving from stability to instability, whether that's through a loss of a job, relationship, family, or home. Such a tropic storyline plays on the reader's fear in order to teach a "lesson." It doesn't showcase the nuanced and diverse experiences of people with substance use disorders.

Body Type

Body type terminology

The word "fat" was long used as an insult toward people with larger bodies. It has become more than a physical descriptor; it is a way for one person to call another person lazy, unintelligent, unattractive, or poor. However, in the last decade, many people have started to use the word "fat" to describe themselves as a means of removing the negative connotation and turning the word back into the neutral physical descriptor it should be.

When writing characters with larger body types, "fat" can be a word for how your character describes themself. If you have some discomfort using the word, it's a good time to dive into unconscious bias around anti-fatness.

As for other terminology, terms like "people with larger bodies" and "plus-size people" are commonly used and generally acceptable. Other terms like "curvy," "thick," "voluptuous," "shapely," or "chubby" are used among different racial communities, ages, gender identities, and in different genres.

Like with any other identity, speak to fat people about how they like to be described. Also, think about the intersections of race, gender identity, sexual orientation, and disabilities when approaching this identity. A Latine woman with a larger body may describe her body differently from a white man who is gay.

The words "obese" and "overweight" are medical terms

that have stigmas associated with them, especially at the intersections of race. Many people use these terms incorrectly and interchangeably with "fat," "plus-size," or "people with larger bodies." I'd advise against this, as they're not the same. "Obese" and "overweight" are technical, medical terms and should be used in relation to medical diagnoses. That said, there might be instances where these words arise in your story. Perhaps one character uses them to describe another character, because you as a writer want to show how a character is fatphobic. I'm not saying don't use these two terms; just do so in a mindful and accurate way.

Lastly, I do not feel the need to talk about terminology, stereotypes, or tropes as it relates to people who are considered straight size—sizes 0–14. People who fall within these sizes benefit from society's belief that thinness is more attractive and better. While they may have stereotypes associated with them and while people within this range might be considered "plump" or "chubby" by some (especially those who are in the 10–14 size range), they do not face the same marginalization that people who are plus-size do.

If you have a character with a larger body, analyze how you describe them lest you other them or unknowingly make fatphobic associations. Some questions to ask yourself:

- Are you excessively describing the plus-size character's body? Did you do the same with thinner characters?
- Did you unknowingly make negative associations to their weight?
- Did you use hyperbole, a metaphor, or a simile to describe how the character looks?

- Does your description of their body size send messages to the reader that they should not like that character or pity them?
- Does the way you describe how a fat person moves or looks have an undertone of disgust?
- Compare how you describe a fat character and a thin character. Do you notice any differences? Associations that are more positive or negative?
- Do you use stereotypical imagery or descriptions related to harmful ideas of fatness and body size?

Stereotypes
- **Laziness:** Larger bodies are associated with laziness and slovenliness.
- **Poor:** Fat people are associated with lower incomes.
- **Gluttonous:** A plus-size person depicted as always eating and drinking excessively. This indicates that people have larger bodies because they can't control themselves.
- **Fat villains:** This is the assumption that a person who has a larger body is more likely to be a bully or a villain because they are upset, angry, or frustrated with their body weight.
- **Insecure:** Fat people are depicted as being extremely insecure about their looks and attractiveness. It is assumed that fat people could never like how they look or be confident in who they are.
- **Unattractive, single, lonely, non-sexual:** This is the assumption that people with larger bodies are unattractive and therefore single and lonely. They're also depicted as not engaging in sexual activity or having a sensual or

sexy style, personality, and body. Sometimes they are described as more maternal or paternal.

- **Dad bod is acceptable, but fat women and genderqueer people are not:** Fat women and genderqueer people are painted in a worse light in terms of attractiveness, worth, and personality than fat men. In many cases, men who have larger bodies are deemed acceptable and more attractive than fat women and genderqueer people.

Tropes

- **The fat best friend:** This is a common trope of making the best friend of the main character plus-size. These characters generally help the main character learn something (like self-love) and/or provide comic relief and immeasurable support to the main character. It sends the message that fat people cannot be the center of the story because of their weight.
- **Stories about their weight:** This is a storyline trope that focuses on a main fat character whose journey solely focuses on weight—usually losing weight, though not always. The story typically ends in one of two ways: the fat character loses the weight, and their life gets better, or the fat character accepts their body.
- **Gaining weight from trauma:** A fat character is depicted as gaining weight because of some traumatic event, usually in their backstory.
- **Bullying or harassment:** While people who have larger bodies may be bullied, harassed, or insulted because of their looks, some writers have harped on it incessantly in storylines of fat people. Not only is it another example of centering a fat character's entire identity on their

weight, it can result in sentimentality and trauma porn. It also sends the message that plus-size people must go through such harassment to become stronger or accept their bodies.

- **Hot, fit, thin savior:** A "mainstream" attractive, thin, and fit romantic love interest shows the fat woman or genderqueer person that they are beautiful and worthy of love. This indicates that a fat person could only believe such a thing if it comes from a "mainstream" attractive and thin love interest.

- **Formerly fat or formerly fit:** A character who is presented as someone who used to be fat or a character who used to be fit and is now fat. Both types of characters are generally obsessed with their weight, whether it's in maintaining their size or losing weight.

I can't recall where I first heard the term "vicarious operant conditioning," but I found it fascinating, especially as it relates to writing other identities. According to a *Book Riot* article by Carole V. Bell, vicarious operant conditioning is when "we learn by watching what happens to others." In her piece, Bell speaks about how romance novels can push fatphobic ideas in the larger population because of vicarious operant conditioning. The same can be said of other identities. If we write historically marginalized identities poorly, stereotypically, or in a misrepresentative way, we may be teaching readers to make negative associations toward historically marginalized communities. Check out this quote from Bell and read the full article to fully grasp this concept:

"What happens when romance others fat people and relentlessly reproduces negative associations and expectations? Given what we know about fiction as a vehicle of social learning and about narrative persuasion—how norms and ideas are passed on through narratives we consume—I worry that a steady diet of these types of stories will become a way of reinforcing fatphobia. It also just feels like an insidious way of vicariously experiencing negative self-talk.

"Vicarious operant conditioning, for example, is a particular kind of social learning that's particularly relevant to romance. Sounds fancy, but it is straightforward. It means that we learn by watching what happens to others. We see certain characteristics and behaviors being rewarded or punished and learn their value."[18]

Read Bell's full article here:

12

TEN REASONS TO LET THAT STORY GO, DIE, OR BE PUSHED ASIDE

As writers, we know that not everything we write will or should go out into the big wide world. Maybe you tried your hand at a different outline or format, and it didn't work. The same can be said for those who want to write identities not their own. Sometimes, no matter how much you want to succeed at something, it doesn't work out how you planned or hoped it would. To help you decide if you need to let a story go, die on your desktop, or be pushed aside in favor of another one, I've created a list of ten red flags.

1. You wrote the piece because you think that publishers (or some other literary or creative organization or company) will only acquire your work if it features people from historically marginalized identities.
2. You didn't put much effort into uncovering and/or working on your biases, or you don't think you have biases.

3. You did not build authentic relationships with people from the community you're depicting.

4. You created a character who is essentially you, a close friend, or a family member, but gave them a historically marginalized identity.

5. If you discover that the biggest issue with your piece relates to the overall storyline, it could be better to start anew.

6. You refuse to make any edits based on suggestions from beta readers, sensitivity readers, literary agents, or editors.

7. You continue to get concerns and questions from beta readers and sensitivity readers related to your depictions of identities not your own.

8. That bad gut feeling about a scene, depiction, or storyline won't go away, no matter how many revisions you make.

9. You have not done any reflection on why you wrote the piece and/or can't explain what it means for you to tell this story.

10. You aren't comfortable with or confident about being critiqued or scrutinized by others—publishers, readers, literary agents, the public, etc.—regarding why and how you wrote the piece.

13

HOW TO CRITIQUE AN IDENTITY NOT YOUR OWN

When I taught Writing an Identity Not Your Own for the Women's Fiction Writers Association in 2022, I had a student reach out to me at the end of the class. She was in a critique partnership with another writer and had found some biases, bias blocks, and misrepresentation in the writer's creative writing piece. Her question to me: How do I speak to the writer about the issues in their work in a way that won't alienate them?

It was a great question. Telling another writer that their work features a racist depiction or harmful ableist language is tricky. It can be uncomfortable to have those conversations. However, I was glad that the writer reached out to me, and it made me aware of something very important: we either don't know how to talk about this subject or we find it too uncomfortable of a topic to broach. Because of that, many of us take the easy route of not speaking up, making suggestions, or holding one another accountable.

I wasn't going to include this chapter originally, but the more I thought about it, the more I realized that as writers we should be helping one another to get this right. I can't count on this book reaching everyone. However, if you have read this book, have done work to recognize biases, have educated yourself on various systems of discrimination, then you have some knowledge on the subject.

Critique partners generally have a trusting literary relationship, one that allows them to discuss this tough topic in a safe and open space. Writers may be more open to their critique partner than they would be to an authority figure like an instructor, editor, literary agent, or even the author of this book.

Below you will find some of my favorite strategies to use in critique conversations related to writing an identity not your own. I hope they help you to feel more confident in discussing this topic with other writers.

WE ARE ON THE SAME SIDE

When I'm giving feedback to anyone who has written something problematic, I like to set up the conversation in a way that puts us both on the same side. Using the words "we" or "you and I" or "us" aligns you and your critique partner. If they believe you have their best interests at heart, it might make them more open to receiving feedback.

Here are some examples:

- "I want us to work together to figure this out."
- "We would never want to do anything that would be misrepresentative."

328 • ALEX TEMBLADOR

- "I know you don't like seeing biased representations in literature as much as I don't."
- "You know as well as I the harm that othering can do."
- "We don't want to put ourselves in a situation where we unknowingly make a mistake, which is why I wanted you to edit my piece and you wanted me to edit yours."
- "If you don't understand what I mean by the critique, please ask me. I probably didn't fully convey it correctly, and I want us to work it out together."

I'VE F'D UP TOO

People are more receptive to feedback when you share instances in which you've made a similar mistake. Be as open and as honest as you can be, even if what you're recounting is embarrassing or shameful to you. Being vulnerable can create a sense of trust between you and the writer.

Here is an example:

"This scene reminded me of something I wrote in my previous manuscript. Another writer pointed out that I was othering my character. I felt so bad that I didn't recognize it but very thankful that my critique partner brought it to my attention. We don't want to publish or share work with the world that is harmful, so when I read this scene in your manuscript, I thought it best to discuss it."

If you tell your critique partner that you've made the same mistake, they'll see that making mistakes is normal and not so "taboo" that it can't be discussed.

PREP THEM FOR A TOUGH-TOPICS CONVERSATION

You may want to discuss bias and bias blocks in a casual way before you get into the critique. That way you can set the stage for when you bring up an instance in the manuscript where the writer's bias is clear. An example:

"I read this book on writing other identities and it talks about how writers can unknowingly write their biases and bias blocks into their creative work. It got me thinking about how I've done that in the past and made me more diligent to spot these things in my work. I've realized that everyone has biases and bias blocks; it doesn't matter who they are or what their identity is."

SOCRATES AND HIS ENDLESS QUESTIONING

The Socratic Method is the practice of asking another person probing questions to discover their underlying opinions, thought process, or beliefs. In doing so, it helps the person to reflect and question their decision-making and/or guide the conversation where you want it to go.

Here is how it can play out. You can start with one question: "What did you mean when you wrote this?"

Then you can ask another question based off the writer's answer, like "That's interesting. I'm curious—how do you want this character to be perceived?" You can keep asking questions until you get to the root of the issue in their work.

330 • ALEX TEMBLADOR

Sometimes the writer won't like their answer or will recognize that it's a weak argument. If they don't have an answer, it might be because they don't want to admit something aloud. With the Socratic Method, you're essentially getting the writer to think about their depictions and question what they've done and why they've done it. This can lead to some exceptional reflection on the writer's part.

Some other questions you might ask during the Socratic Method:

- "Do you think that if you did this instead, it might make this character a little more rounded out?"
- "Did you mean for that scene to come off that way?"
- "I don't think you wanted the character to seem like that, but I wanted to make sure. What did you intend or what do you want readers to understand?"

WHAT DO YOU THINK ABOUT _____ ?

If you want to make a suggestion, frame it as *"What do you think about [enter suggestion]?"*

By framing the suggestion as a question, it should foster conversation between you and the writer. From there, you can talk through the writer's choices and why they work or don't work. In having a longer conversation, you may help the writer see that the scene or characterization is problematic and not doing what they hoped it would do.

"I" INSTEAD OF "YOU"

Rather than use "you" (e.g., you did this, you did that) in your critique, use "I." I know that seems counterintuitive, but it'll give the writer space to see what they've done and will sound less accusatory to them.

For instance, you might say:

- "I think that this character is being othered here and I don't think that's what was intended."
- "I feel like the characterization isn't as authentic or as nuanced as it could be."
- "I think this is coming off in a negative way toward the non-binary community and I know you would never intentionally do that, so I wanted to point it out."

WHAT AN AMAZING OPPORTUNITY

Show another writer all the opportunities they have to improve their piece by using the word "opportunity" or a synonym of it in your critique.

Here are some examples:

- "This scene is a good opportunity to showcase . . ."
- "You have the opportunity here to help your character grow by depicting how they were being biased to this other character . . ."
- "This is the perfect chance to . . ."

By using the word "opportunity," you're showing the writer that an edit isn't something to be upset, ashamed, or concerned about, but a positive, great, and excellent chance to improve their work and make their piece more dynamic and authentic.

THE OREO METHOD

Have you heard of the "Oreo" critique method? It's the process by which you give a writer a compliment related to their work before you point out a mistake they made. You then follow it up with another compliment, and so on. Using compliments to buffer the critique can go a long way.

THIS COULD COME OFF AS . . .

"This could come off as . . ." is a good phrase to use when giving a critique. Remind the writer that other people could perceive something in a poor light if the scene or character is left the way it is currently written. You could follow it up with "I don't think that's how you meant for it to come off."

CONNECT THE ISSUE TO THE PLOT

When you find a stereotype, trope, or misrepresentation in a scene, you can usually find ways in which it harms the overall storyline or plot. If you can explain how certain scenes or depictions are harmful to big elements of the story like plot, setting, or character development, the writer can see how one decision can make a wider impact than they intended.

"I WAS PULLED OUT OF THE STORY"

Writers seem to respond to this critique: "When I read this, I was pulled out of the story." Most writers know that if the reading experience is interrupted, something about that scene needs to be re-examined and possibly reworked. You can help your critique partner by explaining what pulled you out of the story, which will hopefully lead them in the right direction during the editing process.

BE DIRECT

I have provided you with many tips and tricks to help make critique conversations about writing other identities go smoothly. However, there will be times when you will need to be direct with your critique partner. If you see a harmful trope, depiction, or portrayal, it is imperative that you make it clear to the writer what the issue is. You'll be doing a disservice to your critique partner and the historically marginalized communities that they're portraying if you are too vague in your critique.

14

WHAT DID I DO TO WRITE AN IDENTITY NOT MY OWN WELL?

I n 2022, while sitting in the audience at a literary festival, a literary agent told a story about an author client of his, a white, straight man who published a creative piece in 2017 that featured, in his words, a "positive portrayal" of a gay couple, people of color, and a woman protagonist.

"He was celebrated at the time for his work. No one said anything about him being a white, straight man writing about people not like him," the literary agent said. "But now my author says that he probably couldn't write that same story today because it has characters that are different than his identity. I don't know. We live in scary times. What do you think?"

The literary agent asked us, the audience, what we thought about the subject of writing identities not our own. You might have imagined that I, the author of this book, actively engaged in the conversation. I did not. I was in the final stages of editing this book, so I was exhausted and wanted to protect my energy. However, I thought about the literary agent's statement in the days following the event.

I hadn't read the work that the literary agent was referring to. For all I knew, it could be a great piece of literature in which the writer wrote outside of his identity well. Whether the author succeeded or not really doesn't matter. It's what the literary agent was inferring that caught my attention.

The literary agent said "we live in scary times." Why is it scary that writers and publishers are held to higher standards when it comes to writing identities not their own? How long is long enough for writers to get it completely wrong and disseminate harmful stereotypes and misrepresentations to the masses?

People of historically marginalized identities (or otherwise) may not have said anything en masse about this particular author's work (and maybe there was nothing to say), but they have always voiced their concerns about the topic of writing an identity not your own. No one listened until recently, thanks to the advent of social media, more writers of historically marginalized identities finally being published, and more society-wide discussions about representation.

At the time in which the author wrote his story, publishers weren't publishing many stories by authors who wrote their own identities, so I'm not surprised that they instead published a white cis heteronormative man's work that featured a gay couple, people of color, and a woman protagonist. His depiction of historically marginalized identities would be safer, more palatable, and more relatable to those whom publishing has perceived to be the most important market of readers: white, straight audiences.

Writing identities not your own, especially historically

marginalized identities, is not something that remains on the page. When you tell our stories, we get to have a say—and you have to be okay with that. For some, like the literary agent and his author (at least, according to the agent), this new world of having their historically marginalized characters analyzed and discussed in a wider conversation related to authentic representation is not comfortable.

It's not meant to be.

When I told writers from historically marginalized identities that I was working on this book, they reacted in two ways. Half of them were excited that someone from a historically marginalized identity would be writing a resource on the topic. The other half looked like deer in headlights; they were not sure if they liked the idea and were rightfully concerned that such a book would give people permission to write other identities in a way that still did not get it right. Their reactions mirrored my own complex and contradictory feelings that I had while writing this book.

I wrote this book so writers who want to write other identities would question themselves, their intent, and their process. I wrote this book so writers would understand how poor misrepresentations of characters from historically marginalized identities can further stereotypes, misinformation, and misrepresentation. I wrote this book so writers could learn that writing identities not your own is not simply about setting pen to paper and writing a short story, poem, novel, or screenplay. It also involves a community, one in which the community provides their feedback on how well you accomplished the task of writing an identity not your own. This will not change.

Some people will not be comfortable with all aspects of the process, especially the public commentary part. There is no getting away from it, at least not until the powers that be even the playing field by publishing more writers of historically marginalized identities, giving us the same marketing, print runs, and PR opportunities as privileged writers, and paying writers from historically marginalized identities as much as those who write our identities.

If you cannot deal with others, especially people of historically marginalized identities, analyzing how you write identities not your own, I don't think this is the path for you.

If you are in a place in your life where you would like to move forward in writing another identity, knowing full well what this process will involve, ask yourself these three questions:

- Why do I want to write a different identity?
- Why should I write this story?
- What did I do to write this story well?

Let's start with the first question: Why do I want to write a different identity? Answering this question requires a lot of internal reflection, pushes you to face your biases and truths, and asks you to examine them in the context of your storytelling. Many people ignore this question, especially when the best answer they have is "I don't know." That answer is not going to cut it. You need to know.

The answers that arise from asking that question may not be exactly what you're looking for. Perhaps you realized that you think publishing only wants to publish diverse stories—which is far from the truth—so you took on the task to fit into this perceived idea of a "trend" (again, this doesn't exist). Maybe you discovered that you tried to take on the role of savior for a community that never asked you to save them, or you realized that you've used characters of different identities in ways that have unconsciously exposed a bias.

Whatever the answer may be, I encourage you to not run from it, but to face it head-on.

The next question to ask yourself is: Why should I write this story?

Again, this is a tough question, but it is one that will be asked of you by readers, journalists, publishers, reviewers, and other writers. Can you stand in the confidence of your answer, or will you get defensive if someone asks you such a question?

The last question is the most important one, in my opinion: What did I do to write this story well?

As I said at the beginning of this book, writing an identity not your own will take a lot of work, and not all writers are willing to do it. Merely reading creative work by writers of that identity is not enough. It requires making human connections with people from the community in which you wish to write. For many writers, their fear, their insecurities, or their inability to put themselves in uncomfortable situations hinders their ability to write a different identity.

I cannot be (and I don't want to be) the gatekeeper of stories by writers who feature identities other than their own—no one can. I wrote this book for you to question yourself throughout the process, and to convey how much it takes to write other identities well. I hope that you put in the work, make connections, get feedback from others, question your biases, and edit your work with fervor.

If there is a troubling thought in your mind that a certain characterization is wrong or you recognize a deep, gut-wrenching truth about the overall storyline, I hope you have the moral and ethical strength to put your work aside. Let it sit. Let it be edited. Let it be there in ten years when you're ready to work on it again. Or let it get lost forever among piles of other great stories you are better equipped to tell.

Writing an identity not your own is a lifelong process for a writer and one that will come with mistakes. I hope this book has helped you to make as few of those mistakes as possible. We must be our own gatekeepers, protecting ourselves from doing something we are not ready to do, and we must live with the understanding that it's better to do as little harm to those of historically marginalized identities than it is to pridefully share our work with the world.

ADDITIONAL RESOURCES

I wrote this book because I couldn't find a comprehensive guide on the topic of writing an identity not your own. That said, there are some additional resources that may still hold some amazing gems that haven't been included in this text. If another writer can explain this topic in a way that's easier for you to comprehend, I'm all for it. Keep in mind that some of these books, articles, and websites were published many years ago and may not have been updated since.

BOOKS

- *The Conscious Style Guide: A Flexible Approach to Language That Includes, Respects, and Empowers* by Karen Yin
- *A Stranger's Journey: Race, Identity, and Narrative Craft in Writing* by David Mura
- *Writing Intersectional Identities: Keywords for Creative Writers* by Janelle Adsit and Renée M. Byrd
- *Writing the Other: A Practical Approach* by Nisi Shawl and Cynthia Ward
- *Craft in the Real World: Rethinking Fiction Writing and Workshopping* by Matthew Salesses
- *A Tale of Two Titties: A Writer's Guide to Conquering the Most Sexist Tropes in Literary History* by Meg Vondriska

- *Imagining Autism: Fiction and Stereotoypes on the Spectrum* by Sonya Freeman Loftis

ONLINE RESOURCES

- Writing with Color, writingwithcolor.tumblr.com
- Writing the Other, writingtheother.com
- We Need Diverse Books, diversebooks.org
- Writers for Diversity Facebook Page, facebook.com/groups /writersfordiversity (Be mindful of who is posting and what they're posting.)
- Desi Books, desibooks.co
- Africa Access Review, africaaccessreview.org
- African American Literature Book Club, aalbc.com
- KiBooka, kibooka.com
- Disability in Kidlit, disabilityinkidlit.com
- Jewish Book Council, jewishbookcouncil.org
- Diverse BookFinder, diversebookfinder.org
- American Indians in Children's Literature, americanindiansinchil drensliterature.blogspot.com
- Rich in Color, richincolor.com

OTHER SUGGESTIONS

- Reference up-to-date articles from respectable sources like the *Atlantic, Writer's Digest, Poets & Writers, Electric Literature,* the *Rumpus,* etc.
- Follow authors and book influencers of historically marginalized identities on social media.
- Attend panels at online or in-person writing conferences. Take a writing seminar or class with other authors through MasterClass, Gotham Writers Workshop, writingworkshops.com, the Writer's League of Texas, etc.

If you want more resources related to writing identities not your own, check out Alex Temblador's website, writinganidentitynotyourown.com.

NOTES

Introduction

1. Cummins, Jeanine, *American Dirt: A Novel*, New York: Flatiron Books, 2020.

2. Gurba, Myriam, "Pendeja, You Ain't Steinbeck: My Bronca with Fake-Ass Social Justice Literature," *Tropics of Meta*, December 12, 2019, tropicsofmeta .com/2019/12/12/pendeja-you-aint-steinbeck-my-bronca-with-fake-ass-social -justice-literature.

3. Schmidt, David J., "'American Dirt' Isn't Just Bad—Its Best Parts Are Cribbed from Latino Writers," *HuffPost*, January 24, 2020, www.huffpost.com/entry /american-dirtbook_n_5e2a11e8c5b6779e9c2fd79f.

4. Cummins, *American Dirt*.

5. Grady, Constance, "The Controversy over the New Immigration Novel American Dirt, Explained," *Vox*, January 22, 2020, www.vox.com/culture/2020/1/22 /21075629/american-dirt-controversy-explained-jeanine cummins-oprah-flatiron.

6. Shapiro, Lila, "The Implosion of American Dirt, by Jeanine Cummins," *Vulture*, January 5, 2021, www.vulture.com/article/americandirt-jeanine -cummins-book-controversy.html.

7. So, Richard Jean, and Gus Wezerek, "Just How White Is the Book Industry?," *New York Times*, December 11, 2020, www.nytimes.com/interactive/2020/12 /11/opinion/culture/diversity-publishing-industry.html.

8. "The State of Racial Diversity in Romance Publishing Report," The Ripped Bodice, www.therippedbodicela.com/state-racial-diversity-romance-publishing -report.

9. We Need Diverse Books, "The Cooperative Children's Book Center Has Released the Results of Their 2019 Survey on Diversity in Kidlit/YA, Linked in

Bio," Instagram, June 26, 2020, www.instagram.com/p/CB5mgWFlils/?utm
_source=ig_web_copy_link.

10. "Where Is the Diversity in Publishing? The 2019 Diversity Baseline Survey Results," *Lee & Low Books*, January 28, 2020, blog.leeandlow.com/2020/01/28 /2019diversitybaselinesurvey/.

11. Kingsbury, Margaret, "The Current State of Disability Representation in Children's Books," *Book Riot*, April 28, 2021, bookriot.com/disability -representation-in-childrens-books/.

Chapter 1: Identity

1. "Identity," *Psychology Today*, https://www.psychologytoday.com/us/basics /identity.

2. "Glossary of Essential Health Equity Terms: Marginalized Populations," National Collaborating Centre for Determinants of Health, 2022, nccdh.ca /glossary/entry/marginalized-populations.

Chapter 2: Unintentionally Writing a Problematic Piece

1. "Unconscious Bias Training," UCSF Office of Diversity and Outreach, 2022, diversity.ucsf.edu/programs-resources/training/unconscious-bias-training.

2. Pronin, Emily, Daniel Y. Lin, and Lee Ross, "The Bias Blind Spot: Perceptions of Bias in Self Versus Others," *Personality and Social Psychology Bulletin*, 28(3), 369–381, 2002, https://doi.org/10.1177/0146167202286008.

3. "What Is a Bias Blind Spot?," Study.com, June 6, 2022, https://study.com/learn /lesson/blind-spot-bias-overview-examples.html.

4. Graves, Joseph L., Jr., and Alan H. Goodman, *Racism Not Race: Answers to Frequently Asked Questions*, New York: Columbia University Press, 2022, 72.

5. "Project Implicit," Harvard.edu, 2011, implicit.harvard.edu/implicit/iatdetails .html.

6. Renken, Elena, "How Stories Connect and Persuade Us: Unleashing the Brain Power of Narrative," NPR, April 11, 2020, www.npr.org/sections/health-shots /2020/04/11/815573198/how-stories-connect-andpersuade-us-unleashing-the -brain-power-of-narrative.

7. Kolbert, Elizabeth, "Why Facts Don't Change Our Minds," *New Yorker*, February 19, 2017, www.newyorker.com/magazine/2017/02/27/why-facts-dont -change-our-minds.

Chapter 3: The "Before You Write" Checklist

1. Leitich Smith, Cynthia, "100 Books," *Kirkus Reviews*, September 25, 2017, www.kirkusreviews.com/news-and-features/articles/100-books/.

2. Martin-Rodriguez, Manuel M., "A Visual History of Chicano/A/X Literatures," faculty.ucmerced.edu, faculty.ucmerced.edu/mmartin-rodriguez/vhcl .htm.

3. Reese, Debbie, "An Oft-Posed Question: 'Who Can Tell Your Stories?,'" *Amer-

ican Indians in Children's Literature (*AICL*), July 31, 2007, americanindians inchildrensliterature.blogspot.com/2007/07/often-posed-question-who-can -tell-your.html.

4. Chee, Alexander, "Alexander Chee on How to Unlearn Everything," Vulture, October 30, 2019, www.vulture.com/2019/10/author-alexander-chee-on-his -advice-to-writers.html.

Chapter 4: Characterization

1. Kolker, Robert, "Who Is the Bad Art Friend?," *New York Times*, October 5, 2021, https://www.nytimes.com/2021/10/05/magazine/dorland-v-larson.html.

2. Conrad, Joseph, *Heart of Darkness*, 1899; New York: W.W. Norton & Company, 2017.

3. Achebe, Chinua," An Image of Africa," *Research in African Literatures*, vol. 9, no. 1 (1978), 1–15, http://www.jstor.org/stable/3818468.

4. So, Richard Jean, and Gus Wezerek, "Just How White Is the Book Industry?," *New York Times*, December 11, 2020, www.nytimes.com/interactive/2020/12 /11/opinion/culture/diversity-publishing-industry.html.

5. Milliot, Jim, "Penguin Random House Authors and Creators Skew Heavily White," *Publishers Weekly*, November 18 2021, https://www.publishersweekly .com/pw/by-topic/industry-news/publisher-news/article/87923-prh -contributors-skew-heavily-white.html.

6. Herndon, Jaime, "Report: 2019 Diversity in Children's and YA Literature," *Book Riot*, June 26, 2020, bookriot.com/diversity-in-childrens-and-young -adult-literature/.

7. "23% Decrease in Black Characters in Children's Bestsellers as BLM Bounce Fades—WordsRated," WordsRated, March 28, 2022, wordsrated.com /representation-childrens-literature/.

8. Dickinson, Kari, "CCBC's Latest Diversity Statistics Show Increasing Number of Diverse Books for Children and Teens," University of Wisconsin-Madison School of Education, June 13, 2023, https://education.wisc.edu/news/ccbcs -latest-diversity-statistics-show-increasing-number-of-diverse-books-for -children-and-teens/.

Chapter 5: Writing Discrimination

1. "Tokenism: Impact of Tokenization," *MasterClass*, November 17, 2022, www .masterclass.com/articles/tokenism.

2. Statista Research Department, "Number of People Killed by Police by Ethnicity U.S. 2013–2023," *Statista*, August 1, 2023, www.statista.com/statistics /1124036/number-people-killed-police-ethnicity-us/.

3. "Black Women over Three Times More Likely to Die in Pregnancy, Postpartum than White Women, New Research Finds," Population Reference Bureau, December 6, 2021, https://www.prb.org/resources/black-women-over-three -times-more-likely-to-die-in-pregnancy-postpartum-than-white-women -new-research-finds/.

4. "Small Business and ADA Readily Achievable Requirements," ADA National Network, adata.org/factsheet/small-business-and-ada-readily-achievable-requirements.

5. Gabbert, Elisa, "Is Sentimentality in Writing Really That Bad?," *Electric Literature*, December 17, 2019, electricliterature.com/is-sentimentality-in-writing-really-that-bad/.

6. The Associated Press, "The U.S. Renames 5 Places That Used Racist Slur for a Native Woman," NPR, January 13, 2023, https://www.npr.org/2023/01/13/1148987754/the-u-s-renames-5-places-that-used-racist-slur-for-a-native-woman.

Chapter 6: Dialogue

1. Chow, Andrew R., "As the Final Season of *Kim's Convenience* Arrives on Netflix, Its Legacy Is Dampened by Claims of a Racist Work Environment," *Time*, June 8 2021, time.com/6072074/kims-convenience-racism/.

2. Verissimo, Jumoke, "On the Politics of Italics," *Literary Hub*, August 28, 2019, https://lithub.com/on-the-politics-of%20italics/.

3. "Definition of 'accent,'" *Merriam-Webster*, https://www.merriam-webster.com/dictionary/accent.

4. "Definition of 'dialect,'" *Merriam-Webster*, https://www.merriam-webster.com/dictionary/dialect.

5. Hurston, Zora Neale, *Their Eyes Were Watching God*, J. B. Lippincott, September 18, 1937, 3.

Chapter 7: Identities and Genre

1. Berlatsky, Noah, "A new 'Lord of the Rings' prequel quietly confronts an uncomfortable legacy," NBC News, September 1, 2022, www.nbcnews.com/think/opinion/new-lord-rings-rings-power-revives racism-debate-rcna45955.

2. Sonya Freeman Loftis, *Imagining Autism : Fiction and Stereotypes on the Spectrum*, Bloomington: Indiana University Press, 2015, 48.

3. Davis, Nicola, "Human Memory May Be Unreliable after Just a Few Seconds, Scientists Find," *Guardian*, April 5, 2023, https://www.theguardian.com/science/2023/apr/05/short-term-memory-illusions-study.

Chapter 8: Writing Historically Marginalized Identities

1. Blackwood, Keri, "What Is My Hair Type?," *Hairstory*, April 5, 2023, https://hairstory.com/blogs/news/what-kind-of-hair-do-i-have?geoRedirect=false.

2. "Obesity, Race/Ethnicity, and COVID-19," Centers for Disease Control and Prevention, September 27, 2022, https://www.cdc.gov/obesity/data/obesity-and-covid-19.html.

3. Lyles, Travis, "Here's the 'Straight Outta Compton' Casting Call That Everybody Thought Was Racist," *Business Insider*, August 13, 2015, www.businessinsider.com/racist-straight-outta-compton-casting-call-2015-8.

4. Boudreau, Sarah, "Beyond Just XX or XY: The Complexities of Biological Sex,"

Visible Body, July 22, 2022, www.visiblebody.com/blog/beyond-just-xx-or-xy -the-complexities-of-biological-sex.

5. "The Extraordinary Case of the Guevedoces," BBC News, September 20, 2015, https://www.bbc.com/news/magazine-34290981.

6. "Sex and Gender Identity," Planned Parenthood, www.plannedparenthood .org/learn/gender-identity/sexgender-identity.

7. "Sex and Gender Identity," Planned Parenthood.

8. Heckel, Jodi, "Tracing the History of Gender-Neutral Pronouns," Illinois News Bureau, College of Liberal Arts & Sciences at Illinois, January 29, 2020, https:// las.illinois.edu/news/2020-01-29/tracing-history-gender-neutral-pronouns.

9. Baron, Dennis, "From They to Tey to Te: Pronoun Mansplaining in the 1970s," *The Web of Language*, blogs.illinois.edu, February 28, 2020, blogs.illinois.edu /view/25/806764.

10. Clarke, Arthur C., *Rendezvous with Rama*, Spectra, December 1, 1990.

11. Vondriska, Meg, "and some men shouldn't be commanders if they're distracted so easily," Twitter, February 5, 2023, twitter.com/menwritewomen /status/1622293446827409410.

12. Adichie, Chimamanda Ngozi, "The Danger of a Single Story," TED, July 2009, www.ted.com/talks/chimamanda_ngozi_adichie_the_danger_of_a_single _story/comments.

13. Sunkara, Lavanya, "Consider Ditching These 11 Words When Talking about Your Travels," *Fodor's Travel*, January 25, 2022, www.fodors.com /news/travel-tips/consider-ditching-these-11-words-when-talking-about -your-travels.

14. "Disability Impacts All of Us Infographic," Centers for Disease Control and Prevention, January 5, 2023, https://www.cdc.gov/ncbddd/disabilityandhealth /infographic-disability-impacts-all.html.

15. Perry, David, et al., "The Ruderman White Paper on Media Coverage of the Murder of People with Disabilities by Their Caregivers," The Ruderman Family Foundation, March 2017.

16. "People First Language," Office of Disability Rights, odr.dc.gov/page/people -first-language.

17. "People First Language," Office of Disability Rights.

18. Okundaye, Jevon, "Ask a Self-Advocate: The Pros and Cons of Person-First and Identity-First Language," *Massachusetts Advocates for Children*, April 23, 2021, www.massadvocates.org/news/ask-a-self-advocate-the-pros-and-cons-of -person-first-and-identity-first-language.

19. The elysian collective, "How Person-First Language Isolates Disabled People," *Medium*, September 22, 2020, elysiancollective.medium.com/how-person -first-language-isolates-disabled-people-61a681a4fac4.

20. Wooldridge, Shannon, "Writing Respectfully: Person-First and Identity-First Language," *National Institutes of Health (NIH)*, April 12, 2023, https://www .nih.gov/about-nih/what-we-do/science-health-public-trust/perspectives

/writing-respectfully-person-first-identity-first-language. Accessed October 21, 2023.

21. "Disability and Health Overview," Centers for Disease Control and Prevention, September 16, 2020, https://www.cdc.gov/ncbddd/disabilityandhealth/disabil -ity.html.

22. "Disability and Health Overview," Centers for Disease Control and Prevention.

23. "Facts about Intellectual Disability," Centers for Disease Control and Prevention, May 10, 2022, www.cdc.gov/ncbddd/developmentaldisabilities/facts -about-intellectual-disability.html.

24. "Disability Evaluation under Social Security," Social Security, www.ssa.gov /disability/professionals/bluebook/12.00-MentalDisorders-Adult.htm.

25. "Social Security Disability," Alzheimer's Association, https://www.alz.org /help-support/caregiving/financial-legal-planning/social-security-disability.

26. Young, Stella, "Inspiration Porn and the Objectification of Disability: Stella Young at TEDxSydney 2014," YouTube, May 13, 2014, https://www.youtube .com/watch?v=SxrS7-I_sMQ.

27. Sonya Freeman Loftis, *Imagining Autism: Fiction and Stereotypes on the Spectrum*, Bloomington, Indiana University Press, 2015, 117.

28. "Diversity of Sexual Orientation," Kinsey Institute, Indiana University, kin- seyinstitute.org/research/publications/historical-report-diversity-of-sexual -orientation.php.

29. Dar-Nimrod, Ilan, "Do You Think You're Exclusively Straight?," The University of Sydney, August 20, 2021, https://www.sydney.edu.au/news-opinion /news/2021/08/20/do-you-think-you-re-exclusively-straight-.html.

30. "Split Attraction Model," Princeton Gender + Sexuality Resource Center, https://www.gsrc.princeton.edu/split-attraction.

31. Loggins, Brittany, "What Is the Split Attraction Model?," Verywell Mind, January 29, 2022, www.verywellmind.com/what-is-the-split-attraction-model -5207380.

32. Shapiro, Lila, "Who Gave You the Right to Tell That Story?" Vulture, October 31, 2019, www.vulture.com/2019/10/who-gave-you-the-right-to-tell-that- story.html.

Chapter 9: The Editing Process

1. Bateman, Jason, Sean Hayes, and Will Arnett, "Octavia Spencer," *Smart- Less*, August 23, 2021, podcasts.apple.com/ca/podcast/octavia-spencer /id1521578868?i=1000532779926.

2. Yohana Desta, "Viola Davis Regrets Making *The Help*: 'It Wasn't the Voices of the Maids That Were Heard,'" *Vanity Fair*, September 12, 2018, www.vanityfair .com/hollywood/2018/09/viola-davis-the-help-regret.

Chapter 11: Terms, Stereotypes, and Tropes

1. *Seattle Times* staff, "Capital-B 'Black' Becomes Standard Usage at the *Seattle*

Times," *Seattle Times,* December 19, 2019, https://www.seattletimes.com/seattle
-news/capital-b-black-becomes-standard-usage-at-the-seattle-times/.

2. Thúy Nguyễn, Ann, and Maya Pendleton, "Recognizing Race in Language:
    Why We Capitalize 'Black' and 'White,'" Center for the Study of Social Policy,
    March 23, 2020, https://cssp.org/2020/03/recognizing-race-in-language-why
    -we-capitalize-black-and-white/.

3. Bauder, David, "AP Says It Will Capitalize Black but Not White," *AP News,*
    July 20, 2020, apnews.com/article/entertainment-cultures-race-and-ethnicity
    -us-news-ap-top-news7e36c00c5af0436abc09e051261fff1f.

4. Appiah, Kwame Anthony, "The Case for Capitalizing the 'B' in Black," *Atlantic,*
    June 18, 2020, www.theatlantic.com/ideas/archive/2020/06/time-to-capitalize
    -blackand-white/613159/.

5. Jackson, Dr. Jenn M., "Tweet Thread: 'Capitalizing the 'W' Is Only a Performa-
    tive Act for White People. The Rest of Us Are Already Aware That Whiteness
    Is *Not* Invisible,'" Twitter, August 2, 2020, twitter.com/JennMJacksonPhD
    /status/1289887251179200512.

6. National Archives, "Treaty of Guadalupe Hidalgo (1848)," National Archives,
    June 25, 2021, https://www.archives.gov/milestone-documents/treaty-of
    -guadalupe-hidalgo.

7. Martinez, Fidel, and Julissa Arce, "Latinx Files: When Mexicans Became
    'White'-Ish," *Los Angeles Times,* May 12, 2022, https://www.latimes.com
    /world-nation/newsletter/2022-05-12/latinx-files-julissa-arce-book-latinx
    -files.

8. "Edward Bing Kan: The First Chinese-American Naturalized after Repeal of
    Chinese Exclusion | USCIS," uscis.gov, July 28, 2020, https://www.uscis.gov
    /about-us/our-history/stories-from-the-archives/edward-bing-kan-the-first
    -chinese-american-naturalized-after-repeal-of-chinese-exclusion.

9. "Dept. of Justice Affirms Arab Race in 1909," Arab American Historical Foun-
    dation, www.arabamericanhistory.org/archives/dept-of-justice-affirms-arab
    -race-in-1909/.

10. Parvini, Sarah, and Ellis Simani, "Are Arabs and Iranians White? Census Says
    Yes, but Many Disagree," *Los Angeles Times,* March 28, 2019, www.latimes
    .com/projects/la-me-census-middle-east-north-africa-race/.

11. Ishisaka, Naomi, "Why It's Time to Retire the Term 'Asian Pacific Islander,'"
    Seattle Times, November 30, 2020, www.seattletimes.com/seattle-news/why
    -its-time-to-retire-the-term-asian-pacific-islander/.

12. African American Literature Book Club, aalbc.com.

13. "Where Does the Term AMEMSA Come From?," AMEMSA Fact Sheet, Civic
    Engagement Fund, November 2011.

14. "Fighting Antisemitism | 2016," Jewish Voice for Peace, September 7, 2016,
    www.jewishvoiceforpeace.org/2016/09/07/fighting-antisemitism/. Accessed
    February 21, 2024.

15. "Our Approach to Zionism," Jewish Voice for Peace, www.jewishvoicefor-
    peace.org/resource/zionism/.

16. "Roma," *Britannica*, 2020, www.britannica.com/topic/Rom.

17. Dowd, Rachel, "Transgender People over Four Times More Likely than Cisgender People to Be Victims of Violent Crime," Williams Institute, 2021, williamsinstitute.law.ucla.edu/press/ncvs-trans-press-release/.

18. Bell, Carole V., "The Troubling Gap between Fat Representation and Fat Acceptance in Romance," *Book Riot*, September 10, 2020, bookriot.com/fat-representation-in-romance/.

ACKNOWLEDGMENTS

Writing an Identity Not Your Own has been the hardest book I've ever written. It was through the love, support, encouragement, and knowledge from others that I was able to go on this journey.

To Blake Kimzey, for asking me to teach a class on writing an identity not your own with Writing Workshops. Without that opportunity, I don't know if I would have truly understood how this topic weighs on the hearts of many creative writers and why they deserve more guidance, insight, and answers. Thanks to that first class, I had the opportunity to teach with so many other wonderful organizations and associations, which gave me the chance to learn more about this subject and ultimately led me to write this book.

I have to give an immense shout-out to my literary agent, Mary C. Moore. You had never sold a nonfiction book, but when I came to you with this idea, you were all onboard and took it out on the market with vigor. I'm so glad we've been working with each other since 2017 and that you've always had my back.

Thank you to Gwen Hawkes for seeing the potential of *Writing an Identity Not Your Own* and how it might impact the creative writing world and the publishing community. I'm so glad you brought it to the St. Martin's Essentials family.

To my editor, Mara Delgado Sánchez—what a joy it was to work with you on this book. I was so relieved to have someone in my corner who knew what it was like to be part of a historically marginalized identity. Thanks for seeing my vision and advocating for me and my book throughout this process. I can't even fully convey what it means to have an editor like you.

I appreciate every single person at St. Martin's Essentials who contributed to this book. Thank you to Carla Benton and Cassie Gutman for catching things I did not see and sharing insight in the copyedits that helped to make this book better. To the design, marketing, and publicity teams—thanks for helping me to spread the word about this book.

As I wrote and edited this book, I struggled a lot with my mental and emotional well-being. I spiraled out often, found myself in tears, lost confidence, and questioned myself constantly. I want to thank the many, many different friends who were there when I needed to talk out my concerns and fears and who gave me new perspectives on this book and what it could mean for writers of different disciplines. Thank you to the friends who reminded me of who I am as a person and a writer. You know who you are, and you know how much I cherish our friendship.

I could not have written this book without my family. My parents and siblings have given me so much insight into different identities beyond the ones that we share. I have learned so much from each of you. You have consistently supported me with each and every book and I'm incredibly grateful for that. Love you, Pops, Mom, Tiff, and Erik.

Throughout the book I reference journalists, researchers, authors, activists, literary agents, professors, students, actors, editors, influencers, writers, and so many other knowledgeable people and sources. Much of the information that I share in this book was sourced from wonderful people who have done great work to advocate for people of historically marginalized communities. Without their knowledge and insight, this book could not be.

Last but not least, thank you to the folks who openly discussed the topic of writing an identity not your own with me. Thank you for sharing different perspectives, for agreeing and disagreeing with me, for offering different opinions or ideas, for challenging me, for questioning me, for asking me to find things you weren't sure about, for admitting your biases, for showing me my biases, and for making me a better literary citizen.

ABOUT THE AUTHOR

Shelbie Monkres

Alex Temblador is the Mixed Latine award-winning author of *Half Outlaw* and *Secrets of the Casa Rosada*. She received her MFA in creative writing from the University of Central Oklahoma and is a contributor to *Living Beyond Borders: Growing Up Mexican in America* and *Speculative Fiction for Dreamers: A Latinx Anthology*. Alex has taught creative writing seminars, workshops, and classes with the Women's Fiction Writers Association, WritingWorkshops.com, the Writers' League of Texas, and more, as well as spoken about diversity and representation in the literary world with the Texas Library Association, Abydos Learning Conference, and at many other festivals, conferences, and universities. She is an award-winning travel, arts, and culture journalist who specializes in diversity, equity, and inclusion, publishing in the likes of *Condé Nast Traveler, Outside,* and *Travel + Leisure,* and speaking about such topics at SXSW, the Society of American Travel Writers, and the World Travel Market. Alex lives in Dallas, Texas, where she runs a literary panel series called LitTalk. Connect with her at AlexTemblador .com and WritingAnIdentityNotYourOwn.com.